The Unity We Have and the Unity We Seek

The Unity We Have and the Unity We Seek

Ecumenical Prospects for the Third Millennium

Edited by
JEREMY MORRIS
and
NICHOLAS SAGOVSKY

T & T CLARK
A Continuum imprint
LONDON • NEW YORK

T&T CLARK LTD

A Continuum imprint

The Tower Building   370 Lexington Avenue
11 York Road   New York 10017–6503
London SE1 7NX   USA
UK

www.continuumbooks.com

First published 2003

ISBN 0 567 08879 0 (Paperback)
ISBN 0 567 8907 X (Hardback)

British Library Cataloguing-in-Publication Data
A catalogue record for this book is available from the British Library

Typeset by Waverley Typesetters, Galashiels
Printed and bound in Great Britain by Bookcraft Ltd, Avon

Dedicated to the memory of
Jean-Marie Roger Tillard OP (1927–2000)

Contents

Notes on the Contributors   ix

Acknowledgements   xi

Abbreviations   xiii

Introduction   xv
Jeremy Morris and Nicholas Sagovsky

Part 1: Unity and Plurality: Reconceiving the Difficulties

1 Identity, Plurality, Unity – What's the Right Blend?
   Some Reflections from an Old Catholic Perspective   3
   Urs Von Arx

2 Anglicans and Roman Catholics: a Joint Declaration
   of Agreement?   27
   Nicholas Sagovsky

3 Methodists and the Ecumenical Task   53
   David Carter

4 The Reformed Tradition and the Ecumenical Task:
   'A Vulnerable Catholicity'   77
   Peter McEnhill

5 The Unity We Seek: Prospects for the Local Church   91
   Jeremy Morris

6 The Future of Ecumenism in Europe   119
   Keith Clements

7 Between Christ and Caesar: the Politics of Mission and
   Ecumenism Encountering African Myths and Realities   135
   Valentin Dedji

                Part 2: Prospects for Ecumenism

8 Once More on the Unity We Seek: Testing Ecumenical
   Models   167
   Michael Root

9 The Goal of Visible Unity: Yet Again   179
   Mary Tanner

10 *Ex Tenebris Lux*: Ecumenism Enters a New Phase   191
   Jean-Marie Tillard

11 Route-Planning the Future Ecumenical Journey   203
   Christopher Hill

Conclusion: 2 Peter and the Third Millennium   221
   Nicholas Sagovsky

Appendix: the *Charta Oecumenica*   227

Index   239

Notes on the Contributors

Urs Von Arx is Professor for New Testament and the History of Old Catholicism in the Department of Old Catholic Theology in the University of Bern. He is a member of the Anglican–Old Catholic International Coordinating Council, the Old Catholic–Roman Catholic Dialogue Commission in Switzerland, and consultant to the international Orthodox–Old Catholic Theological Commission.

David Carter is a Methodist local preacher, active in several spheres ecumenically. He is an associate lecturer and research associate in the Religious Studies Department of the Open University.

Keith Clements is a Baptist minister, and has been Secretary of the Conference of European Churches since 1997.

Valentin Dedji is Minister in charge of St Mark's Methodist Church in London. He is an ordained Methodist minister from Benin, West Africa, holds a PhD from the University of Cambridge, and formerly taught ethics and philosophy at the Protestant Theological Seminary in Porto-Novo, Benin.

Christopher Hill is the Anglican Bishop of Stafford, an Area Bishop within the Diocese of Lichfield, and is in regular contact with a wide range of Christian and other faith communities. Formerly he worked in the Secretariat for Ecumenical Affairs at Lambeth Palace, and had wide-ranging contact at both diplomatic and theological levels with the spectrum of Christian churches throughout the world.

Peter McEnhill is Tutor in Systematic Theology at Westminster College, Cambridge, and in the Cambridge Theological Federation. He is a minister of the Church of Scotland, and has served on the Reformed–Oriental Orthodox Theological Commission. Formerly he was a parish minister in Glasgow, where he also taught at the university.

Jeremy Morris is Dean and Robert Runcie Fellow in Ecclesiastical History at Trinity Hall, Cambridge. He is an Anglican priest, and has specialized in modern British church history and Anglican theology, serving on the staff at Westcott House as Vice-Principal until 2001.

Michael Root is Edward C. Fendt Professor of Systematic Theology at Trinity Lutheran Seminary, Columbus, Ohio. He has been involved in Lutheran dialogues with Methodists, Anglicans and Roman Catholics both in the USA and internationally.

Nicholas Sagovsky is Professor of Theology and Public Life at Liverpool Hope University College. He has been a member of the Anglican–Roman Catholic International Commission (ARCIC) since 1992. His most recent book is *Ecumenism, Christian Origins and the Practice of Communion* (Cambridge: Cambridge University Press, 2000). A parallel study of ecumenism and social justice is shortly to be published.

Mary Tanner served as the General Secretary of the Church of England Council for Christian Unity from 1991–98. She was Moderator of the World Council of Churches' Faith and Order Commission from 1991–98, and a member of the Anglican–Roman Catholic International Commission from 1982–91.

Jean-Marie Tillard OP, who died in 2000, was Professor of Dogmatic Theology at the Dominican College of Theology, Ottawa, and Vice-Moderator of the Faith and Order Commission of the World Council of Churches. He was a member of the Orthodox–Roman Catholic Commission, of the Roman Catholic dialogue with the Disciples of Christ, and, from the beginning, a member of the Anglican–Roman Catholic International Commission (ARCIC). His published works included *The Bishop of Rome* (London: SPCK, 1984), *Church of Churches* (Collegeville, Minnesota: Liturgical Press, 1987) and *L'Église locale* (Paris: Editions du Cerf, 1995).

Acknowledgements

We would like to acknowledge a particular debt to Westcott House, Cambridge, both for hosting the conference in September 1999 at which many of the contributions to this volume were presented, and for its generosity in making available financial support towards the publication of the conference papers. Jeremy Morris would like to add a personal note of gratitude for the support and friendship of the Principal, staff and students there over five years, including the period in which the Centre for Ecumenical Studies was established. Thanks also go from both of us to friends and colleagues in the Cambridge Theological Federation, which has been instrumental for years in presenting a model for ecumenical cooperation in the field of theological education, and as such an inspiration to many.

We would of course like to thank our contributors for their patience in bearing with the somewhat extended process of putting this volume together. Both our families have also had their role to play, and deserve our gratitude.

Abbreviations

AACC	All Africa Conference of Churches
ACC	Anglican Consultative Council
AEAM	Association of Evangelicals of Africa and Madagascar
AICs	African Independent churches
ARCIC	Anglican-Roman Catholic International Commission (I & II)
BEM	*Baptism, Eucharist, Ministry* (Geneva: WCC, 1982)
CCBI	Council of Churches of Britain and Ireland
CCEE	Council of Catholic Episcopal Conferences in Europe
CEC	Conference of European Churches
CPI	Church Publishing Incorporated
CTE	Churches Together in England
CTS	Catholic Truth Society
EATWOT	Ecumenical Association of Third World Theologians
EECCS	European Ecumenical Commission for Church and Society
Ep.	Epistles (Cyprian of Carthage; Augustine)
ESP	Ecumenical Sharing of Personnel
ET	English translation
EU	European Union
GA	*The Gift of Authority* (ARCIC II)
IMC	International Missionary Council
LC	*Life in Christ* (ARCIC II)
LG	*Lumen Gentium* (Vatican II)
LWF	Lutheran World Federation
NIRC	Nigeria Inter-Religious Council
OSCE	Organization for Security and Cooperation in Europe

Phld.	Letter to the Philadelphians (Ignatius of Antioch)
SC	*Salvation and the Church* (ARCIC II)
UR	*Unitatis Redintegratio* (Vatican II)
WARC	World Alliance of Reformed Churches
WCC	World Council of Churches
WMC	World Methodist Council

Introduction

The essays in this book are the fruit of a conference on 'The Unity We Have and the Unity We Seek', held at Westcott House, Cambridge, in September 1999. The conference marked the launch of the Centre for Ecumenical Studies, which has now become a focus for ecumenical research within the Cambridge Theological Federation, an association of training institutes almost unique in Western Europe for its ecumenical diversity.

The task of the conference was retrospective and prospective. It sought to draw in a wide range of confessional perspectives, in order to celebrate and review significant developments in church unity over recent decades. It also sought to look forward to developments that will take place in coming years. Perhaps inevitably, given the location of the Centre in an Anglican theological college, there was a certain Anglican 'tinge' to the conference, and something of that has remained in this volume. But the invited speakers represented a broad cross-section of the denominational traditions with which the Anglican churches are in longstanding ecumenical relationships. Some omissions from the conference programme have been addressed in this volume: we are pleased to include additional essays from Methodist and Reformed perspectives by David Carter, Valentin Dedji and Peter McEnhill. Other lacunae remain, and we look forward to the work of the Centre embracing perspectives such as those of the Pentecostal churches or Eastern Orthodoxy which could not be included here. We hope that the breadth of the contributions is sufficient to indicate the breadth and complexity of the ecumenical task, and the variety of perspectives sufficient to indicate the stimulating interactions generated by the conference and the work of the Centre.

A conference on the eve of the Millennium was obviously a good time to take stock of 'the unity we have'. The deep roots of the contemporary ecumenical movement can readily be traced to the founding of the Faith and Order and the Life and Work movements between the two world wars, and the founding of the World Council of Churches in 1948. The second half of the twentieth century saw the emergence of United and Uniting Churches, the Second Vatican Council (1962–65), which marked a new ecumenical openness in the Roman Catholic Church, the setting up of a whole range of bilateral and mutilateral ecumenical dialogues, of which the most important was perhaps the one leading to *Baptism, Eucharist and Ministry* (1982), and the creation of ecumenical instruments such as national and local councils of churches and local ecumenical projects.

In the last two decades, there have been further signs of progress towards the ecumenical goal of full, visible unity. Lutherans and Roman Catholics have agreed a declaration of the doctrine of justification and rescinded their mutual anathemas. In America, Anglicans and Lutherans have reached full agreement on relations of communion. United and Uniting churches, bringing together different strands of Protestantism, have come into being in various parts of the world. New ecumenical instruments which allow for Roman Catholic participation have been created, particularly in Western Europe and America. The All Africa Conference of Churches has continued to play a crucial role in strengthening African church life. The body of authoritative ecumenical texts has continued to grow and to form the mind of the Church. A major encyclical, *Ut Unum Sint* (1995) has reaffirmed the commitment of the Roman Catholic Church to the ecumenical journey. Theological insights, such as those surrounding the understanding of *koinonia*, have been developed and used in a way which has led some to see a new, emergent ecumenical consensus on issues of church order, authority and life.

Yet, despite these signs of new life, there are those who see this as a time of ecumenical 'winter'. In contrast with the heady enthusiasm for schemes of organic church unity in the 1960s and 1970s, ecumenism may be seen as something of a bore, a sort of necessary but dull adjunct to the 'real' task of Christian mission. Something of this attitude – common enough in local church circles in Britain – undoubtedly derives from a certain cynicism after the failure of particular schemes for unity, such as the Anglican–Methodist proposals of the 1970s, and the British churches' covenant scheme in the 1980s. It may also have been fed by different confessional reactions to the various ways in which churches have sought to respond and adapt to the challenges of modernity – one can think, for example, of the way in which the ordination of women to the priesthood and the episcopate in many of the Anglican and Lutheran churches has raised deep concerns for Roman Catholics and the Orthodox churches. People do ask, especially around the Week of Prayer for Christian Unity, how much that really matters has changed. Added to this, in Britain certainly, is the pressure of a growing secularism and multiculturalism which has placed the churches on the defensive, making them less confident about taking imaginative new initiatives.

Trying to assess the unity we have, and to reassess the unity we seek, is no easy task. The signals are contradictory and the information available continues to grow at an alarming rate. Ecumenism is perhaps best served when it is a permanent dimension of daily practice – the severed part always being implicitly conscious that it belongs to an integrated whole – but there is clearly a need for interpretative clarity, and for the power to discern what the Spirit is saying to the churches. What kind of *kairos* is this? What are the new opportunities and points of growth which lie ahead of the churches?

These are some of the questions which the newly launched Centre for Ecumenical Studies will address. Westcott House, by foundation an Anglican theological college, has, for over a hundred years, stood for excellence in theological education and for the openness of the Church to the world – a vision inspired by its founder, Brooke Foss Westcott, Bishop of Durham. It has throughout its history maintained a close and fruitful relationship with the Faculty of Divinity in the University of Cambridge, and in the last 30 years has become an integral part of the Cambridge Theological Federation. Teaching in the Federation takes place ecumenically, with students and teachers from Anglican, Roman Catholic, Methodist, United Reformed and Orthodox churches working together in the study of common traditions, and with respect for the diversity of Christian structures and practice among them. Westcott House and the Federation thus seemed an ideal context in which to create a resource centre for the study of the ecumenical movement. The collection in the Centre for Ecumenical Studies aims to make available to research students all the relevant documentation on ecumenical initiatives – local, national and inter-national – and to support teaching and learning about the movement for Christian unity.

It is impossible, in a volume of essays published after the event, satisfactorily to capture the flavour of a conference. We remember it as a lively and goodhumoured occasion, which drew together over 60 theologians, ecumenical officers and ecumenical enthusiasts from across the world. As a reminder that this was a time not only to study but also to worship together, we have included in this volume the sermon that was preached at the closure of the conference. To those who knew Jean-Marie Tillard (1927–2000), one of the main speakers, it was clear he was not in good health, but few can have guessed that his address at the conference was to be one of his last. The contribution he made to the ecumenical movement, drawing on his own Roman Catholic tradition, to which he was deeply loyal, and on his unstinting commitment to the work of the World Council of Churches, latterly as a Vice-Moderator of the Faith and Order Commission, was unique. So also were his expansive personality, his idiosyncratic use of the English language and his gift for personal friendship. When taking stock of the ecumenical movement on the eve of a new millenium, we had not envisaged that it would go forward without the stream of new ideas which sprang from Jean's theological genius. His work, however, has been done with tremendous thoroughness and energy. There are doubtless rich new insights to be drawn from his many books and articles, and further progress to be made along the lines he so clearly indicated.

Amongst the many memories of Jean later shared by those who had been at the conference was his reaction to a speech by the Dean of Windsor welcoming the Anglican–Roman Catholic International Commission back to St George's House, Windsor, in 1992, after some eleven years, and expressing the hope that St George's House would have the pleasure of welcoming ARCIC again after another suitable interval. Jean was not at all pleased by the Dean's gracious words. He had hoped last time round that visible unity would be achieved before

1992, and he saw no reason to anticipate a return of ARCIC to Windsor yet again. Jean's ire provided a salutary reminder to new members as to what 'seeking unity' was really all about. Being a true ecumenist, he never lost the hope that, despite all setbacks, the unity he discerned in the tradition and in Christ would surely be realized by the power of the Spirit in the Church. Whereas at the Eucharist other presidents would in the conventional way bless those who refrained from communion, it was Jean's habit, at that most sacred point of unrealized unity, to proclaim to each non-communicant personally: 'There is one Lord, one Faith, one Baptism.' In thankfulness for what he showed us about the unity we have in Christ, and for his commitment to the unity we seek, we dedicate this book to him.

Jeremy Morris
Nicholas Sagovsky

Part 1

Unity and Plurality: Reconceiving the Difficulties

1

❦

Identity, Plurality, Unity – What's the Right Blend? Some Reflections from an Old Catholic Perspective

Urs Von Arx

Introduction

The title of this chapter may make you think of a recipe: how much identity, plurality and unity, and of what kind, are to be blended in order to get the desired result? What result?

There is a worldwide discussion of how to conceive the unity of the Church, how to discover and live it. In this discussion there is much talk of unity, identity, plurality, also of uniformity and diversity – and this in varied contexts and from different perspectives: we come across phrases like unity in faith, identity of the faith, unity in diversity, limits of plurality or dangers of uniformity, maintenance of ecclesial identity, etc. They refer to elements that are deemed relevant for the being of the Church and for its unity. If this is correct, the desired result of my cookery metaphor is the unity of the Church. So it is necessary to have a certain idea of this unity and then to define the constitutive elements in their interrelation. Not being a professional ecumenist nor a systematic theologian I dare to offer some reflections from an Old Catholic perspective.

I have to explain what I mean by this. The Old Catholic Church and theology emerged in opposition to a conception of the Catholic

3

Church and its unity that found its expression in the papal decrees of the First Vatican Council. In order to justify their opposition as well as their ideas of church reform and their initial steps to restore its unity, the Old Catholics always referred to the ancient Church, however this term and entity was specified (the undivided church of the first millennium, i.e. before the great and lasting divisions with their diverging developments, or the church of the seven ecumenical synods) and however it was being used as a regulative idea in concrete terms. What is to be stressed is that the ancient Church as the basic element of reference is *a reality of communal life* characterized *inter alia* by certain structures for a community spreading in time and space (the Eucharist, the ordained ministry with episcopacy serving to represent and maintain the unity of the Church at various levels, as well as synodal elements) and by certain theological clarifications of its belief (Christological and Trinitarian dogma). The Old Catholic Church considers these community structures and fundamental definitions binding and appropriate.

It should be noticed, however, that I speak of the ancient Church as a basic element of reference, which is to be distinguished from imitating it in a slavish or anachronistic manner – this would lead to a 'parrot theology' and foster a tendency to petrification. To live in an historical continuity must not be a jail, but a *Grundorientierung* that is open for the Spirit of God who leads the Church on its pilgrim way. Thus the Old Catholic appeal to the ancient Church moves in a tension between being tied and being free. The task of theology is to offer the necessary discernment and by doing so exercise theological tactfulness.

I see in this approach a certain difference to the Reformation of the sixteenth century and the later revivalist movements, in that they chose as their basic point of reference Holy Scriptures as the inspired Word of God and operated with a book. I do not want to overstress the difference, but taking the Bible as a fundamental point of reference in connexion with a biblicist use of the *sola scriptura* principle or in connexion with its modern variation (the 'canon in the canon' and *Frühkatholizismus* as its negative counterpart) may easily lead to another view on how the Church of a single generation is linked with the Church as an entity comprehending ages and generations,[1] and thus to another ecclesiology.

4

May I add another preliminary remark. It is well known that the New Testament is without a single, unified ecclesiology. What we find is a number of rudimentary ideas about the being, function and shape of the Church.[2] Even more: a critical reading of the New Testament writings reveals strong tensions, if not divisions, among the various Christian groups of the first generations.[3] Should we draw the conclusion that the search for common ways to live and manifest local and supralocal unity is unnecessary, dangerous, or even prohibited by the Bible? I do not think so. After all, we may discern in the many ecclesiological statements in the New Testament a sufficient number of convergent convictions: those who are won by the proclamation of the Gospel form a community of which unity in various range and expression is an essential element.[4] From this we might rather deduce the task to translate this spiritual experience of fellowship and unity into somewhat stable, institutionalized forms of manifestations of unity.

This is what happened in the early Church, fundamentally in its pre-Constantine period and later on within and outside the Roman empire – a remarkable fact. Of particular importance are the elements I deem relevant for my paper: the Eucharist and the episcopal ministry for the local church, and a synodical network for the supralocal communion of churches.[5] Incidentally, the tendency to unite plurality and diversity in a unity can also be discerned in the formation of the scriptural canon. That is why I think the post-New Testament Church, i.e. the ancient Church, has a right to be heard, since essential aspects of its history – which, of course, reveals dubious things as well – may be understood as a continuous effort for unity in new situations and in the face of new questions and challenges. It is precisely when we refrain from seeing the ancient Church as an harmonious entity and an idealistic *consensus patrum* as it may appear in textbooks that we may learn something about unity and communion in diversity.

What I call an Old Catholic perspective is not universal, but neither is it denominational in a narrow sense. It belongs to a wider tradition where being in historical continuity with the pilgrim Church throughout the ages is deemed relevant and where the basic forms of visible church ordering are a consequence of a 'realistic' ecclesiology. In any case it places itself in a line with recent ecclesiological efforts

5

of the Commission on Faith and Order of the World Council of Churches.[6] This is especially true with regards to the concept of *episkope*, as will become clear later.

Some Preliminary Ecclesiological Reflections

Hardly anybody will deny that the unity of the Church is a given reality.[7] The Church (and so its unity) has its foundation in the triune God who through the mission of the incarnate Logos and the Holy Spirit makes humans participate in his life and so become a new creation (see especially the Pauline tradition). Men and women who in the process of justification and sanctification participate in God become and are a *koinonia*.[8] This communion is the manifestation of God's reconciling himself with humans and of the reconciliation of humans among themselves. Through the proclamation of the Gospel and through service the Church participates in a process that is grounded in the Christ event and dynamized by the Holy Spirit and which will find its fulfilment in the perfection of the creation in God. The Church proleptically lives the reality of the new creation in the Eucharist. *Martyria* (the witness of faith in all its possible concrete articulations), *leitourgia* (worship as a fundamental expression of being oriented to God as the source of life) and *diakonia* (the task of looking after and healing people in their spiritual and material distress, i.e. a holistic understanding of charity) are the fundamental manifestations of the life of the Church which as a whole has a sort of priestly responsibility for the creation. It is on a pilgrim way to judgement and perfection in God. Its proper limits should be seen as no less than the limits of creation that is called and destined to be transformed in the power of the kingdom of God.

This is the reality that is called in the Niceno–Constantinopolitan Symbol of Faith the One, Holy, Catholic and Apostolic Church. It is a reality to be believed and confessed.

But where is this reality of the Church and its unity to be discovered, if at all? Does it remain fundamentally invisible, because it is realized only eschatologically or because its foundation cannot be verified by 'objective' methods or because it is exclusively an object of belief? Many answers have been given in the history of theology, especially in the West, and they differ in their ways of how to correlate the divine and the human reality. It is either denied or asserted that the human, the material, can be a manifestation or bearer of divine presence. The answer has repercussions on ecclesiology. An idealistic conception of the Church will tend to devalue the Church that can be described with sociological methods and to suspect the sacraments and the ordained ministry to be instruments for a magic use of the grace of God. This tendency is not, however, to be identified with the important distinction between the true or hidden and the visible Church.[9]

I plead for a type of 'incarnational' theology where it is possible to define the Church and the four *notae ecclesiae* as a reality that can somehow be demonstrated with all the inherent ambiguities. Consequently, the Church on its pilgrim way 'in the world' will have structures by which to live and manifest its unity. These structures must be in a coherent relation to what is constitutive for its being and mission.

The ineluctable ambivalence of the Church makes it necessary to speak of the *mysterium* of the Church (e.g. *Lumen Gentium*, 1) or of its *Verborgenheit* (Luther), but it does not preclude on the other hand the legitimacy of developing a structured shape and of subjecting it to a phenomenological analysis. (I assume that ambivalence qualifies every theological statement about the real Church that takes into consideration its foundation and goal in God, the Lord and Creator.)

Now, such a phenomenological analysis offers the picture of a Church that is united and divided at the same time. On the one hand we see churches that are distinct from each other and separated according to their denominational identity, but within the denominational identity they manifest unity with varied degrees of organization (and common theological interpretation). But the prevailing perception is disunity, and this from a universal and a local perspective – as the various Sunday morning services in a particular town of our society show.

The theological interpretation of this phenomenological fact seems to be controversial. Many ecumenical statements coming from a Western (and for that Augustinian) context presuppose some sort of ecclesiality in the various denominations – the walls between the churches do not extend to the heavens. So it may be stated that a particular denomination is a 'part', all the different churches are 'parts' of the One Church of the symbol of faith. Or it may be said that the *Una Sancta* is (only) subsisting in the local church, and consequently also being somehow present in other Christian bodies.[10] The obvious intention is to avoid an exclusive identification of the local church with the One Church or to deprive other denominations of all ecclesiality. There is a difficulty, however. If the Oneness, the unity of the Church is an essential aspect of its nature as it is stated in the authoritative expression of the Apostolic faith in the creed of 381, the question arises whether the assumption of the Church being divided into 'parts' gainsays the reconciliation in Jesus Christ for which the *One* Church is the 'proof' and thus compromises the work of God. Or can the unity of the Church be discerned only in such a way that the reality of the One Church is once again pushed into the realm of the invisible?

This leads me to the frequent assertions from the Eastern Orthodox side that only the Orthodox Church is a representation of the One Church. To be sure, this assertion would be less offensive if the word 'only' (*solus*), in theology a highly risky term, were shunned. It then could be said: every church may believe, even ought to believe itself to be a representation of the One Church, but refrains from an ecclesiological judgement on another church (to be consequential here I should use another term) as long as it is not in communion with it. It exercises ecclesiological *epoche*, but it is animated by the strong expectation that other communities that confess the triune God are also a representation of the One Church – otherwise ecumenical dialogues do not make sense – and this will become manifest when churches mutually discover and recognize themselves as (theologically) identical and live in unqualified communion.[11]

My queries concern the application of the distinction true and visible Church on the situation of denominationally divided churches.

The Visible Unity of the Church – an ecclesiological outline

How are we to speak of those elements of the unity of the Church that are liable to be manifest? What is constitutive for the manifestation and maintenance of the unity that is a God-given reality? I can mention a few points only in connection with the terms 'identity' and 'plurality'. I propose to do this by discussing them in the context of an ecclesiology I have now to outline in the first place. I shall try to describe how the unity of the Church is to be manifested in varying geographical dimensions. The following ecclesiological blueprint stands in a loose relation to certain elements of the ancient Church which serves as a model.

To speak of various geographical dimensions puts before us the question of how to see the relation of the local and the universal Church, a question that is often reflected on in ecumenical dialogues.[12] I take the local church as a point of departure for my ecclesiological outline because it is in the local church and not in a worldwide organization that ecclesial communion is lived in a sort of primary concreteness; this is true even if the liturgy of the terrestrial Church is bound up with the liturgy of the heavenly one. By the term 'local church' I refer to a eucharistic community of baptized people living in a particular 'place' that has its foundation in God's activity and is able to realize the basic elements of ecclesial life and service with a sufficient degree of self-reliance. This requires a certain geographical dimension and numerical strength which will usually transcend the single eucharistic congregation (i.e. the parish). So the 'place' is more than a particular locality. The local church thus circumscribed might be traditionally termed 'diocese'. The bearer of the personal *episkope* traditionally called the bishop – is a personal focus and sign of the unity of the local church and has a primary responsibility for it, though not solely, as he or she is fundamentally integrated in a synodical network of the local church. The principle underlying the communal structures of the local church could be expressed – in a slightly anachronistic manner – with the words of Cyprian of Carthage and Ignatius of Antioch: the bishop is not to act without the counsel of the presbytery and the assent of the people (Ep. 14:4); the people are not to act without the bishop (Phld. 7:2). Or else the maxim stemming from the Roman law *Quod omnes tangit ab omnibus tractari et approbari debet*[13] may be the guiding principle for the elaboration of ways of how to ensure the participation of the baptized in the process of decision-making in the local church.[14]

What I have outlined very briefly is a variation of eucharistic ecclesiology that tries to integrate the ministry of the bishop as a focus

9

of unity for a synodically structured community.[15] In this ecclesiology of the local church the recently discussed concept of *episkope* plays an important role (see below).

Now the local church is a realization and representation of the One Church of the Symbol of Faith. This becomes manifest in its being in communion with the other local churches. This point of view will qualify the term 'catholicity'. Each local church is catholic because on the one hand it participates in the whole reality of salvation and truth and finds its unity in this very reality that encompasses heaven and earth, and because on the other hand it is linked in unity and communion with other local churches it recognizes as identical. The soteriological–trinitarian identity of the local churches (the triune God makes humans participate in the reality of salvation in a concrete community) is to be distinguished from other (sociocultural, etc.) identities of the local churches, which are diverse and must be so – thus we have to do with identity in plurality *and* unity in diversity. This specification of the term 'catholicity' does not primarily nor exclusively place it in the realm of geographical universality. So I make a terminological distinction between the catholicity and universality (or ecumenicity) of the Church, although the two aspects are closely interrelated. The fact that the Eucharist is the central christological–pneumatological event in the local church will imply that the local churches are ontologically not 'secondary' to the universal Church or a 'part' of it, but that the local and universal Church – to be more precise: the local church and the universal communion of local churches – are both a representation and realization of the One Church and are thus to be seen as standing in a relation of theological simultaneity and identity.[16]

Each local church being the entity where the fundamental acts of *martyria, leitourgia* and *diakonia* take place and where the sacramental participation in the God-given reality of the pilgrim Church is lived – each local church is in its inner life and administration autonomous. But it also carries responsibility for the maintenance and strengthening of communion with other local churches. To act with an intention for the supralocal or universal communion of churches represents an important self-obligation. Whatever concerns the maintenance of this supralocal communion must consequently be made an object of common consultation, witness and decision-making. So we need certain structures that manifest the supralocal unity and communion of local churches. This supralocal unity and communion of churches is also a realization and representation of the One Church – not as a super-diocese or as a district of the universal Church being taken as the basic ecclesiological unit, but rather as a communion of local churches. This communion may have a regional, national, continental or universal extension (the criteria for a circumscription of these purely territorial entities are contingent).[17]

So in the ecclesiological conception I present here there are inter-mediary stages between the local and the universal aspect of the Church – and this is an important element in the whole approach. As I said they are representations of the *Una Sancta*, communions of local churches, or communions of communions of local churches.

In order to maintain the supralocal communion there will be various ways of common consultation and witness. The bearers of personal *episkope*, i.e. the bishops, being the representatives of the local churches and witnesses of their faith, will have an indispensable responsibility. They are at the intersection of the local church and the communion of local churches. As single bishops they are a focus of unity within the local churches and as a group they are a focus of unity for the communion of local churches. As they are tied on to a synodical net-work in the local church, so they will be part of a supralocal synod. One of them has a specific responsibility as *primus inter pares*. His or her overall task is to see that the unity and communion of local churches becomes manifest using the synodical, conciliar structures of the Church.

In respect of the first 'stage' of the supralocal communion of local churches the *primus inter pares* may be called a metropolitan (following a frequently used terminology of the Ancient Church), the corres-ponding communion a province.[18] For wider extensions of supra-local communions of the Church other terms may be used,[19] but the structures serving the manifestation and realization of the God-given unity of the Church are the same. What matters is that the inter-related responsibility of the one and the many, the interplay of primacy and synodality, brings to bear the unity and communion of local churches.[20]

11

I cannot go into any details concerning the rules of decision-making. I assume a qualified consensus will be necessary. A decision of the respective primate alone is excluded. On the other hand I have my doubts whether majority decisions analogous to the parliamentary system of modern democracies are appropriate for matters (of faith or other) where the communion of local churches is at stake. If the mechanism of a *per se* submission to a majority or primatial decision is not a required virtue in the ecclesiology of communion, should we then be prepared to give a more dignified status to schism, taking it as a possible sign that the common discernment of truth is yet out of reach?

Another element of the present ecclesiological outline I have to mention is the process of reception.[21] It is to ensure that the participation of the baptized is as *pneumatophoroi* and so the *sensus fidelium* comes into play in the widest and informal sense. Reception, being a pneumatological process in the last resort, cannot completely be put into juridical mechanisms.[22] Strictly speaking, the process of reception accompanies all the stages of decision-making, not only the ultimate phase. Reception thus understood corresponds to an understanding of the Church as a communion with a relational ontology (if I may say so), and this within the local church and among the local churches. In this respect we may say that the life of the Church is an analogy of the life of the triune God and we may cautiously speak of 'trinitarian' ecclesiology.

From this perspective we may also make use of the term 'dispersed authority' in the sense that the structured Church of all the baptized is the place of ecclesial authority (authority, however, also resting in tradition with Scripture as the prime witness of God's saving act).

The ecclesiological outline of the unity of the Church as a communion of local churches in various extensions does not as far as I see correspond fully to an existing reality. It is not realized in the guise of a denominational universality. The Orthodox Church as a communion of autocephalous churches may come rather near to it; in a certain sense also the Anglican Communion. The Roman Catholic conception of the unity of the Church in a universal perspective differs, as becomes manifest in its conception of the universal (i.e. papal) primacy.

Let me address this in an excursus on the role of the primate in the universal communion of local churches. The interplay of primate and synod (of bishops in the first place) on various supralocal levels is an important element in the ecclesiological concept I have sketched. Now for Old Catholics it is self-evident for historical reasons that the Bishop of Rome is the primate in the universal communion of local churches. But the conception of the papal primacy as it was developed in the course of history and dogmatically defined in 1870 presents great problems. The Pope as universal primate is a *primus* without *pares*, and so this particular form of primacy has become something that ought to be called 'unicity'. It is not in his capacity as (the or the first) patriarch of the Latin Church that he exercises his primacy for the universal communion, but in his capacity as the sole head of the universal Church who possesses an immediate and episcopal jurisdiction in every local church, i.e. an authority that obliges all the pastors and faithful to submission and obedience. I have difficulties in seeing how such a primacy can organically be integrated in an ecclesiology of communion of local churches. In my view this conception of (universal) primacy is part of an another ecclesiology that moreover is not really compatible with the ecclesiology of communion as it appears in various documents of the Second Vatican Council. In this other ecclesiology it is clearly the universal Church that is the basic entity, not the local church (with its indispensable reference to supralocal unity and communion).[23] It is an encouraging sign that in his encyclical *Ut Unum Sint* (1995) Pope John Paul II has invited the *oikoumene* to reflect with him on how his primacy can serve the unity of the Church in a really universal way (para. 95f.). But is it realistic to expect something like an unambiguous redefinition of the dogmatically fixed primacy of jurisdiction and universal episcopacy of the Bishop of Rome in such a way as to become a primacy in the sense of the intimated understanding (better preserved in the East) that seems far more acceptable?[24] Time will tell.

In outlining an ecclesiology of the visible unity of the Church I have tried to take up suggestions from my own[25] and various other traditions, ecumenical dialogues and individual authors.[26] I have to concede, however, that the 'Catholic' traditions seem to dispose of more ecclesiological conceptions with universal outreach and of more corresponding experiences than the traditions stemming from the Reformation. It is true that Protestant denominations have forms of a universal network, i.e. the worldwide Christian communities, but I must not put a claim on their ecclesiological self-understanding (a federation of churches) for my outline.

I add a concluding caveat: I do not plead for a bureaucratic giant organization or a global ordinary church government. As the essential manifestations of the life of the Church will happen in the local or the first supralocal context I plead for the general observation of a rule of subsidiarity in decision-making whenever the maintenance of communion allows for this.

Elements of Identity and Plurality

In the network of ecclesial representations of the One Church there are elements that testify to and manifest the theological identity of the local churches and thus their catholicity. Such an element is faith inasmuch as it can be articulated, say in a confession of faith or in liturgical prayer. Another element that is closely linked with faith is the liturgy or a certain practice of Christian life. However, these elements of identity will always exhibit aspects of diversity and difference. This is a consequence of the phenomenon of the inculturation of faith and church. So we have to do with unity in diversity. The question is: where and when does plurality begin to make no longer recognizable, and even to destroy the underlying identity? In this case plurality or diversity may be Church-dividing instead of being a legitimate, pertinent and enriching diversity.[27] A further element is the conception of the Church, particularly as to the ministry.

I shall make some general remarks concerning faith and worship and go somewhat more into detail with respect to the ordained ministry. I end up with asking questions as to the status of denominational identity in the local (and supralocal) church. The methodological objective of my attempt is to discuss questions of identity and plurality (or uniformity and diversity) in regard to a model of the unity of the Church and not in isolation from it.

Faith, as it has come to be articulated in view of the self-revelation of God in Jesus Christ and the experience of the Holy Spirit from

14

the Apostolic time onwards, is an important aspect of the manifestation of the God-given reality of the Church. The New Testament in connexion with the first point above is the prime and fundamental witness which, however, is open for interpretation and clarification in view of the life of the Church moving in space and time on its pilgrim way to its goal in God. As faith refers to the mystery of God and has to be stated in various and changing cultural situations, there will be no strictly definitive, i.e. for ever exhaustive statements. Diversity may communicate a deeper understanding of the mystery and make plain that truth is not simply identical with an articulated belief, but rather with God.

If faith cannot be expressed in a definitive compendium of statements,[28] but is in need of restatement and ascertainment in a sort of dialogue with various and changing cultural situations, it will probably be necessary from time to time to ask for the essentials or the essence of faith, or whatever other formulation is more appropriate. This will already happen within a specific denominational tradition, and even more so when separated traditions endeavour to discover and define the common basis of faith. The distinction of essentials or *necessaria* and *adiaphora* or *dubia*, or of *dogma* and *theologoumena*[29] can probably only be made in a process of dialogue and common consensus-finding, not by doing it unilaterally nor by using an allegedly neutral methodology.[30] Such a process of consensus-finding will more than once show that one partner of a dialogue will evaluate an element as non-theological and 'only' of cultural relevance, whereas for the other it is a matter of theological necessity because this partner lives in a different cultural situation. It may be added that a process of common consensus-finding may by way of feedback lead to an enrichment of the local tradition, unless this is suppressed for the sake of keeping the confessional identity pure.[31]

The common consensus-finding as to the essentials of the faith that figure as elements of uniformity and identity is one thing; it will be necessary to have a number of texts that may serve as recognized common elements of reference and thus manifest a certain historical continuity of faith. Apart from Holy Scriptures there will be further common and shared testimonies of faith like the well-known symbols of faith of the ancient Church or the definitions of the ecumenical

15

synods. They represent an element of identity (or 'uniformity'); their interpretative exposition an element of diversity.

More difficult is the integration of confessions of faith or other statements claiming a high degree of authority into the common stock of basic elements of reference if they were set up by a single denomination, possibly with the goal to formulate a denominational identity in strict distinction from another identity. Such is the case with many of the confessions of the sixteenth and seventeenth centuries. Can they be integrated into the complex reality of the one faith in diversity or not?[32] What is their status if they cannot be recognized as an element of diversity within the foundational identity of the faith?[33]

Still another element in strengthening and facilitating the process of recognizing the identity of faith in diversity and of passing it on in a modern context could be a common collection of texts from religious writers from various traditions.

A special and primary form to express the faith is worship, particularly the Eucharist (with the proclamation of the Gospel and the Lord's Supper as focal points, together with other sacramental acts that are deemed relevant for the entering and remaining in the relation with God). It has been stressed over and over again that differences in the liturgy are not Church-dividing. This is a remarkable fact in view of the rule *lex orandi–lex credendi*.[34] It is possibly the result of an isolated understanding of faith as doctrine.

The modern liturgical movement has given many impulses for renewal and has contributed to a deeper understanding of the fundamentally doxological character of the confession of faith and indeed of theological reflection.[35] For our purpose it is important that the ecclesial relevance of the Eucharist as making and expressing the *koinonia* (cf. 1 Cor. 10:16f.) has been recognized in various traditions[36] and has corrected too strong an individualistic understanding of the act of eucharistic communion. The structure (though not the wording) of the eucharistic liturgy is now seen as an important element in the quest for and restoration of identity among the various Christian traditions. Ecumenical *rapprochement* has taken place and thus identity in diversity has to some extent been recovered.

'Mutual recognition of ministry remains the single greatest need to be met on the way to full visible and Eucharistic unity.'[37] Mutual recognition presupposes that there are elements that are comparable and thus possibly identical. As to the theology of the ordained ministry, this is notoriously difficult since strongly divergent views seem to separate what can be termed the 'Catholic' and the 'Protestant' side (e.g. concerning the threefold ministry, form and understanding of ordination, the minister being a representative of Christ,[38] the question of Apostolic Succession and the historic episcopate, etc.).[39] Could it be that it is easier to recognize identities if we look at what is done in the various denominations to ensure that the Gospel is proclaimed, the community built up and its unity preserved? I think we would then see that practically everywhere there are people who have a special respon-sibility for this, a responsibility of some duration and acknowledged by the community. They have an office, in the major denominations conferred by an act of ordination.

There are different forms of the ordained ministry: one type is more or less a continuation of the threefold ministry of the ancient Church (bishops, presbyters/'priests', deacons); other forms were established in the time of the Reformation following biblical data and the particular view of Jerome with regard to the relation of bishop and presbyter.[40] If there are problems of comparability, it might help to discuss their respective responsibilities in the context of an ecclesiological blueprint of the local church and the various levels of supralocal communion up to the universal communion of local churches, even if there is as yet no such reality for a number of traditions.[41] This might facilitate the discovery of *functional* identities as a first step to further investi-gation of identities within the more controversial field of a *theological* understanding of the ordained ministry.

In this respect important preliminary work has been done with the concept of *episkope* with the distinction of its personal, collegial and communal dimensions.[42] I think it could be a help to bring together elements that developed in divergent ways in the different denomi-nations. In the 'Catholic' traditions, the personal dimension has been overstressed to the detriment of the other aspects. In monarchical episcopacy (not to be confused with monepiscopacy, as witnessed to by Ignatius or Cyprian) the relationship between the bishop and the college of priests and other collaborators in the service of Christ has suffered for a long time, and the correlation of local church and bishop as it is presupposed by the eucharistic liturgy of the early Church has often disappeared. In the traditions of the Reformation it is the personal dimension that has found a low profile – for whatever reasons and regardless of the 'non-episcopal' terminology that is being used.[43]

I perceive in the concept of *episkope* a certain analogy to the Old Catholic insistence that epicopacy as the central element of the (three-fold) ordained ministry[44] is necessary for the unity and communion of the Church on the various levels of its extension, but that it needs to be integrated in a synodical network of the local church and the supralocal communion. I hope the debate on *episkope* will be an encouragement that forms of personal *episkope* will be developed and tested by those churches which were not able to do so because of historical circumstances and inherited aversions to (sometimes disfigured) episcopacy.

The exact position of the laity in the synodical network of the local church (and the supralocal communion of local churches) will probably depend on the various cultural situations. Whatever form of participation is considered best, it should reflect the irreducible dignity of the laity by virtue of their initiation into the body of Christ through baptism.[45] The primary responsibility of the bearer of personal *episkope* and the co-responsibility of others should not be destroyed by mechanisms of unqualified majority decisions; possible tensions may enforce a deeper search for consensus on supralocal levels of the communion of churches.

To conclude I address some questions as to the denominational iden-tity in the local and supralocal church. How is it possible to integrate the various denominations into the ecclesial outline of a universally united church in the form of a communion of local churches? In my view this is one of the most difficult questions, as the problems of identity and plurality turn up again with additional force. There is after all such a thing as an ecclesial, i.e. confessional identity which is manifest not only in specific theological positions, but perhaps even more in cultural peculiarities; churchmanship may be further deter-mined by social and ethnic considerations.[46] The constitutive factors of denominational identity leave their traces in the articulation of faith, in worship and piety and in the ethos of exercising the ministry. What

18

is the place of such identities in the worldwide communion of united local churches?

I think we have to distinguish two fundamentally different situations. First, wherever denominations which may exist as supralocal communions do not live in the same 'place', i.e. do not share the same territory, denominational identity can be maintained and lived as a legitimate enriching diversity in the unity of supralocal communion as long as these identities are not considered to be a denial of the universal message of salvation and do not prevent the manifestation of unity on supralocal levels on account of the discerned and confessed identity as representations of the One Church. Local and supralocal loyalty to the confessional identity need not contradict loyalty to the wider communion as a representation of the One Church.[47]

Second, wherever different confessions live in the same 'place' (where the denominations are manifest as local or nation-wide organized churches) – and this is the normal state of affairs in our societies characterized by mobility and migration – we are confronted with the question of how the future 'multidenominational' unity of the Church is to be realized. Are the various denominations like local churches – as some ecumenical statements seem to imply?[48]

If the various denominations living in one 'place' (locality, country or whatever circumscription) are so to speak local churches which recognize each other as a representation of the One Church and as such continue to exist, they would – in my terminology – form a province or a larger unit, but they would not be strictly territorial entities but personal communities organized along denominational affiliation and each having an *episkope* of its own. This is a form of reconciled diversity. But the problem of how to manifest the unity of the Church on the strict local level and the wider extensions of supralocal communion would not be solved. If the old rule holds good that there is only one bishop in each place, i.e. one community comprising all the baptized, a transformation of the denominational churches toward a sort of united church[49] would be the consequence. This corresponds to the model of reunion that has been termed 'organic union'[50] and seen as a final stage in the process of recovering Christian unity.

But how can denominational identity survive in the structured communion of a local church without preventing this *one* communion to come in existence and live? Could 'rites' (cf. the uniate churches in communion with Rome and having their own liturgy and canon law), or could monastic orders serve as a conceptual analogy to denominations? Or do we have to think of non-territorially defined (denominational) communities (*Personalgemeinden*) that together form a territorial local church? But what would be the eucharistic liturgy of this local church, who would be the bearer of (permanent or temporary) personal *episkope*?

How is the balance between loyalty to the local confessional tradition in its supralocal manifestation and the loyalty to the multiconfessional tradition in the local church as a realization of the *Una Sancta* to be found and lived? What about groups of ethnic minorities in diaspora situations who look for their national identity manifest in their confessional church and who want to maintain a close relationship to their country or to the mother church respectively?

If long-term processes of mutual influence take place, will this lead to a loss of enriching diversity in the local church? Or will other identities come into existence that bring to bear unity in diversity of a new kind in a universal context?

Conclusion

Identity, plurality, unity – what's the right blend? I obviously cannot give a comprehensive answer, but had to end with asking questions. I am convinced, however, that it is a good sign that ecclesiology has been resolutely put on the ecumenical agenda, as is shown by recent documents of the Commission on Faith and Order such as *The Nature and Purpose of the Church*. The 'ecclesiological neutrality'[51] advocated in Toronto in 1950 and afterwards has been given up. This should present a challenge to all the churches to come up with their vision of a universal communion of churches visibly manifesting what it is to be a given reality in the mind of God. This vision should have a double perspective: it should be a vision of universal unity irrespective of the denominational division of the Church, and set out for the unit equivalent to what I have called the local church the interplay of being self-relying *and* being under the obligation to be in communion with other entities ('local churches'), thereby trying to determine the elements that must be recognized and shared as identical. It should specify the human agents responsible for the Church to remain true to the Gospel and to manifest its unity at the local and various supralocal levels. Secondly, it should show ways of integrating the denominational churches into this vision. This is a conceptual problem. The discernment of the status of a particular denominational identity, however, is dependent on a mutual bilateral or multilateral assessment.

Notes

1. Here different options in seeing the history of the Church may play a certain role, which ranges between two extremes: the Church offers the picture of a continuous breaking away from the Gospel, a process that may have started already in New Testament times; or, the Church reveals a steady progress that may be discernible in the development of dogma. A question I cannot address is: how much is the concern for a certain historical continuity dependent on a particular denominational perspective? Is it a particular European point of view that is not to be forced on younger churches in the Third or Fourth World or on pentecostal groups? On the other hand, is a straight appeal to the Bible sufficient, if as a consequence the relatively recent history of these churches is directly linked with the 'history' of Israel and the apostolic generation as described in the two Testaments? For the phenomenon of a varying usage of the Bible see the concluding report 'Schriftverständnis und Schriftgebrauch' of the 'Ökumenischer Arbeitskreis evangelischer und katholischer Theologen', in Theodor Schneider and Wolfhart Pannenberg (eds), *Verbindliches Zeugnis*, Vol. III, *Schriftverständnis und Schriftgebrauch* (Dialog der Kirchen 10; Freiburg: Herder/Göttingen: Vandenhoeck, 1988), pp. 288–389, and the contribution by Otto Hermann Pesch, 'Schriftauslegung – kirchliche Lehre Rezeption. Versuch einer Zusammenschau in Thesen', ibid., pp. 261–87.

2. Cf. Jürgen Roloff, *Die Kirche im Neuen Testament* (Grundrisse zum Neuen Testament 10 (Göttingen: Vandenhoeck, 1993), p. 311.

3. Cf. Ernst Käsemann, 'Begründet der neutestamentliche Kanon die Einheit der Kirche?', *Exegetische Versuche und Besinnungen* I (Göttingen: Vandenhoeck, 1960), pp. 214–23; well known is his dictum that denominational divisions have a better foundation in the New Testament canon than the unity of the Church; idem, 'Einheit und Vielfalt in der neutestamentlichen Lehre von der Kirche', *Exegetische Versuche und Besinnungen* II (Göttingen: Vandenhoeck, 1964), pp. 262–7; James D. G. Dunn, *Unity and Diversity in the New Testament. An Inquiry into the Character of Earliest Christianity* (London: SCM Press, 1990); Raymond Brown, *The Churches the Apostles Left Behind* (London: Chapman, 1984). Concerning the phenomenon of 'orthodoxy' we have a similar problem, as Walter Bauer made clear a long time ago, even if he overstated the case.

4. Cf. the list of Kevin Giles, *What on Earth is the Church? An Exploration in New Testament Theology* (Downers Grove, IL: InterVarsity Press, 1995), pp. 182–9. The Christian community is one, the true Israel, the body of Christ, the *ekklesia*: it creates specific communities, it always has leaders and an institutional form. The Christian community as a whole and particular Christian communities are interrelated (e.g. baptism is not repeated when moving from one community to another). It is distinct from the world.

5. Cf. Werner Elert, *Abendmahl und Kirchengemeinschaft in der alten Kirche hauptsächlich des Ostens* (Berlin: Lutherisches Verlagshaus, 1954 [reprint: Fürth 1985]); Joseph Anton Fischer and Adolf Lumpe, *Die Synoden von den Anfängen bis zum Vorabend des Nicaenums* (Konzilien-geschichte Reihe A; Paderborn: Schöningh, 1997); also Hermann Joseph Sieben, *Die Konzilsidee der Alten Kirche* (Konziliengeschichte Reihe B; Paderborn: Schöningh, 1979).

6. Cf. *Baptism, Eucharist and Ministry* (Faith and Order Paper 111; Geneva: WCC, 1982); *Confessing the One Faith. An Ecumenical Explication of the Apostolic Faith as it is Confessed in the Nicene-Constantinopolitan Creed (381)* (Faith and Order Paper 153; Geneva: WCC, 1991); *The Nature and Purpose of the Church. A stage on the way to a common statement* (Faith and Order Paper 181; Geneva: WCC, 1998).

7. Cf. e.g. Harding Meyer, *Ökumenische Zielvorstellungen* (Bensheimer Hefte 78 = Ökumenische Studienhefte 4; Göttingen: Vandenhoeck, 1996), pp. 17–25.

8. Cf. Josef Hainz, *KOINONIA. 'Kirche' als Gemeinschaft bei Paulus* (Biblische Unter-suchungen 16; Regensburg: Pustet, 1982). Today the term is used in an inflationary way.

9. Since Augustine the distinction between true or invisible and visible Church is being made in the context of the discussion of the holiness of the Church – it is a *corpus permixtum*. It became an urgent issue for the Church, which now included the totality of society and so lacked the clear social contrast to the 'world'. I think the stress on the (essential) invisibility of the Church was even intensified in the great schism of the West, where the Church had been seen as a comprehensive *corpus Christianum* – in these circumstances churches not in communion with Rome, i.e. with the majority, could only see themselves as churches when using this conception.

10. Thus both the Dogmatic Constitution on the Church of the Second Vatican Council, *Lumen Gentium*, para. 8. The Decree on Ecumenism, *Unitatis redintegratio*, para. 3, speak of 'separated Churches and Communities'. The expression *vestigia ecclesiae* was an earlier attempt at granting some ecclesiality to other churches.

11. Judgements on the degree of ecclesiality of a particular 'Church' outside the ecclesial communion to which one belongs are very difficult. Does the Holy Spirit, the source of all ecclesiality, stick to our theological assessments? To take an example: baptism is mutually recognized in large areas of Christendom, but not the Eucharist or the ministry. If the Holy Spirit is present and active in the baptisms performed in a particular church, why not also in the eucharistic celebration? Is the mutual recognition of baptism a rash judgement or an act of ecumenical politeness? In other words, if according to the theology of a particular church Christ is being made present in the eucharistic gifts by the Holy Spirit, why should the same Spirit refrain from doing it in another church whose theologians are denying the real presence? (Of course, the argumentation could be reversed.)

12. Cf. e.g. the study commissioned and received by the Joint Working Group between the Roman Catholic Church and the World Council of Churches, *The Church: Local and Universal* (Faith and Order Paper 150; Geneva: WCC, 1990); see also Gillian R. Evans, *The Church and the Churches. Toward an Ecumenical Ecclesiology* (Cambridge: Cambridge University Press, 1994), pp. 18–120.

13. Cf. Yves Congar, 'Quod omnes tangit ab omnibus tractari et approbari debet', *Revue historique de droit français et étranger* 36 (1958), pp. 210–59.

14. 'Participation' is in my view a more appropriate motto than 'democratization of the church'. If the Church is neither a monarchy nor a (hierarchic or clerical) oligarchy, it is still far from being a democracy. The dimension of the *familia Dei*, of brothers and sisters in Christ, requires other metaphors.

15. The historical development of the early 'congregational' to the later 'regional' local church (= diocese) and the concomitant assumption of a priestly, i.e. an episcopal, function of the members of the presbytery when presiding at a Eucharist in local separation from the Eucharist

presided at by the bishop should not be a major obstacle to an ecclesiology that takes the episcopally and synodically ordered local church to be its basic unit.

16. Cf. John Zizioulas, 'Christologie, Pneumatologie und kirchliche Institutionen aus orthodoxer Sicht', in Giuseppe Alberigo *et al.* (eds), *Kirche im Wandel. Eine kritische Zwischenbilanz nach dem Zweiten Vatikanum* (Düsseldorf: Patmos, 1982), pp. 124–40, 132; idem, 'The Local church in a Perspective of Communion', in *Being as Communion. Studies in Personhood and the Church* (Crestwood, NY: St Vladimir's Seminary Press, 1993), pp. 247–60; differently on the one hand Nicolas Afanasieff, *L'Eglise du Saint-Esprit* (Cogitatio Fidei 83; Paris: Cerf, 1975), and on the other Joseph Cardinal Ratzinger, *Kirche, Ökumene und Politik*, quoted in Evans, *Church and the Churches*, pp. 108–17.

17. Historical or other practical reasons may be relevant. The term 'national church' as it is used in Old Catholic perspective is to be defined in strictly geographical or territorial terms as a church – even a minority church – organized within a particular country. It would be highly problematic, to say the least, to see it as the church of the dominant nationality or ethnic population programmatically excluding the baptized of other, 'foreign' groups.

18. Cf. Canon 4–6 of the Council of Nicaea in 325; Canon 9 of the Synod of Antioch 341, Canon 34 of the so-called Apostolic Canons (*Ap Const* VIII 47). Incidentally, the province is autonomous, insofar as the consecration of a bishop by (at least three) neighbouring bishops – the sign of the communion of local churches – is effected within this circumscription.

19. E.g. exarchates, patriarchates, etc.

20. Cf. the Faith and Order study document *The Nature and Purpose of the Church*, discussing 'supralocal links for the eucharistic communities' in paras 107–10, in a section entitled 'Conciliarity and Primacy'. See already 'Authority in the Church I', paras 21–3, and 'Authority in the Church II', paras 9 and 19, in Anglican–Roman Catholic International Commission, *The Final Report* (London: CTS/SPCK, 1982). See also paras 32–50 of the recent study of ARCIC II, *The Gift of Authority. Authority in the Church III* (Toronto: Anglican Book Centre/London: CTS/New York: CPI, 1999).

21. Cf. Yves Congar, 'La "Réception" commé réalité ecclésiologique', in *Eglise et papauté* (Cogitatio Fidei 181; Paris: Cerf, 1994), pp. 229–66.

22. The idea that a synodal decision of representatives of a particular communion of local churches should be submitted to a ratification in the local churches in order to become 'valid' is foreign to the conception of reception.

23. Slightly overstating the case one might say that the Church universal is seen as a world diocese governed by the responsible bishop – the bishop of the Church of Rome (as *caput, fons et origo* of the others – cf. Yves Congar, 'Romanité et catholicité. Histoire de la conjonction changeante de deux dimensions de l'eglise', in *Eglise et papauté*, pp. 31–64), to whom the rest of the bishops are assigned as the college of 'presbyters' who are responsible for their 'parishes' as parts of the world diocese. I wonder if the conception of a college of bishops in modern Roman Catholic communion ecclesiology is in fact an element in an ecclesiology that still has its starting point in the so-called universal Church (which is conceptually not identical with the universal communion of local churches), not in the local church. Cf. Gavin White, 'Collegiality and Conciliarity in the Anglican Communion', in Stephen W. Sykes (ed.), *Authority in the Anglican Communion. Essays presented to Bishop John Howe* (Toronto: Anglican Book Centre, 1987), pp. 202–20.

24. Cf. ARCIC II, *The Gift of Authority*, paras 25 and 62 concerning the phenomenon called 're-reception'. Incidentally, I cannot suppress my exegetical scepticism against the (widespread) conviction that some of the New Testament writings know of such a thing as a Petrine ministry for the unity of the (universal!) Church, a ministry (consequently *iure divino*) that has to be continued by a single responsible person after the death of St Peter. However, recent Old Catholic statements on the role of the papal primacy do speak of such a Petrine ministry.

25. For an account in English see my 'The Old Catholic Churches of the Union of Utrecht', in Paul Avis (ed.), *The Church in Ecumenical Perspective* (London: SPCK, 2000), pp. 157–85.

26. Cf. e.g. the contributions of Nikos A. Nissiotis, John Meyendorff, (Metropolitan) John Zizioulas and Anastasios Kallis; furthermore Jean-M. R. Tillard, *Eglise d'eglises*. *L'ecclésiologie de communion* (Cogitatio Fidei 143; Paris: Cerf, 1987); idem, *L'Eglise locale*. *Ecclésiologie de communion et catholicité* (Cogitatio Fidei 191; Paris: Cerf, 1995); Yves Congar, 'Le Pape, patriarche d'Occident', in *Eglise et Papauté*, pp. 11–30; Jean Rigal, *L'Ecclésiologie de communion*. *Son évolution historique et ses fondements* (Cogitatio Fidei 202; Paris: Cerf, 1997); Edmund Schlink, *Ökumenische Dogmatik*. *Grundzüge* (Göttingen: Vandenhoeck, 1983), especially pp. 537–724; Ferdinand Gahbauer, 'Patriarchalstruktur als Angelpunkt der Wiedervereinigung', in idem (ed.), *Primum Regnum Dei . . . Die Konzilsrede von Abt Johannes Hoeck*, s.l. and s.a. (Ettal, 1987), pp. 37–201; idem, *Die Pentarchietheorie*. *Ein Modell der Kirchenleitung von den Anfängen bis zur Gegenwart* (Frankfurter Theologische Studien 42; Frankfurt a.M.: Knecht, 1993); Terence L. Nichols, *That All May Be One*. *Hierarchy and participation in the Church* (Collegeville, MN: Liturgical Press, 1997).

27. Cf. Michael Kinnamon, *Truth and Community*. *Diversity and its Limits in the Ecumenical Movement* (Grand Rapids, MI: Eerdmans/Geneva: WCC, 1988).

28. Issues such as the correlation of individual belief and 'the Faith of the Church', the privatization of religion and the formation of an '*à la carte*' Christianity must be passed over.

29. Cf. the Pseudo-Augustinian motto: '*In necessariis unitas, in dubiis libertas, in omnibus caritas.*' The necessary distinctions may sometimes refer to faith and discipline (Aug. *Ep*. 54, 2.2; Gregor I, Reg 1, 57,16; differently Damasus of Rome, *Decretum ad Gallos*). Another differentiation concerns *Traditio–traditiones* as elaborated in the Faith and Order Assembly of Montreal in 1963. For the whole subject see Yves Congar, *Diversités et communion*. *Dossier historique et conclusion théologique* (Cogitatio Fidei 112; Paris: Cerf, 1982), pp. 71–80, 155–83.

30. Attempts at establishing essentials of the faith in dialogues of churches with different theological traditions are difficult. It seems that such efforts turn out rather differently according to the dialogue partner. The Anglican–Old Catholic Agreement of Bonn in 1931 states the implication 'that each [communion] believes the other to hold all the essentials of the Christian faith', which is the basis of the mutual recognition of the catholicity (and independence) of the churches involved. But the agreement does not make clear what are 'all the essentials of the Christian faith', and the minutes of the conference show that there were a number of unresolved divergencies; see *Report of the Meeting of the Commission of the Anglican Communion and the Old Catholic Churches Held at Bonn on Thursday, July 2, 1931* (London, s.a.); cf. Harald Rein, *Kirchengemeinschaft*. *Die anglikanisch–altkatholisch–orthodoxen Beziehungen von 1870 bis 1990 und ihre ökumenische Relevanz*. Vol. 1: *Allgemeine Einführung. Die anglikanisch–altkatholischen Beziehungen* (European University Studies XXIII/477; Bern: P. Lang, 1993), pp. 168–351. On the other hand, in the dialogue with the Orthodox the Old Catholics seemed to advocate a rather fuller theological programme already during 1931, and during 1975–87 they went to great lengths in manifesting a common teaching in the classical topics of theology, without, however, saying that all the essentials of the faith are thereby touched upon and fixed. The aim of the dialogue, ecclesial communion, is still distant; cf. Urs von Arx (ed.), *Koinonia auf altkirchlicher Basis*. *Deutsche Gesamtausgabe der gemeinsamen Texte des orthodox–altkatholischen Dialogs 1975–1987 mit französischer und englischer Übersetzung* (Beiheft zu IKZ 79, 1989); idem, *Der orthodox–altkatholische Dialog. Anmerkungen zu einer schwierigen Rezeption* (IKZ 87, 1997), pp. 184–224. In the first case the Old Catholic bishops would have preferred to have something more explicit, whereas in the second it was the Orthodox partner who insisted on common statements covering large areas of dogmatics. Churches that conduct dialogues with even more partners may face even greater problems of knowing what is held to be essential on all sides. In

this situation, the work of the Faith and Order Commission operating on a multilateral level may be of great help.

31. The conception of a hierarchy of truths is not to be confused with the distinction between essentials and non-essentials or *adiaphora*. The first may be a help in discovering the place of a particular theological statement in a conceptual system. If the doctrinal system of one particular church is confronted with other traditions, a new reflection on what is essential may be initiated. This, however, requires the art of leading a true dialogue, i.e. to call into question one's own position, to recognize the foreign in one's own tradition and vice versa, and to thus discover unity in diversity.

32. Cf. e.g. the *Confessio Augustana* as the foundational document of the Lutheran reformation. Another example is taken from the Orthodox–Oriental–Orthodox dialogue: after having discovered and stated the common christological faith, it is now confronted with the difficult problem of whether or not the ecumenical synods later than Chalcedon have to be formally integrated into the (liturgical) tradition of the Oriental–Orthodox Churches.

33. Relevant examples are the papal decrees of Vatican I (confirmed by Vatican II). The often quoted statement of Joseph Cardinal Ratzinger (in 1977), that with respect to the primacy of the Pope Rome is not to ask of the Eastern churches more than what has been said and lived in the first millennium, raises some questions (cf. 'Die ökumenische Situation – Orthodoxie, Katholizismus und Reformation', in Ratzinger, *Theologische Prinzipienlehre. Beiträge zur Funda-mentaltheologie*, Munich: Wewel, 1982, pp. 203–14). Does he assume that the doctrine of primacy as dogmatically defined in 1870 has been a living and acknowledged reality in the first millennium, not only in the primatial claims of Rome since Leo I at the latest, but in a general way in the East? Or does he think that the the papal dogmas of Vatican I should not commit the Eastern churches (and even other non-Roman Catholic Christians in the West?) so that it would be a regional dogma – which surely is no dogma at all?

34. The rule of prayer is the norm of belief according to the initial meaning of the phrase 'legem credendi lex statuat supplicandi'. In the context of the modern liturgical renewal one might prefer to speak of an interrelation between worship and doctrine as a form of faith. Cf. the report of the Ditchingham Consultation in Thomas F. Best and Dagmar Heller (eds), *So We Pray, So We Believe. Towards Koinonia in Worship* (Faith and Order Paper 171; Geneva: WCC, 1995).

35. Cf. Geoffrey Wainwright, *Doxology. The Praise of God in Worship, Doctrine and Life. A Systematic Theology* (London: Epworth, 1980). The relevance of the eucharistic prayers in the ancient Church for the articulation of belief has been brought out by Hans-Joachim Schulz, *Ökumenische Glaubenseinheit aus eucharistischer Überlieferung* (Konfessionskundliche und kontroverstheologische Studien 39; Paderborn: Bonifacius, 1976).

36. Cf. also Paul McPartlan, *The Eucharist Makes the Church. Henri de Lubac and John Zizioulas in Dialogue* (Edinburgh: T&T Clark, 1993).

37. G. R. Evans, *Church and the Churches*, p. 234.

38. Cf. the noteworthy statement of the Leuenberg Fellowship that 'according to the understanding of the Reformation the ordained office rests upon a *particular commission of Christ* and at the same time stands together with the whole congregation in his service under the word of God' (2.5.1.1 – my italics), in *The Church of Jesus Christ. The Contribution of the Reformation towards Ecumenical Dialogue on Church Unity* (Leuenberger Texte 1; Frankfurt a.M.: Lembeck 1995), p. 99. This rules out another understanding, i.e. the ordained ministry is only a commission or delegation on the part of the congregation.

39. One issue seems now to be generally clarified: the historic succession of the (episcopal) ministry is to be seen as an element within the apostolic succession of the whole Church and its faith, not as something beside or above the Church.

40. Cf. Jerome, *Tit.* 1, 5; *Ep.* 146.

41. Again, it would be a great help and also a challenge if those denominations who traditionally have a weak understanding of universal communion put forward such a vision.

42. I confess that when I first came across it I had suspected the term to be a sort of trick to get round the requirements of the historic episcopate. Cf. *Baptism, Eucharist and Ministry* (Faith and Order Paper 111; Geneva: WCC, 1982), para. 26 (without the term *episkope*); *The Nature and Purpose of the Church. A Stage on the Way to a Common Statement* (Faith and Order Paper 181; Geneva: WCC, 1998), paras 89–106. See further Peter C. Bouteneff and Alan D. Falconer (eds), *Episkopé and Episcopacy and the Quest for Visible Unity. Two Consultations* (Faith and Order Paper 183; Geneva: WCC, 1999).

43. Concerning the problem of how the episcopacy of the early Church relates to the ministry advocated by the Reformers – apart from terminological differences – cf. Jean Jacques von Allmen, *Le Saint Ministère selon la conviction et la volonté des réformés du XVIe siècle* (Neuchâtel: Delachaux et Niestlé, 1968), especially pp. 168–91.

44. In presiding at the Eucharist the 'priests' as commissioned collaborators of the bishop assume an episcopal function. It is more difficult to show why the diaconate belongs to the threefold ministry.

45. In modern Old Catholic theology the relationship between the ordained ministry and the laity is often paralleled with the relationship between Christ and the Holy Spirit, implying the same dignity and a mutual interdependence without the difference being effaced.

A particular problem is the fact that the necessary knowledge of tradition as a manifestation of the historical continuity and identity of the Church is very often the exclusive domain of members of the ordained ministry thanks to their theological formation.

46. I should add that a strict distinction between theological and non-theological factors does not always seem possible, indeed that every theologically relevant statement is made in a particular cultural context.

47. It is in this perspective that the reunion of East and West has usually been envisioned. The same can be said of the Full Communion between Anglicans and Old Catholics, although the fully or partial overlapping of jurisdictions in the USA and Europe renders this view somewhat unconvincing. Possibly the relationships of younger churches of the Third and Fourth Worlds to those in other areas of the globe is a further analogy.

48. Cf. e.g. the statement in the report of the 4th General Assembly of the World Council of Churches at Uppsala in 1968 or the 5th General Assembly at Nairobi in 1975, 'The one Church is to be envisioned as a conciliar fellowship of local churches which are themselves truly united', quoted after Günther Gassmann (ed.), *Doc:...entary History of Faith and Order 1963–1993* (Faith and Order Paper 159; Geneva: WCC, 1993), p. 3. Another model is favoured by Oscar Cullmann, *Einheit durch Vielfalt. Grundlegung und Beitrag zur Diskussion über die Möglichkeiten ihrer Verwirklichung* (Tübingen: Mohr, 1990), pp. 28–9, who tries to apply the Pauline view of the baptized as members of the Body of Christ (1 Cor. 12:12–27) to the confessional churches.

49. United churches seem mostly to exist within the Reformed tradition. Do they belong to a specific worldwide fellowship?

50. Cf. Meyer, *Ökumenische Zielvorstellungen*, pp. 88–121, who outlines three models of reunion: corporate federation, mutual recognition and organic union.

51. Lesslie Newbigin, quoted by Kinnamon, *Truth and Community*, p. 78.

2

Anglicans and Roman Catholics: a Joint Declaration of Agreement?

Nicholas Sagovsky

Introduction: a Joint Declaration

From the meeting of Anglican and Roman Catholic Church leaders in May 2000 at Mississauga, Canada,[1] has come a new initiative in the search for visible unity. Pairs of bishops from thirteen countries, led respectively by Cardinal Cassidy, President of the Pontifical Council for Christian Unity, and George Carey, the Archbishop of Canterbury, met to reflect on ways in which they could work more closely together in various parts of the world. The statement from this meeting, *Communion in Mission*, contained the following words:

> We believe that now is the appropriate time for the authorities of our two Communions to recognise and endorse this new stage [of communion in mission] through the signing of a Joint Declaration of Agreement. This Agreement would set out our shared goal of visible unity; an acknowledgement of the consensus in faith that we have reached, and a fresh commitment to share together in common life and witness. Our two Communions would be invited to celebrate this Agreement around the world.[2]

A commission is now to prepare the text of the proposed joint declaration of agreement. What that declaration might contain and how it might carry us forward in the search for visible unity, I intend in this paper to explore.

In speaking of a joint declaration of agreement, the bishops at Mississauga would have been well aware of the remarkable joint declaration on the Doctrine of Justification signed by Lutherans and

Catholics in Augsburg on 31 October 1999.[3] The declaration begins with a preamble enumerating the convergent statements that have preceded this joint declaration, followed by a study of the relevant biblical material. At its centre there is 'A Common Understanding of Justification', expressed in four paragraphs, each of which begins, 'In faith we together hold . . .'. There are then seven further confessional statements, explicated with respect to Lutheran and Catholic tradition. It concludes:

> The understanding of the doctrine of justification set forth in this declaration shows that a consensus in basic truths of the doctrine of justification exists between Lutherans and Catholics. In light of this consensus the remaining differences of language, theological elaboration and emphasis in the under-standing of justification described . . . are acceptable . . . Thus the doctrinal condemnations of the 16th century, in so far as they relate to the doctrine of justification, appear in a new light. The teaching of the Lutheran churches presented in this declaration does not fall under the condemnations from the Council of Trent. The condemnations in the Lutheran confessions do not apply to the teaching of the Roman Catholic Church presented in this declaration.[4]

Since our aim is to offer a preliminary sketch of what a joint Anglican–Roman Catholic declaration of agreement might contain, we may begin by asking to what extent the Roman Catholic–Lutheran joint declaration could act as a model.

Only to a limited extent. It was an advantage for those involved in the Roman Catholic–Lutheran dialogue on justification that their subject was so clearly focused by the targeted confessional state-ments of the Reformation and of the Council of Trent. If the teach-ing of the two traditions on this central doctrinal issue, which for Lutherans is 'the first and chief article' and 'the ruler and judge over all other Christian doctrines',[5] can be no longer regarded as church-dividing, this is a huge step forward towards unity. On the other hand, so much has been said and written on this particular issue that almost any joint declaration is likely to be regarded as in some measure inadequate, and it still remains to be seen to what extent this statement will actually be received by the Lutheran churches[6] and in Rome.

The issues that have divided Anglicans and Roman Catholics have been no less deep than those which divided Lutherans and Roman

Catholics, but whilst justification was a key issue for the English Reformers, there was in England no Luther to focus the broad dispute about authority, the mediation of salvation, the sacraments, and Church–state relations on this one issue. The only specific anti-Anglican condemnation on the part of Rome has been of Anglican Orders (1896),[7] but the Articles of Religion contain specific condemnation of 'The Romish doctrine[8] concerning Purgatory, Pardons, Worshipping and Adoration, as well of Images as of Reliques, and also invocation of Saints' as 'a fond thing vainly invented, and grounded upon no warranty of Scripture, but rather repugnant to the Word of God' (XXII). Similarly, they affirm that 'Transubstantiation (or the change of the substance of Bread and Wine) in the Supper of the Lord, cannot be proved by Holy Writ; but is repugnant to the plain words of Scripture, overthroweth the nature of a Sacrament, and hath given occasion to many superstitions' (XXVIII). They also specify that 'The Bishop of Rome hath no jurisdiction in this realm of England' (XXXVII). Other contradictions of Catholic doctrine in the Articles (such as the affirmation that 'concupiscence and lust hath of itself the nature of sin' (IX)) are made less pointedly. The shape of the problem is thus rather different from that so far confronted in Roman Catholic–Lutheran dialogue. There are indeed mutual condemnations to be addressed, Roman Catholic definitions of doctrine (Papal Infallibility, the Immaculate Conception and bodily Assumption of Mary) which Anglicans do not receive, and Anglican developments (the ordination of women to the priesthood and episcopate), which Roman Catholics reject, but they are not directly related to one central strand on which there have been mutual condemnations. An Anglican–Roman Catholic joint declaration would need to be less focused on justification than the Lutheran–Roman Catholic declaration and, to cover the grounds of explicit communion-breaking division, would have to take in the Eucharist, ministry, authority, justification and the communion of saints, including Mary – topics which (with the exception of justification) the Lutheran dialogue will now have to cover, but in a secondary way. It is to be hoped that by the end of the current round of dialogue, the second Anglican–Roman Catholic International Commission (ARCIC II) will have ensured there are texts to draw on in all these areas.

The 'Deep Structure' of a joint declaration

In two respects the 'deep structure' of any Anglican–Roman Catholic joint declaration is likely to be similar to that between the Roman Catholics and the Lutherans. The first is that it will be supported by a body of texts showing the extent of the consensus between the two communions. It hardly needs saying that Roman Catholics and Anglicans share a common rootedness in the Scriptures, in the authoritative teaching of the first four ecumenical Councils, and in the Western Christian tradition. Beyond this, the texts in *The Final Report* (1982) of ARCIC I demonstrate a convergence in understanding of Eucharist, ministry and authority. Though the Anglican response was to see the statements on eucharist and ministry as 'consonant in substance with the faith of Anglicans',[9] the Roman Catholic response was more guarded:

> The Catholic Church judges . . . that it is not yet possible to state that substantial agreement has been reached on all the questions studied by the Commission. There still remain between Anglicans and Catholics important differences regarding essential matters of Catholic doctrine.[10]

It would be easy, taking this out of context, to read it as wholly negative, but the Commission itself never claimed agreement on *all* the questions studied, and the further work that has been done on Petrine ministry and the exercise of authority in *The Gift of Authority*[11] clearly addresses some of the Vatican concerns. On the Eucharist and ministry, *Clarifications* were produced, after which Cardinal Cassidy wrote, 'The agreement reached on Eucharist and Ministry by ARCIC I is thus greatly strengthened and no further study would seem to be required at this stage.'[12] The Vatican itself expressed the hope that their response would 'contribute to the continued dialogue' by indicating areas where further work needed to be done, as has happened. Though the ARCIC I texts cannot be taken, especially from the Catholic point of view, as an adequate statement of the faith, and though there has been no full official response on either side to the texts of ARCIC II,[13] the official Anglican and Catholic responses to ARCIC I suggest that this whole body of material could confidently be used to draft a joint declaration which would address a number of the communion-dividing issues.

Apart from a common body of agreed texts, building on a common rootedness in the Western Christian tradition, there is another reason why an Anglican–Roman Catholic joint statement would probably be similar in method to that between the Catholics and the Lutherans: the close attention to Scripture. The Catholic–Lutheran statement speaks of a 'common way of listening to the word of God in scripture', showing itself attentive to divergent emphases in different scriptural texts, and to a rich variety of metaphorical language in speaking of salvation. The same could be said of the documents of ARCIC,[14] though here the starting point is often trinitarian rather than immediately Scriptural.

This brings us to one sharp difference of method between the Roman Catholic–Lutheran joint declaration and the ARCIC texts. The ARCIC texts are marked by an increasingly powerful systematic use of the notion of *koinonia* (communion). This is made evident in the introduction to *The Final Report*: 'This theme of *koinonia* runs through our Statements. In them we present the eucharist as the effectual sign of *koinonia*, *episkope* as serving the *koinonia*, and primacy as a visible link and focus of *koinonia*.'[15] The influence of Vatican II (especially the Constitution on the Church, *Lumen Gentium*) may be seen behind this, though it is modified by the context in which it is deployed. As *Church as Communion*[16] shows, the ecclesiology that has inspired the work of ARCIC is an ecclesiology of *communio/koinonia*, which has real similarities with that in *Lumen Gentium*, though it is used more flexibly, and includes no discussion of 'hierarchical communion'.[17] What such an ecclesiology allows for, which is not allowed for in the theological thinking behind either the Decrees of the Council of Trent or the Articles of Religion, is the notion of 'some, though imperfect' communion, which may grow into full communion as impediments to communion between 'separated brethren' are removed.[18] This turn to an 'ecclesiology of communion' is much indebted to renewed patristic study, and to a renewed understanding of the way the Fathers read Scripture. It has enabled ARCIC creatively to go behind specific instances of division to a deeper level of unity.

If it proves possible to move to a joint declaration, the work of ARCIC will surely be seen as a necessary backdrop to such a declaration. It will not be necessary for ARCIC statements to have

31

been accepted in their entirety by both communions for them to be of use, since the aim is to quarry from them the raw material for specific confessional expressions of shared understanding which relativize or 'bracket' the polarized understandings of the past. As discursive, theological texts, the ARCIC statements have undoubtedly prepared the ground for a more sharply focused joint declaration, helping us towards the position where some of the differences that have been seen as communion-dividing begin to be seen as within the range of legitimate diversity.

An Anglican–Roman Catholic joint statement might, I suggest,[19] contain the following elements, though not necessarily in this order. By contrast with the Decrees of the Council of Trent or the Articles of Religion, it would not seek to define truth over against error, but rather, positively to enunciate, as far as possible, communion in truth. It would in this sense represent a reconciling 're-reception'[20] of the tradition which has been handed down to Christians of the West. Such a 're-reception' might cover the following areas:

1. A brief review of what Anglicans and Roman Catholics are known to share in common, concentrating on Scriptures, creeds, and the decisions of the first four ecumenical Councils, all of which bear witness to a common understanding of authority.

2. A common understanding of justification.

3. A common understanding of the Eucharist.

4. A common understanding of ministry, including the ministry of the Bishop of Rome.

5. A common understanding of moral teaching.

6. A common understanding of the communion of saints and of Marian teaching.

Such might be 'building-blocks' in a joint declaration, so I shall now turn to each in turn, trying to show how texts that have been agreed in common might be adapted to serve this new purpose. Since my aim is to offer a preliminary sketch of what an Anglican–Roman Catholic joint declaration might contain overall, what follows will inevitably be something like a collage made up of extracts from ARCIC statements. In trying to frame such a declaration, it is clear that only selected extracts can be used. There would have to be careful discussion of the precise extracts chosen, and the order in which topics are covered. However, it seems to me worth the attempt, precisely to sketch how the next step might be taken in the search for visible unity between the two communions.

A Common Understanding of Authority

ARCIC has devoted more attention to authority than to any other topic. Of the statements on authority,[21] it is the first which is most amenable to adaptation for use in a joint declaration. Paragraph 1 could be adapted to read:

> [1][22] We believe that the confession of Christ as Lord is the heart of the Christian faith. To him God has given all authority in heaven and on earth. As Lord of the Church he bestows the Holy Spirit to create a communion of men and women with God and with one another. To bring this *koinonia* to perfection is God's eternal purpose. The Church exists to serve the fulfilment of this purpose when God will be all in all. (cf. Authority I.1)

Paragraph 2 brings out the place of Scripture:

> [2] The inspired documents of the Old and New Testaments came to be accepted by the Church as a normative record of the authentic foundation of the faith. To these the Church has recourse for the inspiration of its life and mission; to these the Church refers its teaching and practice. Through these written words the authority of the Word of God is conveyed. Entrusted with these documents, the Christian community is enabled by the Holy Spirit to live out the Gospel and so to be led into all truth. (cf. Authority I.2)

We might add some words from the Elucidation to Authority I, quoted in *The Gift of Authority*:

> Since the Scriptures are the uniquely inspired witness to divine revelation, the Church's expression of that revelation must be tested by its consonance with Scripture. (Authority I, Elucidation, 2; cf. *GA* 19)

The authority of the whole body of baptized believers is expressed in the following words from *The Gift of Authority*:

[3] The meaning of the revealed Gospel of God is fully understood only within the Church. God's revelation has been entrusted to a community . . . Believers are together the people of faith because they are incorporated by baptism into a community which receives the canonical Scriptures as the authentic Word of God . . . The faith of the community precedes the faith of the individual . . . Word of God and Church of God cannot be put asunder. (*GA* 23)

Authority I moves from the authority of the whole body of believers to the authority of bishops within the body:

[4] The Holy Spirit . . . gives to some individuals and communities special gifts for the benefit of the Church . . . Among these gifts of the Spirit for the edification of the Church is the *episcope* of the ordained ministry. There are some whom the Holy Spirit commissions through ordination for service to the whole community. They exercise their authority in fulfilling ministerial functions related to 'the apostles' teaching and fellowship, to the breaking of bread and the prayers' (Acts 2:42). This pastoral authority belongs primarily to the bishop, who is responsible for preserving and promoting the integrity of the *koinonia* in order to further the Church's response to the Lordship of Christ and its commitment to mission. (Authority I.5)

In *The Gift of Authority* there is a substantial account of Apostolic tradition,[23] which enables the collegiality of the bishops to be expressed in the following way:

[5] The duty of maintaining the Church in the truth is one of the essential functions of the episcopal college. It has the power to exercise this ministry because it is bound in succession to the apostles, who were the body authorised and sent by Christ to preach the Gospel to all the nations. The authenticity of the teaching of individual bishops is evident when this teaching is in solidarity with that of the whole episcopal college. The exercise of this teaching authority requires that what it teaches be faithful to Holy Scripture and consistent with apostolic Tradition. (*GA* 44)

The role of councils is made clear in Authority I:

[6] Ever since the Council of Jerusalem (Acts 15) the churches have realised the need to express and strengthen the *koinonia* by coming together to discuss matters of mutual concern and to meet contemporary challenges. Such gatherings may be either regional or worldwide. Through such meetings the Church, determined to be obedient to Christ and faithful to its vocation, formulates its rule of faith and orders its life. In all these councils, whether of bishops only, or of bishops, clergy, and laity, decisions are authoritative when they express the common faith and mind of the Church. The decisions of what has traditionally been called an 'ecumenical council' are binding upon the whole Church; those of a regional council or synod bind only the churches it represents. Such decrees are to be received by the local churches as expressing the mind of the Church. (Authority I.9)

The *Gift of Authority* speaks of the circumstances in which the authoritative decisions of councils are preserved from error:

[7] In its continuing life, the Church seeks and receives the guidance from the Holy Spirit that keeps its teaching faithful to apostolic Tradition. Within the whole body, the college of bishops is to ... discern and give teaching which may be trusted because it expresses the truth of God surely. In some situations, there will be an urgent need to test new formulations of faith. In specific circumstances, those with this ministry of oversight (*episcope*), assisted by the Holy Spirit, may together come to a judgement which, being faithful to Scripture and consistent with apostolic Tradition, is preserved from error. (*GA* 42)

It is because both communions see these conditions fulfilled in the decrees of the first four ecumenical councils that they accept them as authoritative.

A joint declaration cannot give a full ecclesiology. What it includes should be enough to act as a basis for subsequent clauses, duly acknowledging the omission of key points – such as the place of the laity, and the implications of this for *synodality* – which have not been the subject of explicit division, though there is divergence of practice (as *GA* shows). There are other key points, such as the relation between the local and the 'universal' church, on which, though they continue to be discussed within and between the communions, ARCIC has said nothing because they have not been explicitly communion-dividing. A selection of quotations, adapted from the statements on authority, such as the one offered here, would be enough to sketch a common ecclesiology – which could be filled out by reference to the full ARCIC statements. Clearly, the order and manner in which interweaving topics are handled is important, so a move to the topic of justification would be only one possible way forward.

A Common Understanding of Justification

The central affirmation in the Lutheran–Roman Catholic joint declaration, 'A common understanding of justification' may well be of help here, as it contains nothing with which Anglicans would want to disagree. There is much to be said for ensuring consistency between ecumenical statements, so it would be well worth considering borrowing from the joint declaration. There might well be useful material in the seven sections where this common understanding is explicated with reference to the complementary but differing emphases of Catholics and Lutherans: human powerlessness and sin in relation to justification; justification as forgiveness of sins and making righteous; justification by faith and through grace; the justified as sinnner(s); law and gospel; assurance of salvation; and the good works of the justified. The ARCIC statement on *Salvation and the Church*[24] covers the same areas, but more briefly. It has sections on Salvation and Faith (dealing with assurance); Salvation and Justification (dealing with the problem of imputed and imparted righteousness); Salvation and Good Works and the Church and Salvation. One of the areas covered by the Roman Catholic–Lutheran statement (complete human dependence on the grace of God for salvation) is picked out early as an area of general agreement:

> [8] It is agreed that the act of God in bringing salvation to the human race and summoning individuals into a community to serve him is due solely to the mercy and grace of God, mediated and manifested through Jesus Christ in his ministry, atoning death and rising again. (cf. *SC* 3)

To this, we might add selected sentences from the sections that follow. On the initiative of God's grace, and the human response of faith:

> [9] When we confess that Jesus Christ is Lord, we praise and glorify God the Father, whose purpose for creation and salvation is realised in the Son, whom he sent to redeem us and to prepare a people for himself by the indwelling of the Holy Spirit. This wholly unmerited love of God for his creatures is expressed in the language of grace, which embraces not only the once for all death and resurrection of Christ, but also God's continuing work on our behalf. . . . The human response to God's initiative is itself a gift of grace, and is at the same time a truly human, personal response. It is through grace that God's new creation is realised. Salvation is the gift of grace; it is by faith that it is appropriated. (*SC* 9)

On the response of faith and the assurance of salvation:

> [10] It is God's gracious will that we, as his children, called through the Gospel and sharing in the means of grace, should be confident that the gift of eternal life is assured to each of us. Our response to this gift must come from our whole being. . . . Living faith is inseparable from love, issues in good works, and grows deeper in the course of a life of holiness. Christian assurance does not in any way remove from Christians the responsibility of working out their salvation with fear and trembling. (*SC* 10)

On justification and salvation:

[11] The term justification speaks of a divine declaration of acquittal, of the love of God manifested to an alienated and lost humanity prior to any entitlement on our part. Through the life, death and resurrection of Christ, God declares that we are forgiven, accepted and reconciled to him. Instead of our own strivings to make ourselves acceptable to God, Christ's perfect righteousness is reckoned to our account. . . . God's declaration of forgiveness and reconciliation does not leave repentant sinners unchanged but establishes with them an intimate and personal relationship. The remission of sins is accompanied by a present renewal, the rebirth to newness of life. (SC 18)

On justification and good works:

[12] The works of the righteous performed in Christian freedom and in the love of God which the Holy Spirit gives us are the object of God's commendation and receive his reward (Matt. 6:4; 2 Tim. 4:8; Heb. 10:35, 11:6). In accordance with God's promise, those who have responded to the grace of God and consequently borne fruit for the Kingdom will be granted a place in that Kingdom when it comes at Christ's appearing. They will be one with the society of the redeemed in rejoicing in the vision of God. This reward is a gift depending wholly on divine grace. It is in this perspective that the language of 'merit' must be understood, so that we can say with Augustine: 'When God crowns our merits it is his own gifts that he crowns' (Ep. 194.5.19). Christians rest their confidence for salvation on the power, mercy and loving-kindness of God and pray that the good work which God has begun he will in grace complete. (SC 23)

A Common Understanding of the Eucharist

The problem about what to include and what to leave out in any joint declaration is particularly acute with the Eucharist. The 1971 statement on eucharistic doctrine turns on the use of *anamnesis* (living memorial) as a reconciling term, but not on the eucharistic ecclesiology which becomes increasingly prominent in later statements. In *The Gift of Authority* (1999) it is especially clear that the eucharistic theme, developed through a strong account of the life of the local church, is integral to the account of the workings of authority at every level, including the ministry of the Bishop of Rome. The drafters of a joint declaration will have to decide how much of this should be made explicit. I have chosen some sentences from *The Gift of Authority* which sketch the local church as a eucharistic community, because this is essential to the understanding of synodality on which the later account of the teaching ministry of the Bishop of Rome is predicated:

> [13] The local church is a eucharistic community. At the centre of its life is the celebration of the Holy Eucharist in which all believers hear and receive God's 'Yes' in Christ to them. In the Great Thanksgiving, when the memorial of God's gift in the saving work of Christ crucified and risen is celebrated, the community is at one with all Christians of all the churches who, since the beginning and until the end, pronounce humanity's 'Amen' to God – the 'Amen' which the Apocalypse affirms is at the heart of the great liturgy of heaven (cf. Rev. 5:14; 7:12). (*GA* 13)

This might be the place to quote from the ARCIC I statement on Eucharistic Doctrine (5) on 'Christ's redeeming death' as taking place 'once and for all in history' and as 'the one, perfect and sufficient sacrifice for the sins of the whole world'. However, a more telling statement of agreement uses new language to reach into the area of eucharistic memorial and eucharistic sacrifice, which was integral to the argument against the recognition of Anglican Orders:[25]

> [14] The eucharistic memorial is no mere calling to mind of a past event or of its significance, but the Church's effectual proclamation of God's mighty acts. Christ instituted the eucharist as a memorial (*anamnesis*) of the totality of God's reconciling action in him. In the eucharistic prayer the church continues to make a perpetual memorial of Christ's death, and his members, united with God and one another, give thanks for all his mercies, entreat the benefits of his passion on behalf of the whole Church, participate in these benefits and enter into the movement of his self-offering. (Eucharistic Doctrine 5)[26]

On eucharistic presence, some words in the original statement, together with the Elucidation (1979), could be helpfully adapted to read:

> [15] (In the Eucharist,) the bread and wine become the body and blood of Christ by the action of the Holy Spirit . . . What is here affirmed is a sacramental presence in which God uses realities of this world to convey the realities of the new creation: bread for this life becomes the bread of eternal life. Before the eucharistic prayer, to the question, 'What is that?', the believer answers: 'It is bread.' After the eucharistic prayer, to the same question he answers: 'It is truly the Body of Christ, the Bread of Life.' (Eucharistic Doctrine 10, Elucidation 6)

At this point we should note the footnote in the statement on eucharistic doctrine, which specifically refers to transubstantiation:

The word *transubstantiation* is commonly used in the Roman Catholic Church to indicate that God acting in the Eucharist effects a change in the inner reality of the elements. The term should be seen as affirming the *fact* of Christ's presence and of the mysterious and radical change which takes place. In contemporary Roman Catholic theology, it is not understood as explaining *how* the change takes place.[27]

The implication of this for the wording of a joint declaration is that a shift away from an understanding of the '*how*' of Christ's presence in the eucharistic elements (or from an interpretation of 'transubstantiation' with this emphasis) towards an emphasis on the *fact* or givenness of Christ's presence suggests that the condemnation of Article XXVIII would no longer apply. The understanding of transubstantiation in 'contemporary Roman Catholic theology' would not 'overthrow' the nature of a sacrament and would not be contrary to 'the plain words of scripture'. There is doubtless more work to be done here (as the Elucidation hints in a short paragraph on 'Gift and Reception'), but this is one of those hopeful points at which a Reformation condemnation might now be judged no longer applicable.

There is a helpful paragraph in the Elucidation which addresses the question of eucharistic reservation:

[16] The whole eucharistic action is a continuous movement in which Christ offers himself in his sacramental body and blood to his people and in which they receive him in faith and thanksgiving. Consequently communion administered from the reserved sacrament to those unable to attend the eucharistic celebration is rightly understood as an extension of that celebration. Differences arise between those who would practise reservation for this reason only, and those who would also regard it as a means of eucharistic devotion. For the latter, adoration of Christ in the reserved sacrament should be regarded as an extension of eucharistic worship, even though it does not include immediate sacramental reception, which remains the primary purpose of reservation . . . Any dissociation of such devotion from this primary purpose, which is communion in Christ of all his members, is a distortion in eucharistic practice. (Eucharistic Doctrine, Elucidation 8)

It is clear that the Roman Catholic Church has commended the devotional use of the reserved sacrament, but the terms in which it has done so need to be studied carefully. For instance, *Eucharisticum Mysterium* (1967), in discussing adoration of Christ in the reserved sacrament, says, 'The mystery of the Eucharist should therefore be considered in all its fullness, not only in the celebration of Mass but also in devotion to the sacred species which remain after Mass and are reserved to extend the grace of the sacrifice.'[28] It seems clear that teaching of this kind is not addressed by Article XXVIII: 'The Sacrament of the Lord's Supper was not by Christ's ordinance reserved, carried about, lifted up, or worshipped.' Interpreted strictly, the Article is non-controversial: eucharistic reservation is palpably not a practice 'ordained by Christ'. Going behind it to the contemporary practices it sought to proscribe, we may doubt its applicability in the wholly different contemporary context, as sketched in the ARCIC corpus, where it is strikingly clear that there is no question of *worship* for 'the *Sacrament* of the Lord's Supper'. This is another area where it can be claimed that former condemnations do not apply, that Roman Catholic practice and the divergent practice that exists within Anglicanism (to which the *Clarifications*[29] also draw attention) fall within the range of permissible diversity.

A Common Understanding of Ministry, including the Ministry of the Bishop of Rome

The second agreed statement of ARCIC I addressed the question of ministry in the Church. Words from that statement can be adapted to read:

[17] The Christian community exists to give glory to God through the fulfilment of the Father's purpose. All Christians are called to serve this purpose by their life of prayer and surrender to divine grace, and by their careful attention to the needs of all human beings. They should witness to God's compassion for all mankind and his concern for justice in the affairs of humanity. They should offer themselves to God in praise and worship and devote their energies to bringing men and women into the fellowship of Christ's people, and so under his rule of love. The goal of the ordained ministry is to serve this priesthood of all the faithful ... This ministry assumes various patterns to meet the varying needs of those whom the Church is seeking to serve, and it is the role of the minister to coordinate the activities of the Church's fellowship and to promote what is necessary and useful for the Church's life and mission. The minister is to discern what is of the Spirit in the diversity of the Church's life and promote its unity. (Ministry and Ordination 7)

[18] An essential element in the ordained ministry is its responsibility for 'oversight' (*episcope*). This responsibility involves fidelity to the apostolic faith, its embodiment in the life of the Church today, and its transmission to the

Church of tomorrow. Presbyters are joined with the bishop in his oversight of the church and in the ministry of the word and the sacraments; they are given authority to preside at the eucharist and to pronounce absolution. Deacons, although not so empowered, are associated with bishops and presbyters in the ministry of word and sacrament, and assist in oversight. (Ministry and Ordination 9)

A key issue to address is that of eucharistic sacrifice and the priesthood – as we have seen, one of the crucial issues lying behind the condemnation of Anglican Orders in 1896:

[19] The priestly sacrifice of Jesus was unique, as is also his continuing High Priesthood . . . Because the eucharist is the memorial of the sacrifice of Christ, the action of the presiding minister in reciting again the words of Christ at the last supper and distributing to the assembly the holy gifts is seen to stand in a sacramental relation to what Christ did in offering his own sacrifice. So our two traditions commonly use priestly terms in speaking about the ordained ministry. Such language does not imply any negation of the once-for-all sacrifice of Christ by any addition or repetition. There is in the eucharist a memorial (*anamnesis*) of the totality of God's reconciling action in Christ, who through his minister presides at the Lord's Supper and gives himself sacramentally . . . Christian ministers are members of the redeemed community . . . Nevertheless their ministry is not an extension of the common Christian priesthood but belongs to another realm of the gifts of the Spirit. It exists to help the Church to be 'a royal priesthood, a holy nation, God's own people, to declare the wonderful deeds of him who called [them] out of darkness into his marvellous light' (1 Pet. 2:9). (Ministry and Ordination 13)

Both communions affirm the teaching role of bishops and the indefectibility of the Church:

[20] In both our traditions the appeal to Scripture, to the creeds, to the Fathers, and to the definitions of the councils of the early Church is regarded as basic and normative. But the bishops have a special responsibility for promoting truth and discerning error, and the interaction of bishop and people in its exercise is a safeguard of Christian life and fidelity. The teaching of the faith and the ordering of life in the Christian community require a daily exercise of this responsibility; but there is no guarantee that those who have an everyday responsibility will – any more than other members – invariably be free from errors of judgement, will never tolerate abuses, and will never distort the truth. Yet, in Christian hope, we are confident that such failures cannot destroy the Church's ability to proclaim the Gospel and to show forth the Christian life; for we believe that Christ will not desert his Church and that the Holy Spirit will lead it into all truth. That is why the Church, in spite of its failures, can be described as indefectible. (Authority I.18)

41

In *The Gift of Authority*, the move is made from indefectibility, through the collegiality of the bishops and the gathering of the bishops in council, to the possibility of the Church giving 'infallible teaching':[30]

[21] In its continuing life, the Church seeks and receives the guidance from the Holy Spirit that keeps its teaching faithful to apostolic Tradition. Within the whole body, the college of bishops . . . is to discern and give teaching which may be trusted because it expresses the truth of God surely . . . In specific circumstances, those with this ministry of oversight (*episcope*), assisted by the Holy Spirit, may together come to a judgement which, being faithful to Scripture and consistent with apostolic Tradition, is preserved from error. By such a judgement . . . the Church is maintained in the truth so that it may continue to offer its 'Amen' to the glory of God . . . Such infallible teaching is at the service of the Church's indefectibility. (*GA* 42)

From this, it is possible to move to primacy in general, to universal primacy and to the teaching ministry of the Bishop of Rome:

[22] In the course of history the synodality of the Church has been served through conciliar, collegial and primatial authority. Forms of primacy exist in both the Anglican Communion and in the churches in communion with the Bishop of Rome. Primacy fulfils its purpose by helping the churches to listen to one another, to grow in love and unity, and to strive together towards the fullness of Christian life and witness; it respects and promotes Christian freedom and spontaneity; it does not seek uniformity where diversity is legitimate, or centralize administration to the detriment of local churches. (*GA* 45; Authority I.21)

The notion of universal primacy as such is one which both Anglicans and Roman Catholics can readily affirm:[31]

[23] The general pattern of complementary primatial and conciliar aspects of *episcope* serving the *koinonia* of the churches needs to be realized at the universal level. The exigencies of church life call for a specific exercise of *episkope* at the service of the whole Church . . . Historically, the Bishop of Rome has exercised such a mission either for the benefit of the whole Church, as when Leo contributed to the Council of Chalcedon, or for the benefit of a local church, as when Gregory the Great supported Augustine of Canterbury's mission and ordering of the English church. This gift has been welcomed and the ministry of these Bishops of Rome continues to be celebrated liturgically by Anglicans as well as Roman Catholics. (Authority I.23; *GA* 46)

The definition in *Pastor Aeternus* at the First Vatican Council (1870), of the Pope's universal jurisdiction and of the conditions under which the Pope may teach infallibly has been central to the rift between

Anglicans and Roman Catholics since that time.[32] This is why a broad statement of agreement covering these areas (and pointing to 're-reception') is such a positive move. *The Gift of Authority* offers the formulation:

[24] Within his wider ministry, the Bishop of Rome offers a specific ministry concerning the discernment of truth, as an expression of universal primacy . . . Any such definition is pronounced *within* the college of those who exercise *episcope* and not outside that college. Such authoritative teaching is a particular exercise of the calling and responsibility of the body of bishops to teach and affirm the faith. When the faith is articulated in this way, the Bishop of Rome proclaims the faith of the local churches. It is thus the wholly reliable[33] teaching of the whole Church that is operative in the judgement of the universal primate. In solemnly formulating such teaching, the universal primate must discern and declare, with the assured assistance and guidance of the Holy Spirit, in fidelity to Scripture and Tradition, the authentic faith of the whole Church, that is, the faith proclaimed from the beginning . . . It is this faith which the Bishop of Rome in certain circumstances has a duty to discern and make explicit . . . The reception of the primacy of the Bishop of Rome entails the recognition of this specific ministry of the universal primate. (*GA* 47)

Since the universal, ecclesiastical jurisdiction of the Bishop of Rome has been a key problem area between Anglicans and Catholics and Article XXXVII specifically affirms that 'The Bishop of Rome hath no jurisdiction in this Realm of England' (where 'jurisdiction' has a predominantly political connotation), it would be a significant step to include a paragraph which affirms the general need for spiritual jurisdiction (the phrase is Hooker's) appropriate to the level of episcopal responsibility:

[25] Each bishop is entrusted with the pastoral authority needed for the exercise of his *episcope*. This authority is both required and limited by the bishop's task of teaching the faith through the proclamation and explanation of the word of God, of providing for the administration of the sacraments in his diocese and of maintaining his church in holiness and truth. Hence decisions taken by the bishop in performing his task have an authority which the faithful in his diocese have a duty to accept. This authority of the bishop, usually called jurisdiction, involves the responsibility for making and implementing the decisions that are required by his office for the sake of the *koinonia* . . . So too,[34] within the universal *koinonia* and the collegiality of the bishops, the universal primate exercises the jurisdiction necessary for the fulfilment of his functions, the chief of which is to serve the faith and unity of the whole Church. (Authority II.17).

A Common Understanding of
Moral Teaching

The Anglican–Roman Catholic dialogue has been the first among the many international dialogues to produce a statement on morals.[35] It was asked to attend to this area because it has been thought that there can be no restoration of communion unless it is possible to bridge the ostensible gap that divides the two communions in their moral teaching. *Life in Christ, Morals, Communion and the Church*[36] speaks of 'a shared vision of Christian discipleship and a common approach to the moral life'[37] even though specific teaching, as, for example on contraception or remarriage after divorce, may be at variance. The statement develops an account of this shared moral vision in somewhat general terms, and then with reference to specific examples where there is disagreement. The link between catholicity and holiness is made in *Church as Communion*:

> [26] The Church is *holy* because it is 'God's special possession' (1 Pet. 2:9–10), endowed with his Spirit (Eph. 2:21–2), and it is his special possession since it is there that 'the mystery of his will, according to his good pleasure' is realised 'to bring all things in heaven and on earth together under one head, Christ' (Eph. 1:9–10). Being set apart as God's special possession means that the Church is the communion of those who seek to be perfect as their Heavenly Father is perfect (Matt. 5:48). This implies a life in communion with Christ, a life of compassion, love and righteousness. (*Church as Communion* 38)

Life in Christ affirms the importance of natural law for moral teaching and practice in both communions:

> [27] Despite the ambiguities and evils in the world, and despite the sin that has distorted human life, the Church affirms the original goodness of creation and discerns signs and contours of an order that continues to reflect the wisdom and goodness of the Creator . . . Reflection on experience of what makes human beings, singly and together, truly human gives rise to a natural morality, sometimes interpreted in terms of natural justice or natural law, to which a general appeal for guidance can be made. In Jesus Christ this natural morality is not denied. Rather, it is renewed, transfigured and perfected, since Christ is the true and perfect image of God. (*LC* 9)

Rather than specifying moral tenets, *Life in Christ* speaks of a common understanding of how the mind of Christ is formed in the Church:

[28] The fidelity of the Church to the mind of Christ involves a continuing process of listening, learning, reflecting and teaching. In this process every member of the community has a part to play. Each person learns to reflect and act according to conscience. Conscience is informed by, and informs, the tradition and teaching of the community. Learning and teaching are a shared discipline, in which the faithful seek to discover together what obedience to the gospel of grace and the law of love entails amid the moral perplexities of the world. It is this task of discovering the moral implications of the Gospel which calls for continuing discernment, constant repentance and 'renewal of the mind' (Rom. 12:2), so that through discernment and response men and women may become what in Christ they already are. (*LC* 29)

[29] In the tradition common to both our Communions, discerning the mind of Christ is a patient and continuing process of prayer and reflection. At its heart is the turning of the sinner to God, sacramentally enacted in baptism and renewed through participation in the sacramental life of the Church, meditation on the scriptures, and a life of daily discipleship. The process unfolds through the formation of a character, individual and communal, that reflects the likeness of Christ and embodies the virtues of a true humanity (cf. Gal. 5:19–24). At the same time shared values are formulated in terms of principles and rules defining duties and protecting rights. All this finds expression in the common life of the Church as well as in its practical teaching and pastoral care. (*LC* 31)

I do not see that it would be possible to produce a declaration which reconciled radically divergent moral teaching, but at least in this area there are no condemnations to be addressed. It may indeed be that for this reason nothing on morals need be included, but some general paragraphs of the sort I have indicated would make a vital point about shared ideas of Christian moral formation, which, of course, hold out the hope of moral convergence, or, at least, further discrimination as to what may be brought within the bounds of legitimate diversity. There may well be paragraphs which could be written to bring out from the rich resources of Catholic social teaching shared understandings in the field of economic justice, political participation, human rights, human sexuality or the environment, but a joint declaration based on a common text like *Life in Christ* may be sufficient to indicate the strong undergirding consensus, the importance of serious continuing moral debate, and areas where further reconciling work needs to be done.

A Common Understanding of the Communion of Saints and of Marian Teaching

There is little that can be added here. The definition of the two Marian dogmas, the Immaculate Conception (1854) and the bodily Assumption (1950), has changed the situation between Roman Catholics and Anglicans from one of legitimate diversity to one of new communion-dividing issues.[38] It is, paradoxically, easier to find a way through an issue where a position attributed to another communion, usually in a sharply polarized situation, has been condemned than where a position has been defined as *de fide* within one tradition. In *Lumen Gentium*, teaching about Mary was significantly included within a document on the Church. Recent Mariological statements from Rome such as *Redemptoris Mater* ('On the Blessed Virgin Mary in the Life of the Pilgrim Church', 1987) have a clear christological focus. In official teaching there has not been developed a 'Mariology' in isolation from central theological themes, so it is to be hoped that a joint agreed statement could find much common ground, in accord with the ARCIC method, but this study is not yet complete. Since the Articles say so little about Mary, though Article XXII explicitly rejects 'invocation of saints', it is to be hoped that there can be some reconciling statement to show in what sense 'invocation of saints' as proscribed by the Reformers does not accord with current Roman Catholic teaching, which has frequently reiterated the importance of Christ's unique place as mediator between God and humanity.[39] As, however, I have tried to use only agreed texts as the basis for a putative joint declaration, without the ARCIC statement which is currently being prepared we can at this point add nothing specific on Mary and the saints.

Conclusion: Choices to be Made

The Mississauga meeting called for a joint declaration of agreement that will set out 'our shared goal of visible unity; an acknowledgement of the consensus in faith that we have reached, and a fresh commitment to share together in common life and witness'. It may be that what was envisaged was something rather short, and that what is sketched here – to which a restatement of the shared goal, and a commitment to future action would have to be added – is too discursive for the task in hand: the provision of something 'to celebrate around the world'. Those who draft a joint declaration will have to decide whether they want to develop a broad account of the consensus that has been developed by ARCIC, knowing it will serve only partially to indicate where mutual condemnations or divergent teaching can be reconciled, or a more targeted declaration, addressed to certain defined issues which have occasioned reciprocal condemnation, or variance in teaching. My preference for the first is because it will gather together the work of ARCIC and, in so doing, should provide a pointer to further sharply focused dialogue. Such a joint declaration would take the pressure off the authorities in both traditions to analyse in detail what would now be the 'background' ARCIC documents, which is obviously difficult, especially where there is a dissonance of theological method between the approach of ARCIC and any official analysis. A statement such as the one I have sketched could not be a balanced or rounded summary of those things the two communions hold in common, since the work of ARCIC has focused on communion-dividing issues. It would, however, show the depth of the consensus that already exists in those areas where there have been explicit or implicit condemnations. It would gather up the fruits of 30 years' ecumenical work and help to clarify the agenda for the next steps towards visible unity. It would indeed be something 'to celebrate around the world'.

Notes

1. The presence of Jean-Marie Tillard, the one surviving member of ARCIC I still on ARCIC II, as a consultant at the Mississauga meeting was vital to its success. The strength of ARCIC's work as a resource for unity is in large measure due to Jean Tillard's extraordinary contribution. 'Visible unity' was always his focus and his goal.

2. 'Communion in Mission', statement from Mississauga meeting, May 2000, available at *www.anglicancommunion.org/acns/acnsarchive/acns2125/acns2137.html*.

3. A convenient place to find this and other ecumenical texts discussed below is J. Gros, H. Meyer and W. G. Rusch, *Growth in Agreement II, Reports and Agreed Statements of Ecumenical Conversations on a World Level 1982–98* (Geneva: WCC/Grand Rapids, MI: Eerdmans, 2000). For the Lutheran–Roman Catholic joint declaration, see pp. 566–82.

4. Joint declaration 40–41; *Growth in Agreement II*, p. 573.

5. These two phrases are quoted from the Smalcald Articles and from Luther's own writings (WA 39, I, 205) in the Preamble to the Lutheran–Roman Catholic joint declaration, *Growth in Agreement II*, p. 566.

6. A statement of opposition to the signing of the joint declaration attracted 251 signatures from German Lutheran teachers of theology.

7. See C. Hill and E. Yarnold SJ, *Anglican Orders: The Documents in the Debate* (Norwich: Canterbury Press, 1997).

8. This article first (1553) condemned 'the doctrine of the school authors'. 'The Romish doctrine' was substituted in 1563.

9. Lambeth Conference 1988, Resolution 8.1.

10. *The Response of the Holy See to the Final Report of the Anglican–Roman Catholic International Commission, 1982* (London: Catholic Truth Society, 1991).

11. Anglican–Roman Catholic International Commission, *The Gift of Authority* (London: Catholic Truth Society/Toronto: Anglican Book Center/New York: Church Publishing, 1999), hereafter *GA*.

12. Anglican–Roman Catholic International Commission, Pontifical Council for Promoting Christian Unity, *Clarifications of Certain Aspects of the Agreed Statements on Eucharist and Ministry* (London: Church House Publishing/Catholic Truth Society, 1994).

13. The Lambeth Conference 1998 encouraged the referral of *Salvation and the Church* (1987), *Church as Communion* (1991), *Life in Christ* (1994) and the anticipated document on authority in the Church (*The Gift of Authority*, 1999) to the provinces for study and for response at the next Lambeth Conference. See Resolution 4.23(d).

14. An important background influence here, not only for Roman Catholics, but also for their dialogue partners, has been *Dei Verbum*, the Dogmatic Constitution on Divine Revelation from Vatican II, which affirms that 'the books of Scripture, firmly, faithfully and without error, teach that truth which God, for the sake of our salvation, wished to see confided to the sacred Scriptures' (II), but will not allow the mediation of the authority of Scripture to be divorced from sacred tradition: 'Sacred Scripture is the speech of God as it is put down in writing under the breath of the Holy Spirit. And Tradition transmits in its entirety the Word of God which has been entrusted to the apostles by Christ the Lord and the Holy Spirit' (9). The influence of *Dei Verbum* is particularly evident in *GA* 14–23.

15. Anglican–Roman Catholic International Commission, *The Final Report* (London: Catholic Truth Society/SPCK, 1982), p. 6.

16. Anglican–Roman Catholic International Commission, *Church as Communion* (London: Church House Publishing/Catholic Truth Society, 1991).

17. Jean Rigal provides a useful survey in *L'Ecclesiologie de communion* (Paris: Cerf, 1997). For a fine comparison of two forms of the ecclesiology of communion (those of J. Ratzinger and J. Zizioulas), see M. Volf, *After Our Likeness* (Grand Rapids, MI/Cambridge, UK: Eerdmans, 1998).

18. See *Unitatis Redintegratio*, the Decree on Ecumenism from Vatican II, especially para. 3.

19. These are purely personal suggestions, put forward to facilitate discussion of what might be in a Joint Declaration and how it might help the cause of visible unity.

20. The term 're-reception' is taken from Y. Congar, *Diversity and Communion* (London: SCM Press, 1984), pp. 171–2 and used in *GA*. See 'Reception and Re-Reception: the Church's "Amen" to the Word of God', *GA* 24.5.

21. 'Authority in the Church I' is printed, with an Elucidation, followed by 'Authority in the Church II', in *Final Report*. *GA* is subtitled 'Authority in the Church III'.

22. I have numbered the paragraphs of the putative joint declaration to facilitate discussion of it as a continuous text.

23. For the meaning of 'Tradition' and 'tradition', see the footnote in *GA*, p. 16. 'Apostolic Tradition' is defined as 'the content of what has been transmitted from apostolic times and continues to be the foundation of Christian life and theology'.

24. Anglican–Roman Catholic International Commission II, *Salvation and the Church* (London: ACC/Catholic Truth Society, 1987), hereafter *SC*.

25. The judgement of *Apostolicae curae* (1896) that Anglican Orders are 'absolutely null and utterly void' was based in part on the lack of specification in the Edwardine Ordinal (1550, revised 1552) of the order to which the candidate was being admitted (a point corrected in 1662) and on the lack of explicit mention of sacrificial priestly intent. Since the ordinals and the eucharistic liturgies now in use throughout the Anglican Communion have moved so far from the 1552 Prayer Book towards a common recognition of the eucharistic memorial as one of *anamnesis* of Christ's once-for-all sacrifice, this is one area where it could be said that the presupposition for a condemnatory judgement no longer applies. I have discussed these issues in a review of Hill and Yarnold, *Anglican Orders*, in *Journal of Theological Studies* 50 (1999), pp. 413–18. The situation is, of course, made much more sensitive by the ordination of women to the priesthood and the episcopate within the Anglican Communion, but though the Pope has judged in the Apostolic Letter *Ordinatio Sacerdotalis* that 'the Church has no authority whatsoever to confer priestly ordination on women and that this judgment is to be definitively held by all the faithful', this need not preclude the recognition of the authenticity of Anglican Orders as such. On the issue of Anglican Orders, see also para. 19 below.

26. There is a valuable restatement of this position in the Elucidation (1979), *Final Report*, p. 20.

27. *Final Report*, p. 14, n. 2.

28. A. Flannery (ed.), *Vatican Council II, The Conciliar and Post-Conciliar Documents*, (Dublin: Dominican Publications, 1975), p. 104.

29. *Clarifications*, pp. 7–8.

30. For Anglicans, the application of the word 'infallible' to the Church's teaching is not impossible. Richard Hooker (*c*.1554–1600), writing about Scripture, says that 'God himself can neither possibly err, nor lead into error. For this cause his testimonies, whatsoever he affirmeth, are always truth and most infallible certainty' (*Laws of Ecclesiastical Polity* II.vi.1). Hooker does not, however, extend his discussion of 'infallible knowledge' to the conciliar teaching of the Church. However, Richard Field (1561–1616), Hooker's contemporary, has a whole chapter entitled 'Of the different degrees of infallibility found in the Church'. First he gives consideration to 'the Church, as it comprehendeth the whole number of believers that are and have been since Christ appeared in the flesh', which is 'absolutely free from all error and ignorance of divine things that are to be known by revelation'. Then he considers the more limited, synchronic picture: 'Touching the Church, as it comprehendeth only the believers that now are, and presently live in the world, it is most certain and agreed upon, that in things necessary to be known and believed expressly and distinctly, it never is ignorant, much less doth err' (*Of the Church*, Book IV, chapter 2, Cambridge, 1849, Vol. 2, pp. 392–6). John Pearson (1612–86), whose exposition of the Creed was compulsory reading for generations of Anglican divinity students, follows Hooker closely: 'It is not imaginable that [God] should intend to deceive any man, and consequently whatsoever he hath delivered for a truth must be necessarily and infallibly true; I readily and steadfastly assent unto them as most certain truths' (*An Exposition of the Creed*, London, 1822, p. 36). William Laud (1573–1645) discusses the infallibility in the Church in *A Relation of the Conference between William Laud and Mr Fisher the Jesuit* (Oxford: Oxford University Press, 1839). In considering the scriptural texts on which the claims to the infallibility of General Councils have been based,

he concludes: 'Suppose these places, or any other, did promise assistance, even to infallibility, yet they granted it not to every general council, but to the catholic body of the church itself; and if it be in the whole church principally, then it is in a general council but by consequence, as the council represents the whole' (p. 200). In the following generation, William Payne (1650–96) was also content to speak of the infallibility of the Church, provided that the authenticity of the church in question was securely demonstrated: 'For it cannot be pretended that Infallibility belongs to any but the true Church, and therefore it must be first known that the present Church agrees with the Primitive, before it can be known that she is an Infallible Guide or Teacher' (*The Notes of the Church as Laid Down by Cardinal Bellarmin Examined and Confuted*, London, 1687, p. 114).

31. It is at this point that the shared approach to universal primacy of Anglicans and Roman Catholics shows itself distinctly Western. The Orthodox would challenge the assertion that there needs to be *episcope* at the universal level. *GA*, however, speaks of a 're-reception' of the exercise of primacy by the Bishop of Rome, 'exercised collegially in the context of synodality', by both Anglicans and Roman Catholics (52, 62). This comes close to the discussion of primacy with specific reference to canon 34 of the 'Apostolic Canons' by Zizioulas and other Orthodox theologians. Zizioulas has written: 'The importance of this model lies in the fact that, through it, synodality and primacy are affirmed in such a way that the fullness and catholicity of each local church, expressed through its bishop, is fully safeguarded . . . Can there be unity of the church without primacy on the local, the regional and the universal level in an ecclesiology of communion? We believe not. For it is through a "head", some kind of "primus" that the "many" . . . can speak with one voice. But a "primus" must be part of a community; not a self-defined, but a truly relational ministry.' ('The Church as Communion', in T. F. Best and G. Gassmann (eds), *On the Way to Fuller Koinonia*, Official Report of the Fifth World Conference on Faith and Order (Geneva: WCC, 1994), p. 108.) One creative way of developing this thinking would be to re-examine the role of the Pope as Patriarch of the West.

32. Writing of re-reception, Congar specifically suggests: 'The primacy that Roman Catholics would require Orthodox and Protestants to recognize would no longer be that of Gregory VII, Boniface VIII and Pius IX which they would find impossible' (*Diversity and Communion*, p. 172). John Paul II himself discusses the exercise of the primacy very openly in *Ut Unum Sint* (1995), asking for a 'patient and fraternal dialogue' with church leaders on the basis of the 'real but imperfect communion' that exists between them. An excellent collection of essays which takes up this invitation is J. F. Puglisi, *Petrine Ministry and the Unity of the Church* (Collegeville, MN: Liturgical Press, 1999).

33. This may be taken as a translation of the Greek term *asphales* (cf. Luke 1:4; Acts 2:36; Heb. 6:19), where the emphasis falls on 'absolute trustworthiness' rather than the easily mis-understood 'inerrancy'.

34. This is a key statement for Anglicans, because it affirms that implicit within the notion of a universal primacy is the recognition of appropriate jurisdiction (with appropriate safeguards). We may compare *The Virginia Report* of the Inter-Anglican Theological and Doctrinal Commission: 'Indeed there is a question as to whether effective communion, at all levels, does not require appropriate instruments, with due safeguards, not only for legislation, but also for oversight. Is not universal authority a necessary corollary of universal communion?' *The Official Report of the Lambeth Conference*, 1998 (Harrisburg, PA: Morehouse, 1999), p. 54. This principle is practised within Anglicanism at diocesan and provincial levels, but currently debated with respect to the role of the Primates as a body and the Archbishop of Canterbury within the Anglican Communion.

35. We might note the suggestion in *Unitatis Redintegratio* (23) that 'the ecumenical dialogue could start with the moral application of the Gospel'. Since public perception of divergences in moral teaching between Christians of different traditions (e.g. over contraception, abortion,

understandings of social justice, pacificism, suicide, divorce and euthanasia) is often one of mutual disagreement rather than of shared moral vision, this is an area where further exploration and clarification is urgent.

36. *Life in Christ, Morals, Communion and the Church* (London: Church House Publishing/ Catholic Truth Society, 1994).

37. Ibid., p. 86.

38. With specific reference to the Marian dogmas of 1854 and 1950, Congar writes, 'Numerous Catholic ecumenists think that one cannot impose dogmas defined without the participation of others and without any root in their tradition as a *sine qua non* for communion' (*Diversity and Communion*, p. 174).

39. See, for example, *Lumen Gentium* 60: 'Mary's function as mother of men [*sic*] in no way obscures or diminishes this unique mediatorship of Christ, but rather shows its power.'

3

Methodists and the Ecumenical Task

David Carter

Methodism has played a prominent part in the modern Ecumenical Movement at all levels. As early as the 1890s the dynamic and innovative Wesleyan leader, Hugh Price Hughes (1847–1902) played a key role in the setting up of the Free Church Federal Council and a prominent one in the work of the Grindelwald Conferences (1891–96), which represented the first serious, though totally unofficial, attempt at *rapprochement* across the Anglican–Free Church divide. Subsequently, British Methodism produced a series of outstanding ecumenical statesmen and theologians. John Scott Lidgett established close contacts with Archbishop Davidson. R. N. Flew played a prominent role in the Faith and Order Conferences of 1937 and 1952. Pauline Webb was one of the first women to play a key ecumenical role, particularly in the context of the World Council of Churches. Today, Geoffrey Wainwright is one of the select band of internationally renowned ecumenical theologians.[1]

On the other side of the Atlantic, John R. Mott played a key role in the early history of the Ecumenical Movement, whilst, since the late 1960s, the United Methodist Church, along with three smaller sister Methodist churches, has played a key role in the Consultation on Church Union. In Canada, Australia and Zambia, Methodism has entered into union with churches in the Reformed tradition, and in the Indian subcontinent with both Anglicans and Reformed.

British Methodism was the one Free church to respond positively to Archbishop Fisher's famous sermon of 1946 by initiating conversations on unity. The Methodist Conference subsequently voted in 1969 and 1972 to accept the scheme for Anglican–Methodist unity that emerged from these conversations. In 1982 it also approved the scheme for a 'Covenant' with the Anglican, United Reformed and Moravian churches which would have established full communion between all four churches concerned. Despite the disappointment caused when these schemes successively failed, by narrow margins, to gain the requisite Anglican synodical vote, Methodism has continued to seek wider unity, and, in 1994, after the ordination of the first women priests in the Church of England, Methodists again proposed talks on closer relationships. These talks issued in *An Anglican–Methodist Covenant* (2001). They recommend steps towards closer cooperation without, however, providing for full reconciliation of ministries or organic unity. Meanwhile, the conference of 2001 reaffirmed its commitment to visible unity and the widest possible ecumenical cooperation.

At the local level, hundreds of Methodist churches are involved in Local Ecumenical Partnerships (LEPs), primarily but not exclusively in-volving Anglicans and Reformed. The last 30 years have also seen the development of many joint URC–Methodist churches.

Finally, mention must be made of the fruitful dialogues in which the World Methodist Council has been involved with other traditions. These dialogues have signally failed to attract the attention that they should, both within Methodism and in other churches. The dialogue with the Lutherans reached the conclusion that nothing need stand in the way of altar and pulpit fellowship between the two communions, and a whole series of such agreements has since been concluded between Methodist and Lutheran churches in particular countries.[2] The dialogue with the Anglicans, issuing in the 1996 report, *Sharing in the Apostolic Communion*, has commended mutual recognition and movement towards a commonly accepted ministry.[3] However, this was not given quite the acclamation for which some hoped at the Lambeth Conference of 1998, though it is clear that Anglican–Methodist relationships are becoming closer, perhaps especially in South Africa and Britain. In the latter, it has been progress in Wales, Ireland and, above all, Scotland, that has been particularly noteworthy. A preliminary

serious exploration and reappropriation of the eucharistic tradition of the Wesley brothers began, the reception of which is still incomplete.[9] The responses of those Methodist churches which responded to the *Baptism, Eucharist, Ministry* document of 1982 (also known as the Lima document) are instructive. The most positive response was that of the United Methodist Church, USA, which acknowledged that in eucharistic faith and practice, it needed to recover the fullness of both Patristic and Wesleyan tradition. Somewhat more varied, and rather defensive of its existing practice, was the British response. The responses of the continental European Methodist churches were much more critical, particularly of anything that seamed to them to veer in too 'catholic' a direction.[10] These last are smallish churches, without the self-confidence of either the American or British connexions. They have also preserved much of the pietistic and evangelical distrust of sacramentalism that was once also so widespread in British and US Methodism.

Methodism, once so strongly 'evangelical' on both sides of the Atlantic in the nineteenth century, has since been widely affected by Liberal Protestantism. The splits and schisms of nineteenth-century Methodism have affected Methodist ecumenical attitudes and preferences for the choice of ecumenical partners.[11] The largest British Methodist body, the Wesleyan Methodist Church, always retained a degree of regard for the 'Old Church' as it called the Church of England. The Anglican order of Holy Communion was used and, in some places, the Order of Morning Prayer. The rise of the Oxford Movement and its dismissive attitude to Methodism turned many Wesleyans against the Church of England, but desire for a renewed relationship with the Church of England, at least when it could be achieved on a basis of equality and mutual respect, was never completely lost. The smaller Methodist groups, such as the Primitive Methodists, developed in a context that was, varyingly, both anti-Anglican and anti-Wesleyan. There was none of the lingering Wesleyan respect for the 'Old Church', nor any retention of Anglican liturgy.

To this day, it would be true to say that some British Methodists regard the Church of England as the obvious major ecumenical partner with which they should seek closer relations. Others would be much happier to see a closer relationship with the other Free churches. The official Methodist position is one of commitment to unity with all Christ's people,[12] but it is clear that Methodists do not share the same views on how far they should go in seeking unity and with which partners. Though Methodism voted for the Anglican–Methodist scheme of 1969–72, and for the Covenant, there was some strong opposition on both occasions, principally from those opposed to historic episcopacy or any suggestion that Methodist ministers might need to be reordained, conditionally or otherwise. Some of it reflected old social as well as theological divisions which, in the 1960s, died hard, particularly in Cornwall and parts of the North. It is clear, from contemporary discussion and comment arising out of the covenant proposals, that though most British Methodists favour more cooperation with Anglicans, some, for a variety of reasons, are still opposed to any unity scheme involving episcopacy.[13] Many Methodists still lack any understanding of the gifts ecumenical partners wish to share with them; puzzlement, as opposed to downright opposition *per se*, is sometimes a Methodist response to URC urging of the value of 'eldership' or Anglican commendations of episcopacy.

Despite these nuanced reservations about empirical Methodist attitudes to the unity of the Church, it can plausibly be argued that Methodism is inherently ecumenical in ethos and orientation. A continuous strand of commitment to the unity of the Church can be traced even through the nineteenth century, in other respects so much a century of competition between churches rather than one of a search for unity. Two Methodist theologians stand out pre-eminently within this tradition: William James Shrewsbury (1785–1866) and Benjamin Gregory (1820–1900).[14] The former was remarkable for his irenicism of attitude towards Anglicanism and Dissent, and this at a time when Wesleyan Methodism was frequently assailed by both. Shrewsbury reproved Methodists who did not understand and affirm the leading role within English Christianity of the Church of England. He called upon Methodists to contribute to the missions and charitable works of the other churches as well as their own. He argued that 'disinterestedness' was the key Wesleyan virtue, by which he meant a willingness to rejoice in the gifts and successes of sister churches; he warned against believing that any good could come from criticism of others and said each church should look always to put its own house in order.

Shrewsbury was aware of the richness of the Wesleyan inheritance. He commented on the debt owed by the Wesley brothers to their High Anglican parents and Puritan grandparents. He stressed their debt to the Lutherans and Moravians. 'The Methodists', said Shrewsbury in 1840, 'are the debtors of all.'[15]

Modern Wesley scholarship has made informed Methodists even more aware of this debt, including that (not recognized by Shrewsbury) to the Eastern Fathers and to Counter-Reformation spiritual writers. Benjamin Gregory, the one great ecclesiologist produced in nineteenth-century Methodism, linked the search for unity to the search for holiness, asserting that 'he who despairs of the unity of the Church despairs of its holiness'.[16] In 1964 Rex Kissack picked up this point, arguing that the search for visible unity within time, as opposed to waiting for it as a purely eschatological gift, was a necessary ecclesiological consequence of the doctrine of Christian Perfection.[17]

John Wesley certainly had no desire to do other than preach 'plain scriptural Christianity' and revive the Church of England, much as some of his actions, particularly towards the end of his ministry, pointed towards schism. His famous sermon 'On the Catholic Spirit' is still a classical Methodist text, though it establishes a basis from which a form of spiritual ecumenism can develop rather than commending ecumenism in the commonly understood twentieth-century sense. In it, Wesley maintains a fine balance between generously recognizing the true Christianity of those in other traditions and deprecating any indifferentism which holds that differences do not matter. Wesley was clear that people should hold to their convictions in such matters as forms of church order and worship, since, though secondary to the core of faith, they were still significant. They should not, however, let these obscure their recognition of each others' common discipleship of the one Christ.[18]

The split between Anglicanism and Methodism on both sides of the Atlantic related not to doctrine, or even to principles of church order *per se*, but to missionary strategy. Wesley continued to believe that the order and liturgy of the Church of England were the most scriptural in Christendom. Indeed, he effectively exported them to the Americas, by providing in 1784 a version of the *Book of Common Prayer* and, with his ordination of Coke, the threefold ministry for the

Americans.[19] The fact that Methodism is *not* committed to a theory of ministry that makes it impossible, or at least very difficult, to adopt episcopacy, should be noted.

In 1820 the Liverpool Conference issued a key statement on its attitude to other Christian denominations:

> Let us ourselves remember, and endeavour to impress on our people, that we, as a body, do not exist for the sake of party; and that we are especially bound by the original principle on which our societies were founded, and by our constant professions before the world, to avoid a narrow, bigoted and sectarian spirit, to abstain from needless and unprofitable disputes on minor subjects of theological controversy, and, as far as we innocently can, to 'please all men unto their edification'. Let us, therefore, maintain towards all denominations of Christians, who 'hold the Head', the kind and catholic spirit of primitive Methodism; and, according to the noble maxim of our fathers in the Gospel, 'be the friends of all and the enemies of none'[20]

It was in the spirit of this declaration that Shrewsbury wrote so cogently twenty years later, emphasizing the spirit of humility and mutual reception that should prevail between Christians of differing traditions.

The concept of catholicity has remained an important one for Methodism since its beginning. The Methodist understanding of it derives from the generous love of God and is integrally linked to its Arminian theology. 'The Church is catholic because of the one universal God who has declared his love for all creation in Jesus Christ', declares the recent British Methodist Conference approved ecclesiological statement *Called to Love and Praise*.[21] In the early twentieth century, the Wesleyan scholar H. B. Workman asserted the catholicity of Methodism in terms of doctrine, life and a distinctive ethos and spirituality that represented an authentic style of Christian life.[22] In 1932 the Deed of Union of the British Methodist Church asserted that Methodism 'claimed and cherished its place within the Holy Catholic Church'.[23] The 1936 Covenant service contained an implicit call to catholicity with its reminder to the Methodist people that they were always to seek 'new ventures in fellowship'.[24] Such catholicity has always been seen as implying rich diversity, a diversity that should be expanding constantly as the faith is proclaimed in new situations and cultures, from whose inculturation in the faith the Church in return receives new perspectives on the Gospel. In 1937 the Conference, issuing the ecclesiological statement, *Nature of the Christian Church*, asserted:

> The Church of Christ is the home of the Holy Spirit, and is therefore a family with a unique and developing life. It is a life of distinctive quality, a life which under the guidance of the Spirit should be richer as time goes on, with fresh manifestations as new nations and races are added to the Church and new apprehension of divine truth is given.[25]

A desire for inclusivity has always characterized the Methodist understanding of 'catholicity'. Some of the strongest Methodist attacks on the Oxford Movement were motivated by a rejection of its narrow interpretation of catholicity in terms that gave almost exclusive weight to a particular form of ministerial order.[26]

A particularly Methodist emphasis in the understanding of catholicity relates to mutual strengthening in faith amongst all the churches of God. James Rigg, the nineteenth-century Wesleyan, and John Paul II, alike cite Rom. 1:12, 'that we may be mutually encouraged by each other's faith, both yours and mine'. The Methodist understanding of catholicity rightly implies ecumenical commitment and is also linked to the ecclesiological self-understanding inherent in the 'Connexional principle' which will be further discussed below.

What Might Methodism Have to Offer?

What contributions, then, can Methodism make to current ecumenical and ecclesiological discussion?

The first key contribution, perhaps, is a breadth of understanding of the theological task which transcends the gulf between evangelical experientialism and the catholic 'dogmatic principle'. Methodism stands for what Geoffrey Wainwright has called a 'generous orthodoxy'.[27] It emphasizes the absolute indispensability of the trinitarian faith as encapsulating the distinctively Christian understanding of God. This it holds in common with all trinitarian churches. It contributes its distinctive understanding that the faith of Scripture and Tradition may then be verified in the living experience of believers; as Ted Runyon, the American Wesley scholar, puts it: Methodism stands for orthodoxy, orthopraxis and 'orthopathy', or 'right experience', all of which reinforce each other.[28] Behind the lyricism of many of Charles Wesley's greatest doctrinal hymns lies a combination of doctrinal confession and individual appropriation by the believer. Thus, in a hymn on the Incarnation, we read, in lines redolent of the Orthodox liturgy:

> Emptied of His majesty,
> Of his dazzling glories shorn,
> Being's source begins to be,
> And God Himself is born.

Then follows the experiential appropriation:

> Knees and hearts to him we bow,
> Of our flesh and of our bone,
> Jesus is our brother now
> And God is all our own.[29]

In an age that values experience, and more than ever questions authority for beliefs of whatever sort, it may be that the Methodist approach of combining the dogmatic and the experiential can be more effective in the common mission to which Christians are all called.

Perhaps in all the debates concerning the relationship between dogma, experience and living Christian faith and practice, which ebb and flow between 'evangelical' and 'catholic', 'liberal' and 'traditionalist', the words of Benjamin Gregory, commenting on the significance of the Greek word *proskaterountes* in Acts 2:42 are worth pondering: 'What is meant by "giving themselves to the Apostles" doctrine' is very plain. They devoted themselves to the learning, to the experimental realisation, and to the assiduous practice of those truths which it was the principle work of the Apostles to teach.'[30] In turn, the recent emphasis in the Anglican–Roman Catholic statement, *The Gift of Authority*, on the need constantly to receive and *re-receive* the Apostolic tradition in its fullness, further amplifies Gregory's point.[31]

The second contribution is the principle of a generous recognition, as sister churches, of those communities within which Methodism discerns the living faith in and service of the trinitarian God. Though John Wesley was deeply critical of many of the practices of eighteenth-century Roman Catholicism, some of which he certainly misunderstood, he nevertheless argued that he could tolerate much superstition, 'yea even gross superstition' on account of the undoubted holiness of life of so many in that communion. He paid many tributes to his Roman Catholic contemporaries, such as 'that excellent man, the Bishop of Cambrai'.[32] Nineteenth-century Methodism declined somewhat from Wesley's standards in this particular respect, but it is interesting to note that the only body which Benjamin Gregory 'unchurched' was the Unitarians on account of their lack of faith in the Lord's deity. Gregory showed great appreciation of the nuances of the Church's catholicity. He warned against the tendency to identify perfectly legitimate emphases within the universal Church with distortions that could arise from their overemphasis in isolation. Thus he said, 'if we find an emphasis on continuity, let us not say, "This is popery". If we find a generous inclusiveness, let us not say, "this is latitudinarianism".' For Gregory, the antithesis of a truly 'catholic' attitude was the refusal to recognize other genuinely Christian bodies.[33]

Gregory, and indeed many Methodists since, recognized that the Spirit of God had engendered many genuine Christian communities, some through 'regular' agency and the established ministry of the Church, but some also 'irregularly'. In his analysis of the early chapters of Acts, Gregory argued that after the first persecution in Jerusalem, and resultant scattering of Christians, many new churches had been formed, not on the direct authority of the apostles, but, apparently, by 'lay' agency. The apostles then visited these churches, and, according to Gregory, 'lost no time in recognising and connecting them'.[34]

Gregory enunciated a doctrine of 'apostolic recognition', which could prove very fruitful ecumenically in discussions of apostolicity. He argued that 'Whensoever, wheresoever and by whomsoever, the Spirit prompted church action, and gave to it his imprimatur of spiritual success, they [i.e. the apostles] at once recognized, reverenced and rejoiced in His work.'[35] To Gregory, this was a key aspect of the apostolic role, to recognize the church-creating activity of the Spirit whether it resulted from their own activity or that of others. It was their *duty* to recognize and draw such new churches into the fellowship of the whole, thereby enabling the greater circulation of catholic love, gifts and insight. Methodists are aware of the irregular but (they would also claim) providential origins of their own movement. Nothing might do more to commend the apostolicity of episcopacy to Methodists, and, indeed, others in traditions lacking the historic episcopate, as an act of fuller and more generous recognition from episcopal churches. In turn, such generosity towards newer churches, clearly in the trinitarian tradition but currently still very much isolated from the ecumenical community, might help integrate them into a wider fellowship. Jean-Marie Tillard seems to hint at such a possibility in his consideration of the Petrine ministry, when he talks of its 'Pauline aspect' as involving 'recognition of the unforeseeable activity of God'.[36]

Methodism may also claim to have anticipated the modern emphasis on apostolicity as a bundle of characteristics, including (but not limited to or totally dependent upon) faithful transmission of ministerial office.[37] In looking for succession in apostolicity, Methodists look primarily for succession in faith, life and mission. Methodism also anticipated modern New Testament scholarship in its emphasis on the variety of forms of order to be found within the New Testament churches and in its affirmation that no one pattern could be regarded as rigidly prescribed by Christ or his apostles. Rather, the Wesleyans argued that the apostles were left free to adapt and develop according to the exigencies of mission. They combined this, however, with an emphasis upon the pastoral office, however structured, as necessary to the Church, and on the need for *episkope*, or oversight, whether exercised by persons in the traditional historical episcopal succession or otherwise.[38] We shall return to the question of ministry later in dealing with the Methodist reception of ecumenical insights.

Methodism continues to accept that no one pattern of church structure was laid down in the New Testament. This does not imply, however, that it sees all systems of church government as equally appropriate. Nineteenth-century Methodists regarded their 'connexionalism', with its linking of churches and its sharing of itinerant ministerial oversight, as closest in spirit to the church relationships of the New Testament, whilst denying that it was or could be an exact replication of a New Testament system. In the nineteenth century, seeing the rapid expansion of Methodism, particularly in America, they also came to believe that their system was the most successful in missionary terms.[39] In the twentieth century, Methodists tended to see connexionalism as a Methodist 'peculiar institution', not really suitable for export elsewhere. The last few years, however, have seen renewed ecclesiological interest in the 'connexional principle' both amongst Methodists and some dialogue partners.[40]

The 'connexional principle' had its origins in Wesley's organization of oversight for the societies 'in connexion' with him. It was a pragmatic device to enable the sharing of resources, allowing Mr Wesley to switch around his preachers to the places where he deemed the need to be greatest. Later, the nineteenth-century Wesleyan ecclesiologists came to see the empirical system of connexional organization, linking societies, circuits and the conference, as embodying a vital ecclesiological principle, that of the *necessary* interdependence and mutual accountability of all churches. All the churches of God should be inter-related, with the strong helping the weak where necessary. Resources, especially ministerial, should be allocated not in accordance with the ability of a local church to pay but in accordance with needs when measured against the total priorities of the Church. For British Methodism and its later daughter missionary churches, connexionalism is practised on a national church scale. American United Methodism takes connexionalism to its logical conclusion and practises global connexionalism. The many daughter churches founded from the USA by American Methodist missions are all represented in the quadrennial 'General Conference'.[41]

The value of the 'connexional principle' may become increasingly ecumenically relevant as churches move towards greater unity both at local and at national and international levels. The Methodist circuit, or group of local churches, similar in size to an Anglican deanery or URC area, involves the sharing of ministerial resources and fellowship. As churches of differing traditions become more closely associated in life and witness, this may prove a pattern for their mutual account-ability; indeed, the concept of a 'maxiparish', being adumbrated in present unity schemes in Scotland, certainly owes something to the circuit example. As part of growing into a greater unity and sharing of gifts, it will be important to ensure that channels of communication and accountability exist which do not allow local churches, however 'ecumenical' in theory, to slip back into the sort of congregational independence that is very far from being limited to local churches of 'independent' order and which certainly threatens some LEPs. At national and international level, there is now much talk of 'unity in reconciled diversity' or 'unity in conciliar fellowship'. Anglicans have proclaimed their intention of seeing that the Porvoo Agreement results in real interchange and sharing between the two traditions involved and does not remain the sort of paper theoretical agreement that was largely the fate of the Bonn Agreement with the Old Catholics in 1931. This will necessitate some form of 'connexional' organization.

The key thing Methodists commend is the principle of 'interconnectedness', not any one exact structural embodiment of it. They see the 'connexional principle' as the practical Methodist appropriation of the ecclesiology of communion. Moreover, the very principle renders Methodism open to ecumenical challenges. Methodism has been strong on geographical connexion, but has it been so strong on historical? Might not the adoption of the sign of the historic episcopal succession encourage Methodists to have a livelier sense of the continuity of the Church across all the ages of Christian history than is the case at the moment? Similar considerations apply to the Petrine ministry. Could it provide a universally focused ministry of unity which would both safeguard and enhance the awareness of the total interdependence and sharing of the Church at every level? These questions, needless to say, will feature prominently in Methodist dialogue with Orthodox, Catholics and Anglicans.

Methodism can also contribute to the ecumenical debate its generous regard for the diversity of the worshipping tradition of the Church. Unlike the churches of 'catholic' order, it has not confined itself to an officially exclusively liturgical pattern of worship, but, equally, unlike many in the Free Church tradition, it has not favoured an exclusively extempore prayer tradition. Rather, it has preserved both key elements of the Anglican liturgical tradition and a large dose of the Free church 'extempore' tradition. Both traditions are in a constant state of development, the enriching of the liturgical one being especially apparent in the 1998 Methodist Worship Book. Methodism believes that there is a richness and flexibility to be found in using both the ancient riches of the praying tradition of the Church and more informal forms that may be particularly appropriate in particular situations and localities.[42]

What Might Methodism Receive?

If the above represent insights that Methodism might contribute for the benefit of the wider Church, others may fairly ask what Methodism should be seeking to receive from the rest of the Church? Perhaps the single biggest question here is that of the sign of the episcopal succession and the consciousness of *koinonia* across time that is linked with it.

Unlike many in the Reformed and Baptist traditions, Methodism has never repudiated the idea of episcopacy. Indeed, American Methodism is episcopally ordered, with a threefold ministry. The nineteenth-century Wesleyans alike repudiated the Tractarian view that episcopacy, within the historic secession, was essential to true churchliness, and any view that it was *not* a legitimate way of ordering the Church.

Methodists fully share the concern of those in the 'catholic tradition' that there should be properly constituted ministries of oversight, keeping all the people of God in communion, and that these ministries should be faithfully transmitted. Indeed, Benjamin Gregory referred to presbyters as 'impersonations of unity'.[43] Methodists believe that their conferences, with their associated ministries, whether episcopally structured as in the American tradition or presbyterally, as in Britain, have proved faithful in the task of oversight. From early on in the Faith and Order movement, Methodists have recognized that the 'coming great Church' will include episcopal, presbyterial and congregational elements within its government. Two matters, however, have caused Methodists to hesitate when faced with the practicalities of receiving the sign of the episcopal succession. The first is a fear that, in accepting episcopacy, Methodism might seem to be repudiating its past and/or repudiating its valued links with other non-episcopal churches. The second is a hesitation as to whether, within a connexional system, the present delicate balance between ministerial leadership and full lay participation in decision-making would be preserved.

The result is that Methodism has pressed, in negotiations with the Church of England, for its full ecclesial status to be recognized; it was only when an assurance to this effect was given in 1955 that the first

'Conversations' began. The second issue surfaced at the time of the Covenant negotiations of the late 1970s and resulted in quite a lot of work being done on what Methodist episcopacy might look like. The matter has recently been re-examined.[44]

Many, though not all Methodists, recognize that in view of the great antiquity of the historic episcopate and its acceptance by the majority of Christians, its continuation in a united Church is inevitable. But is such a pragmatic acceptance response enough to the gift that is being offered? Can we say anything further?

In its Lima response of 1985, the British Methodist Conference stated that it awaited the moment 'when it would be appropriate to recover the sign of the episcopal succession'.[45] This 'moment' has usually been assumed as likely to occur within the context of a unity scheme involving an episcopally ordered church, though there have been occasional suggestions that British Methodism might consider adopting episcopacy unilaterally. What is significant is that the conference was prepared to adopt the phraseology of 'sign' in the context of Lima. The recent emphasis on apostolicity as involving a whole series of strands, of which ministerial succession is but one, has helped the discussion. It is perhaps a pity that the suggestion that Anglicans might recognize the American Methodist episcopate as a variant of the historic succession locally adapted was dropped from the interim report of the Anglican–Methodist dialogue. The American Methodist ministry derives its succession in exactly the same way as the Danish and Norwegian Lutheran ministries, from a presbyteral ordination.[46]

The early American Methodist bishops were seen supremely as leaders in mission, their own feats of itinerancy being prodigious even in comparison with those of the other circuit riders. To an extent, they followed in the traditions of the sub-apostolic *apostoloi* recounted in the *Didache* and in the later tradition of the early Celtic bishops, a point that might receive exploration in American Methodism's dialogue with Anglicans and Catholics. The 1992 revision of the Book of Discipline placed a new emphasis on the teaching office of the bishops, showing convergence with modern Roman Catholic emphasis on the teaching function of bishops.[47]

Understanding of the episcopal office is no more frozen and static than anything else in Christian theology, and what both Methodists

and their partners need to do is to seek for a common reappropriation of the Apostolic tradition in this as in other matters. Much
recent Anglican and Roman Catholic thinking on episcopacy should
appeal to Methodists. The Church of England's definition of itself
as 'episcopally led but synodically governed' should satisfy Methodists
that personalized, historic episcopacy could exist within a framework within which conference was still, unambiguously, the supreme
authority in Methodism.[48] The emphasis on the duty of bishops to
listen to and transmit the concerns of their local churches to the wider
Church and their duty to listen to and articulate the *sensus fidelium*
should also satisfy those Methodists who wish to be assured that all
ministry, including episcopal, is exercised within the Church and not
above it or separately from it.[49] The ecclesiology of *koinonia*, which
has proved so fruitful in the last couple of decades of ecumenical
work, resonates with Methodists who discern within it that sense of
total interdependence and communion at every level that they seek
to embody within the structures of connexionalism. Such an
ecclesiology of *koinonia* would seem to be inconsistent with extremes
either of hierarchicalism or independency, and to point rather to the
essential and interactive partnership of lay people and their pastors,
all of which points are consistent with the Methodist participative,
connexional way. Despite this, there are still those in Methodism
strongly opposed to the adoption of the historic episcopate. For some,
their opposition is based on a fear of 'prelacy' and an image of how
Anglican bishops behave which is at least a generation out of date.
There are other Methodists who, while anxious to please 'others unto
their edification' in the spirit of the Liverpool Declaration, still do not
see the point of the historic episcopate. It has perhaps to be said that a
full understanding of its value can come only within the context of its
reception and experience. This was certainly the experience of such
Methodists as Marcus Ward, who became presbyter in the Church of
South India at its inauguration. Ward later recorded his experience of
the great practical value to the Church in each place of having a true
'Father in God' and made it clear that no one in the Church of South
India, including the former members of non-episcopal churches, would
wish to go back on it.[50] What has been particularly persuasive for this
Methodist writer in commending the sign of the succession is the

recognition that in episcopal churches in general, there is a stronger sense of the continuity of the Church across all the ages. Methodists, apart from some interest in the Wesleys, too frequently lack appreciation of their own history, let alone that of the rest of the universal Church.

Though the sign of the episcopal succession may be the strategically most important question with which Methodists have to grapple ecumenically, it is certainly not the only one. In a recent article, Geoffrey Wainwright reminds Methodists that they have yet to complete their reception of *Baptism, Eucharist and Ministry* and to return to the Wesleyan ideal of the Sunday service, complete with the sacrament of the Lord's Supper and the preaching of the Word.[51] It is only fair to point out that the present supply of ministers in full connexion measured against the number of local congregations would make this ideal unattainable except in a few places. However, it is also true that many Methodists do not yet accept the case for a weekly Eucharist being the norm, even if the logistic problem did not exist. There is certainly greater appreciation of the importance of the Eucharist in current Methodism than was the case two generations ago. There is also a richer and more celebratory theology of the Eucharist, one closer to the Lima consensus than was probably the case a generation ago. These developments owe something both to internal Methodist factors and to ecumenical contact and example.[52]

One might conclude these reflections on Methodism's need to 'receive' by saying that it is in the same position as all other churches in this respect. It is a 'pilgrim church' *in via*. It experiences the same temptations as all other churches, to rest content with its present position, to define itself overly against the legitimate emphases of others. It has the same capacity to neglect or distort aspects of the tradition that it then needs to recover if it is to press on to a more fully balanced understanding and practice of the faith. Methodists, in common with other English Christians, need to heed again the call of the Nottingham Conference in the 'Not Strangers but Pilgrims' process that 'unity comes alive as we learn to live in one anothers' traditions'.[53] They also need to heed the advice of William Shrewsbury that Methodism is characterized, above all, by the disinterested search for the truth of Christ and the work of the Holy Spirit wherever they may be found.[54]

The corollary of this is that Methodism has a duty to receive into its life such new understanding and practice as may assist the Methodist people to 'press on to full salvation'. Not to do so flies in the face of the specifically Methodist vocation as well as the call to unity.

Shrewsbury's disinterestedness is effectively Jean-Marie Tillard's call for 'collective conversion to the Apostolic Faith'. There can be no ecumenical progress for any of us without this, though Methodists perhaps especially need to learn that the reception of new truth does not involve disloyalty to the past; rather it is part of that growing into an ever fuller appreciation of the truth that should characterize every age in the Church's life. From the mutual witness of sister churches, testifying to the work of God amongst them, the Universal Church is built up until that day when, as the decree *Dei Verbum* of Vatican II teaches 'all the promises of God are fulfilled in her'.[55]

W. J. Shrewsbury rejected all confrontationalism as contrary to the essential Methodist spirit:

> The Wesleyans have not so learned Christ. It becomes them everywhere to 'rejoice in the truth', and whenever they meet with it . . . to honour it and to observe its silent and gradual working with gladness of heart; and it should be their joy to take every fit occasion of speaking of whatever will give the most favourable impression, consistently with the truth, of every Christian community, and of all Christian ministers.[56]

There can be no better guide as to the spirit in which Methodists, who wish to honour their forebears in the faith, should approach the ecumenical task.

Looking to the Future

A final question remains to be addressed. What is to be the future of Methodism within a reunited Church? Methodists cannot deny that the Church of God existed for seven-eighths of its history without Methodism. On the other hand, many would wish to say that Methodism has contributed some features to the life of the Church that should become part of the ongoing endowment of its tradition regardless of whether a separately identifiable Methodism continues to exist.

Some have taken the view that the ultimate vocation of Methodism is to become a missionary order within the Church Universal, as the Wesleys intended that it should so remain within the Church of England. Many key British Methodist ecumenists of a generation ago agreed with Lesslie Newbigin that organic unity was the unity demanded by Scripture and that such unity must involve the willingness of any participating tradition to die to itself in order that a new church might rise. This view still has its defenders and certainly a value in reminding us that ecumenism is not about 'cheap grace'. Today, though, we are less sure it is the only reasonable option. The concepts of 'unity in reconciled diversity' and 'conciliar fellowship' have come onto the scene. It is far from certain how well the exact nuances of these concepts are appreciated within contemporary Methodism. A survey carried out in the course of the 'Called to Be One' process revealed that many Methodists were attracted by the concept of 'unity in reconciled diversity'. However, it is also revealed that the concept was being variously understood. Some took it to imply little more than the present level of ecumenical commitment. Others took it to involve genuine mutual accountability.

A flexible approach involving real unity in reconciled diversity with mutual accountability might well seem the best way forward, at any rate in England in the shorter term. It might calm the fears of some Methodists who fear their tradition could be swallowed up, at least in a union involving Anglicans, by a church much more powerful in numbers and resources. It would, however, provide for structures of mutual accountability and the creation of a closeness of life in partnership that should make it impossible for either Methodists or their ecumenical partners to slip back into denominational isolationism. It is here that the commendation of the 'connexional principle' made earlier in this chapter becomes particularly relevant. The aim of past and present Methodist connexional structures is to keep all the local churches in living communion, mutual awareness and support, enabling them to learn from each other and to receive all that is best. Connexionalism, in its final rationale, looks beyond Methodism itself, to the communion of all the churches and the assimilation of all that is of permanent value in the Christian heritage from wherever it may come.

The recently proposed Anglican–Methodist Covenant presents a challenge to Methodists in terms of growing into a much closer relationship with a sister church out of which, it is to be hoped, full unity will develop. Both churches are challenged to approach each other in a spirit of penitence 'for all that human sinfulness and narrowness of vision have contributed to our past divisions . . . and in a spirit of thanksgiving and joy' for the developing cooperation of more recent years. Both are called to harvest their diversity and 'share their treasures'.[57]

Methodism has always lived with a large and generous Arminian vision. It has always believed the Gospel is for all humankind. It has always commended the search for Christian holiness, at its best not in a narrow and legalistic or over-pietistic sense, but in the sense of a Christian wholeness, based on the recognition of the dynamic and varied work of the Spirit. Whether the name Methodist continues to appear on any church notice boards is scarcely here or there; what is important is that the sense of mission, the joyful sense of praise of the people of God in pilgrimage and the sense of universal interdependence in Christ become the common property of all the Churches of God. It may be that in some areas, as already in some countries, separate Methodist congregations and particular churches will disappear entirely into a greater whole. In others they will continue to exist but in the closest degree of communion with those of other traditions. It should be the joy of Methodists to await the ecumenical future with enthusiasm. As Charles Wesley wrote, 'the gift that he on one bestows/ We all delight to prove'.[58]

These words were originally written to fit the context of the local Methodist society, but there is no reason why they should not be reinterpreted on a broader ecumenical and ecclesiological canvas.

Notes

1. The best introduction to Methodism and ecumenism historically is J. M. Turner, *Conflict and Reconciliation: Studies in Methodism and Ecumenicalism, 1740–1982* (London: Epworth, 1985).

2. Lutheran World Federation (LWF)/World Methodist Council (WMC), *The Church: Community of Grace* (Lake Junaluska, 1984), cited also in J. Gros, H. Meyer and W. Rusch, *Growth in Agreement*, Vol. 2 (Geneva: WCC, 2000), pp. 200–18.

3. *Sharing in the Apostolic Communion* (London/Lake Junaluska: Epworth, 1996); also in Gros, Meyer and Rusch, op. cit., pp. 55–76.

4. *Orthodox and Methodists* (Lake Junaluska, 1996). A key 'diplomatic' problem was the appointment of a United Methodist bishop for Russia, based in Moscow.

5. For the first three reports of the Roman Catholic–Methodist Commission, see H. Meyer and L. Vischer (eds), *Growth in Agreement* (Geneva: WCC, 1984), pp. 307–88. The later reports are *Towards a Statement in the Church* (Lake Junaluska, 1986), *The Apostolic Tradition* (Peterborough, 1991), and *The Word of Life* (Lake Junaluska, 1996). They are now contained in J. Gros, H. Meyer and W. Rusch (eds), *Growth in Agreement II* (Geneva: WCC, 2000), pp. 583–646. See also the seventh report, *Speaking the Truth in Love – Teaching Authority Among Catholics and Methodists* (Lake Junaluska, North Carolina: WCC, 2001).

6. M. Evans (ed.), *Mary Sign of Grace, Faith and Holiness* (London: Methodist Publishing House/Catholic Truth Society, 1995).

7. For Wesley and Catholics, see D. Butler, *Methodists and Papists* (London: SCM Press, 1995).

8. R. Maddox, *Responsible Grace* (Nashville, TN: Kingswood Books, 1994), and T. Runyon, *The New Creation* (Nashville, TN: Kingswood Books, 1998).

9. See especially J. E. Rattenbury, *Eucharistic Hymns of John and Charles Wesley* (London: Epworth, 1948), and L. Stookey, *The Eucharist, Christ's Feast with the Church* (Nashville, TN: Kingswood Books, 1993).

10. M. Thurian, *Churches Respond to BEM*, Vol. 2 (Geneva: WCC, 1986): see pp. 177–254 for the main Methodist responses.

11. See Turner, op. cit. For fuller treatment of British Methodist history, see R. E. Davies and G. Rupp (eds), *A History of the Methodist Church in Great Britain* (London: Epworth, 1963).

12. Conference agenda, 2001.

13. *Commitment to Mission and Unity*, jointly published by Church House Publishing and Methodist Publishing House (London and Peterborough, 1996).

14. Their main ecclesiological works are, respectively, W. J. Shrewsbury, *An Essay on the Scriptural Character of the Wesleyan Methodist Economy, with an Appendix, Containing Reasons in Favour of a Scriptural Liturgy* (London, 1840), and B. Gregory, *The Holy Catholic Church, the Communion of Saints* (London, 1873).

15. Shrewsbury, op. cit., pp. 89–90.

16. Gregory, op. cit., p. 211.

17. R. Kissack, *Church or No Church* (London, 1963), p. 145.

18. A. Outler (ed.), *The Works of John Wesley*, Vol. 2 (Nashville, TN: Abingdon, 1986), Sermon no. 39, pp. 45–57.

19. B. Gregory, *Handbook of Scriptural Church Principles*, Vol. 2 (London, 1988), pp. 96–103.

20. Cited in J. S. Simon (ed.), *Summary of Methodist Law and Discipline* (London, 1923), pp. 268–9.

21. *Called to Love and Praise* (Peterborough: Methodist Publishing House, 1999), para. 2.4.4.

22. H. B. Workman, *Methodism in the Catholic Church* (London, 1921).

23. Cited in G. T. Brake, *Policy and Politics in British Methodism, 1932–82* (London: Edsall, 1984), p. 829.

24. *Methodist Book of Offices* (London, 1936), p. 129.

25. *Statements of the Methodist Church on Faith and Order, 1933–83* (London: Methodist Publishing House, 1984), p. 7 (hereafter *Statements*).

26. For example, Gregory, op. cit., p. 76.

27. G. Wainwright, *Methodists in Dialog* (Nashville, TN: Abingdon, 1995), pp. 231–6.

28. Runyon, op. cit., pp. 146–67.

29. *Hymns and Psalms* (London: Methodist Publishing House, 1983), no. 101.

30. Gregory, op. cit., p. 76.

31. ARCIC II, *The Gift of Authority* (London: Church House Publishing/Catholic Truth Society, 1999), paras 25 and 31.

32. See Butler, op. cit., p. 148, for a tribute to Fenelon.

33. Gregory, op. cit., pp. 4–5.

34. Ibid., p. 50.

35. Ibid., p. 49.

36. J. M. Tillard, *L'Eglise locale* (Paris: Cerf, 1995), p. 540.

37. See, for example, W. A. Quick, *Methodism, A Parallel* (London, 1891), in which the Wesleyan author makes extensive comparisons between the life and experience of the Apostolic Church and later Methodism.

38. For a classical statement of this view, see J. H. Rigg, *Connexional Economy of Wesleyan Methodism* (London 1852 and 1878), p. 25.

39. Ibid., pp. 37–54.

40. See the seminal article of Brian Beck, 'Some Reflections on Connexionalism', in *Epworth Review* (May/September 1991). See also the general appraisal, dealing with both American and British styles, 'Connexionalism and Koinonia' by B. Robbins and D. Carter, in *One in Christ* (1998), pp. 320–36.

41. For US Methodism in general, see T. E. Frank, *Polity, Practice and Mission of the United Methodist Church* (Nashville, TN: Kingwood, 1997).

42. For a general global survey of Methodist worship, see K. Westerfield-Tucker (ed.), *The Sunday Service of the People Called Methodists* (Nashville, TN: Kingswood, 1995).

43. Gregory, op. cit., p. 103.

44. For statements issued in the later 1970s and early 1980s, see *Statements*, op. cit., pp. 207–37. A new statement was duly accepted by the British Conference in 2000. See *Statements of the Methodist Church on Faith and Order*, Vol. 2 (1984–2000), (Peterborough: Methodist Publishing House, 2000), part 1, pp. 383–411.

45. Thurian, op. cit., p. 215.

46. See the interim statement, *Sharing in the Apostolic Communion* (1994), para. 77b, and D. Carter's evaluation in *Epworth Review* (1995), pp. 110–16.

47. Frank, *Polity, Practice and Mission of the United Methodist Church*, pp. 111–16 for the episcopal office in US Methodism.

48. M. Reardon (ed.), *Called to be One* (London: CTE, 1996), p. 55.

49. Tillard, op. cit., pp. 314–66; ARCIC II, op. cit., paras 34–40.

50. M. Ward, *The Pilgrim Church* (London: Epworth, 1953), p. 73.

51. G. Wainwright, 'Ecumenical Challenges for Methodism', in *Epworth Review* (2000), no. 1, pp. 69–76.

52. For an excellent account of the changing 'ethos' of eucharistic worship within British Methodism over the last half century or so, see J. A. Newton, 'The Eucharist in Methodism', *Methodist Sacramental Fellowship Bulletin* (1996), pp. 6–16.

53. Statement of the 1987 Nottingham Conference in the 'Not Strangers but Pilgrims process', para. 2.

54. Shrewsbury, op. cit., pp. 296ff.

55. The decree *Dei Verbum*, para. 8, in W. M. Abbott (ed.), *Documents of Vatican II* (London: Geoffrey Chapman, 1966), p. 116.

56. Shrewsbury, op. cit., p. 291.

57. *An Anglican–Methodist Covenant. Common Statement of the formal Conversations between the Methodist Church of Great Britain and the Church of England* (London: Methodist Publishing House/Church House Publishing, 2001), pp. 15 and 60.

58. *Hymns and Psalms*, no. 753.

4

The Reformed Tradition and the Ecumenical Task: 'A Vulnerable Catholicity'

Peter McEnhill

It has to be readily admitted that the churches of the Reformed tradition present a somewhat troubling and schizophrenic appearance to their ecumenical partners in relation to the question of ecumenism and church unity. On the one hand they are, in the words of an English Orthodox theologian of my acquaintance, 'fissiparous in the extreme', and this tendency towards fragmentation has to be, and is, readily conceded. Indeed, the most cursory perusal of recent statements by the World Alliance of Reformed Churches (WARC) on this matter would yield a plethora of admissions of guilt in relation to the divisive nature of the Reformed and Protestant traditions.

Yet, whilst admitting and lamenting this tendency, it is also clear that the converse is true in that churches in the Reformed tradition have often been in the vanguard of the modern ecumenical movement's attempts to promote greater unity between the separate Christian communions. The World Council of Churches was in its inception a largely Reformed and Anglican enterprise, and so strong was the Reformed contribution to the foundation of the WCC that its first general secretary was moved to remark that 'without the Reformed Alliance, there would have been no world Council'. Its second secretary was moved to describe the Council as 'the child of the Reformed Alliance'.[1] Merely to list some of the central figures of the early days of the ecumenical movement further demonstrates the scale and scope of the Reformed contribution: William Paton, W. A. Visser't Hooft, John Mackay, John Baillie, Norman Goodall and Lesslie Newbigin to name but a few.

And this is not a new or fleeting phenomenon of Reformed churches, for the formation of their earliest international associations were not attempts to retreat into confessional isolation but were from the first imbued with the sense of a larger ecumenical vision. Thus Philip Schaff speaking at the first Presbyterian Council in 1877 could say that: 'The problem of Christian union and brother-hood is one of the great problems of the nineteenth century, and will work itself out in various ways until the great prophecy of the one Shepherd and one flock be fully realised.'[2] Schaff was, of course, simply reiterating a fundamental theme of Reformed theology that can be traced back to the earliest reformers, and this is the deep conviction that there is only *one* Church catholic. Neither Calvin, Zwingli nor Bucer would have understood themselves to be found-ing a new church gathered around a new polity or a new set of theo-logical insights. They regarded themselves as seeking the reform of the Church catholic in accordance with the truths of scripture. The fact that a separate Reformed 'church' exists and therefore the unity of the Church is broken (forgetting for the moment the prior great schism), represents the failure of the Reformed enterprise and is a 'frightful mutilation of Christ's body' (Calvin). This has always been a matter of considerable regret to informed Reformed Christians everywhere and has been the spur that has prompted all their efforts in this century to overcome the fragmentation of the Christian Church.

These efforts have not been inconsiderable, and Reformed churches have been eager participants in the move towards the formation of transconfessional united churches that has been such a feature of twentieth-century ecumenism. Reformed churches have been at the forefront of some of the most significant church-uniting movements of this century. Often this has meant forming unions and healing divisions within the Reformed family itself, but it has also involved union with other traditions such as the Methodist, Disciples of Christ and Anglican churches as well. Consequently, Reformed churches are now part of united churches in Germany (nineteenth and twentieth centuries), Austria (1891), the Czech republic (former Czechoslovakia) 1918), Canada (1925), China (1927), South India (1947), United Church of Christ, USA (1957), Church of North India (1970), Australia (1977) and, of course, here in Britain in the formation of the United Reformed Church in 1981.[3]

So strong is this impulse towards union that many Reformed churches have a statement in their founding documents committing them to seek the greater unity of the Christian Church. Thus the United Reformed Church states in its Basis of Union that it 'sees its formation and growth as part of what God is doing to make his people one, and as a united church will take, wherever possible and with all speed, further steps towards the unity of all God's people'.[4] So much one might expect from a relatively recent 'united' church, but we find the same impetus towards Christian unity in that rather more venerable and stuffy organization north of the border – the Church of Scotland. We find that the seventh declaratory article of the constitution of the Church of Scotland maintains that:

> The Church of Scotland, believing it to be the will of Christ that His disciples should be all one in the Father and in Him, that the world may believe that the Father has sent him, recognises the obligation to seek and promote union with other Churches in which it finds the Word to be purely preached, the sacraments administered according to Christ's ordinance, and discipline rightly exercised; and it has the right to unite with any such Church without loss of its identity on terms which this Church finds to be consistent with these articles.[5]

In this stress upon the oneness and catholicity of the Church, and of the need for that to be visibly expressed, these documents are fully in accord with the purpose and intent of the original reformers. Calvin himself wrote to Cranmer in the following terms: 'The members of the Church, being severed, the body lies bleeding. So much does this concern me that, could I be of any service, I would not grudge to cross even ten seas, if need were, on account of it.'[6] The conviction of the early Reformed churches that they remained part of the one Church catholic is a constant theme in all the early confessions of the Reformed Church and is succinctly expressed in the 54th question of the Heidelberg Catechism:

q. What do you believe concerning the holy Catholic Church?

a. I believe that from the beginning to the end of the world, and from among the whole human race, the Son of God, by His Spirit and his Word, gathers, protects and preserves for Himself, in the unity of the true faith, a congregation chosen for eternal life. Moreover, I believe that I am and forever will remain a living member of it.

If this stress upon the Reformed emphasis upon the catholicity of the Church seems pedantic and pedestrian then perhaps I could be forgiven an apologetic task. The charge of having an inherent tendency towards fragmenting the body of Christ is a serious one and so any Reformed theologian will wish to stress the strong impulse towards Christian unity that has also been such a feature of the life of Reformed churches. The theological source of this deep and unswerving commitment to unity is a fundamental belief in the catholicity of the Church.

Whilst all this is true we have also to acknowledge the troubled Reformed history of fragmentation and the difficulty that this poses for our brothers and sisters in other Christian communions in discerning where this commitment to 'catholicity' lies. This is where the 'vulnerable' element of the Reformed concept of catholicity is found. An examination of the statements made in Reformed confessions on the catholicity of the Church reveals that the central thrust of Reformed thinking is to define this in Christological rather than structural terms. The Church is called into being by Christ and is maintained by Christ and participates in the mission of God to the world through the power of the Spirit. The catholicity or universality in question is not, therefore, so much of the Church, but of the Gospel concerning Christ's work and its universal scope which embraces the whole world. The Church is catholic in the sense that it is people called together in Christ to embody, confess and participate in his work as a sign to the world until its consummation in the kingdom still to come.

Hence the strong emphasis on the word faithfully preached (and heard) and the sacraments administered according to the word as marks of the Church. These marks do not define the Church but are evidences of its presence and its constitution by Christ. As Lovell Cock said to the seventh Congregational Council in 1953:

When we are asked what is the objective, the massive, unchanging fact which manifests the reality of the Church, we point to the Word preached and the sacraments administered. For behind the Word so preached and acted stands the Incarnate Word . . . The Word that creates and guarantees the Church can be no other than the object of the Church's faith and the content of its message . . . The objectivity of the Church is the objectivity of the Gospel it proclaims and to which its life is conformed . . . And as for their [Church, word and sacraments] authority, warrant or title deed, where can there be authority more decisive, guarantee more secure than the promises of God declared in His Word.[7]

This conception of the relationship between Christ and the catholicity of the Church is in essential agreement with a more recent statement by WARC in its pamphlet *Called to Witness to the Gospel Today*:

Proclaiming the Lordship of Jesus Christ implies a vision of and a commitment to the catholicity of the church. The church is catholic because Jesus Christ, the Saviour of the whole world is present in its midst. It is catholic by witnessing to the work of salvation. It is catholic by embodying in its life the message addressed to all people: be reconciled with God. It is catholic by being a sign of the communion to which all people are called. To this catholicity the church is committed. Its vision embraces the promise of God in Christ for the whole world. It may not be concerned with itself. It must be open to all people in their aspirations and in their sufferings. The church is a wandering people who look forward to the fulfilment of history in the kingdom of God.[8]

Many of our partner churches would, of course, find themselves expressing similar sentiments to this, but would also want to ask if there is not a further dimension to 'visible catholicity' through the bestowal of ideal patterns and structures of ministry upon the Church in its historical form. Such structures and forms of ministry are visible expressions that manifest and guarantee the Church's unity and faithfulness to the Gospel. This, it is contested, would meet the difficulty that has always faced Reformed churches in discerning what constitutes a 'faithful preaching and hearing of the Word and the faithful administration of the sacraments'. Again it has to be admitted that much acrimony, division and hurt have arisen down through the centuries over difficulties in this regard.

In no small measure the promotion and adoption of confessions of faith by Reformed churches was an attempt to provide summaries of the essential Gospel message in order to maintain a common measure of judgement in relation to the faithfulness of the message being preached. However, the profusion of confessions and the strong Reformed conviction that each church in its own geographical location and social context had the responsibility for drawing up its own confession meant that ultimately, despite the high degree of agreement that exists between the various confessions, they were self-relativizing. Consequently, there is no equivalent to the Augsburg Confession in the Reformed tradition.

It has to be remembered that non-theological factors played their part too in the shaping of the ethos and understanding of the Reformed tradition. The politically discrete and separate location of the Swiss cantons encouraged an early stress upon the local and contextual nature of the church community that was to militate against attempts to create a stronger sense of unity despite the best efforts of the early Reformers. In relation to the later tendency towards fragmentation it is simply an historical and sociological fact that Reformed churches were to find themselves located largely in those countries which were to nurture a strong emphasis on voluntarism and the autonomous rights of the individual in relation to the larger community. The free believer before God became the autonomous citizen of Western democracy, and although it is a moot point as to whether Reformed theological concepts were the source of the Western stress upon the freedom of the individual or were themselves the products of a larger movement of thought that would have taken place anyway, there is no doubting the fact that the social and cultural locatedness of many Reformed churches in Western civilization has been such as to encourage and fan the tendency towards fragmentation.

But I digress. This vulnerability in discerning a catholicity that is Christologically defined provides both opportunity and threat. If the history of division and fragmentation amply testifies to the reality of the threat, then it has to be admitted that the Reformed tradition's ability to discern what Christ is saying to the contemporary context is evidence of its ability to grasp the opportunity horn of its dilemma. Its willingness to think and rethink the Gospel in the light of the contemporary situation has been admirable and often courageous.

By resorting to 'the word faithfully preached' as an evidence of the Church, Reformed Christians are not simply searching for the comfortable repetition of theological truisms. It is nothing less than the attempt to find the mind of Christ and the meaning of the Gospel in the light of the contemporary situation. This means that the Church is never a settled possession, never a cosy accommodation with received tradition or past structures, but is a creation of the Word itself and often a disturbing and uncomfortable gift.

With this radical emphasis upon the freedom of the Gospel the Reformed tradition has found itself freer than some of its ecumenical partners to respond to new situations and new insights and it is therefore not surprising that the challenge of church unity has often found a positive response from Reformed churches. In their refusal to raise matters of polity, ministry or order above the Gospel imperative of unity, Reformed churches have often been able to embrace dialogue, share communion and achieve full church union more quickly than many of their partners. In so doing they manifest their faithfulness to the 'marks' as evidences of the existence of the true Church. For although it is often forgotten, Calvin and his contemporaries were profound opponents of needless schism and he forcefully contended that:

> The pure ministry of the Word and pure mode of celebrating the sacraments are, as we say, sufficient pledge and guarantee that we may safely embrace as a church any society in which both these marks exist. The principle extends to the point that we must not reject it so long as it retains them, even if it otherwise swarms with many faults.[9]

In the polemical spirit of the age many churches were of course judged to be unfaithful. (Interestingly, Roman Catholic churches were not *per se* judged to be unfaithful, it was conceded that they could retain the true marks – though admittedly this would be difficult.) However, in our situation today it could be argued that the Reformed churches are not justified in raising anything above these marks as evidence of the presence of the true Church, and that we are therefore committed to unity (though not necessarily absolute uniformity) with all Christian communities which bear them.

Despite these positive remarks it is still the case that a noted Reformed theologian writing on the Church can say, 'neither in their understanding of the Church nor in their spirituality or the structures that they have developed are Reformed churches equipped to locate their ongoing struggles over new insights within a broader unity'.[10]

Undoubtedly this is true and the Reformed churches are especially vulnerable at this point, and it is perhaps the ecumenical movement and moves towards unity which will help us solve this problem.

The Hungarian theologian Janos Pasztor has argued that it is a dualistic misunderstanding of the visible/invisible distinction, inherited from St Augustine, that is responsible for this devaluation of the physical/visible Church in favour of a hidden/spiritual Church.[11] He argues that the doctrine of the mixed community has been interpreted hellenistically and dualistically in favour of the supposedly purer or higher spiritual/doctrinal/invisible reality in order to legitimate division and separation. Although I substantially agree with Pasztor in this assessment there is no overlooking the profound 'psychological' impression of the validity of 'righteous dissent' that inculturation into the Reformed faith imparts to individual believers. Often weaned on stories of heroic figures of the faith who broke with oppressive church authority in order to keep faith with the essential Gospel message, there is no doubt that Reformed Christians imbibe an attitude that regards separation for the sake of doctrinal purity as not only possible but on occasion necessary. Indeed, there is a strong theme in Reformed teaching and preaching that constantly reads the Bible itself in these terms. The prophets and the remnant are faithful to God's message over against unfaithful Israel, the apostle Paul over against Judaizing Christians and so on down through history to Luther, Calvin, the Puritans and early pilgrims over against the established Church, the Confessing Church over against the unfaithful German Christians, and so on. It is almost impossible to overstate the psychological power and force of the image of God's 'faithful outcast' in the Reformed *Zeitgeist*.

However, this favouring of the 'invisible' Church is, as we have seen in the quote from Calvin, antithetical to the original Reformed assertion of invisibility which does not regard the Church as two entities – one pure, one compromised – but rather as one entity viewed from two aspects. The invisibility of the Church is primarily an eschatological category that refers to the invisible Church's hidden nature in the knowledge and purpose of God. The English Reformed theologian Martin Cressey is in substantial agreement with Pasztor on this point, arguing that invisibility originally and primarily applies to the elect in God's purposes and that the deficient understanding of the invisibility of the Church (in that it prioritizes the internal faith attitude of the believer over against the visible structures of the Church) was the product of an amalgam of nineteenth-century liberalism with pietism. Cressey approvingly cites Barth's paradoxical description of 'the Christian community as the visible object of that faith which penetrates to its invisible, spiritual reality – one, holy catholic and apostolic'.[12] Nevertheless, the Reformed conviction that 'The Catholic Church hath sometimes been more, sometimes less visible', that particular churches are more or less pure and that the 'purest churches under heaven are subject both to mixture and error' has tended, in its assertion of the proleptic and eschatological nature of the catholicity of the Church, to minimize the authority of the visible Church as itself a penultimate reality according to the Reformed tradition.

The commitment to catholicity has led to a certain vulnerability in relation to Reformed identity too. For it is the case that there is no single set of Reformed doctrines that belong solely to all the Reformed churches throughout the world (although one doubts that this is true for any Christian communion in this postmodern age, but nevertheless it remains manifestly true for the Reformed tradition). Indeed Alan Sell doubts if there are as many as *five* doctrines that are specifically Reformed in the sense that they belong to no one else.[13] Perversely, this is itself an outcome of the Reformed conviction that they were seeking to express not 'Reformed truths' but catholic doctrine. The Reformers never claimed to be inventing new doctrines but to be rediscovering scriptural truths that belonged to the whole Church.

If there are no distinctive doctrines that distinguish the Reformed churches from other churches then neither, as our discussion has shown, is there a single confession that commands the allegiance of every church that claims to be Reformed. Admittedly, David Willis has argued that every confession gains its validity from its agreement with the first four ecumenical councils of the Church and it is this which safeguards the catholicity of Reformed doctrine.[14] Nor is there uniformity of worship and liturgy, nor is there a common approach to polity or structures of ministry that unites all member churches. In face of such diversity it is easy to see why our ecumenical conversation partners ask us what it means to be Reformed? And wherein does this catholicity of which we speak lie?

The issue of Reformed identity is a live one in Reformed circles. By claiming no new or original doctrines save those that can be demonstrated from Scripture we find that there are no doctrines that can be claimed as uniquely defining what it means to be Reformed. If the likely candidates of the sovereignty of God and the doctrines of grace and predestination suggest themselves, then Luther, Aquinas and Augustine might like to claim those doctrines as catholic truth as well. Similarly, the refusal to accord a certain polity or order of ministry to define the essence of the Church means that Reformed communities will take many different forms in response to the situation and context in which they are placed. In this sense Reformed identity can be a very nebulous and vulnerable concept, and it can be an exasperating experience for our ecumenical dialogue partners to try to get a clear answer from us as to what it means to be Reformed.

In response to this difficulty we should perhaps point out that it is not always easy from the inside to specify what it means to be Reformed. For to be Reformed is a matter of tenor and tone. It is a way of holding a certain constellation of doctrines rather than the unique possession of them. It is a way of inhabiting a certain commitment to the absolute freedom and sovereignty of God that refuses to accord any penultimate system or structure absolute authority.

This ambiguity surrounding what it means to be Reformed pervades Reformed structures from local to national and international level. Often high-level dialogue partners will be frustrated by the inability of WARC to speak for the whole Reformed community. For the results of each dialogue have to be ratified by each member church before they can truly claim to be representative of the Reformed communion. However, this failure to develop an organ of effective communication at the international level is itself the result of a strong commitment to ecumenism. For very early on in the life of the WCC, WARC decided to follow the Lund principle as far as possible and to integrate as much of its activity as it could with the larger work of the WCC. Laudable as this may have been, it has certainly led to a certain diminishment of the standing, role and function of WARC as the international body of the Reformed churches. It is a decision that will prove to have even more serious consequences for Reformed churches if the current speculative plans to change the nature of the WCC so that it more faithfully represents blocks of Christian communions and families should win the day.

In spite of the limitations WARC experiences due to its commitment to the larger ecumenical scene it has embarked upon a series of bilateral dialogues. (After some initial hesitation due to a fear of being seen as going down the confessional route – again a sign of a commitment to a larger vision.) These dialogues have had varied results. Discussions with the Disciples of Christ led to the 1986 statement that 'there are no theological or ecclesiological issues which need to divide us as churches'. This statement has been accepted by both churches and joint participation in decision-making now takes place and in many countries church unions have taken place. In 1973 the Leuenberg agreement between Reformed and Lutheran churches created pulpit and table fellowship and the mutual recognition of ministries between these two traditions. This recognition, based on a common understanding of the Gospel, led to the establishment of full communion between the two traditions. In 1994 the Methodist churches in Europe also affirmed the agreement. Major dialogues have taken place with the Roman Catholic Church and though no formal agreements have been reached much mutual understanding has been achieved. The 1981–84 dialogue with the Anglican communion entitled 'God's Reign and Our Unity' focused primarily upon the missiological task of the Church and urged both sides to consider seriously steps towards union. Admittedly, it did not come to agreement on the question of episcopacy as an essential feature of church order. Similar, engagements have taken place with the Baptists, the Eastern Orthodox churches, the Oriental Orthodox churches and the Pentecostals.

With such a variety of partners what is in sight in each dialogue is different and their relative success has to be measured differently. Discussions with the Roman Catholic Church obviously have a lot of shared history to clear up, whereas discussions with the Oriental Orthodox are not encumbered with the same degree of baggage. (Here the baggage is contemporary as Reformed = Protestant = evangelical = well-funded American who is trying to proselytize their flock). One criticism of such dialogues is that they are not sufficiently aware of each other's conclusions in that the different participants often offer slightly different perceptions of the Reformed understanding of the Church, or salvation, or baptism, etc. Whilst this is true it is not uniquely a Reformed problem, as the comparison of the understandings of the Church given in the Anglican–Reformed discussions and the ARCIC discussions will reveal. This is to some degree inevitable, as any discussion will inevitably focus on where the shoe pinches, but it does point to the need for multilateral as well as bilateral conversations.

What then of a vulnerable catholicity? It is clear that Reformed churches are committed to seeking the greater visible unity of the one Church of Christ. It is clear also that in this desire for unity Reformed identity is uniquely vulnerable. For in claiming no specific doctrine other than catholic truth, in prioritizing no church structure or form of ministry above the *kerygma*, Reformed churches may simply be dissolved and absorbed in unions which might take place with churches that do have a formal commitment to abiding church structures. This may or may not be a bad thing and it may be the peculiar witness of the Reformed churches to be willing to lose their lives in order to regain them in a larger, broader, deeper understanding of catholicity. And perhaps this would represent the culmination of the Reformed enterprise. But such an assertion might puzzle Christians in other traditions who have not experienced Reformed churches in this humble and accommodating way – what of the refusal to countenance episcopacy say? I think enough has been written elsewhere to substantiate the claim that the Reformed tradition has no intrinsic hostility to episcopal forms of government *per se*.

All that I have said previously indicates that we do not privilege any one structure above another, although there is a clear preference for conciliar and collegial forms of government. However, we reserve the right to refuse to concede on biblical, historical, and more importantly theological grounds, that episcopal forms are somehow constitutive of the essence of the Church and its ministry.[15] The difficulty here is not a rejection of authority, nor is it simply the fact that we are unpersuaded by the historical veracity of the apostolic succession (though we may take some persuading). It is rather that we reject it as an unwarranted restriction on the freedom of God's grace. In the words of Bernard Lord Manning: 'We decline still, as we have always declined, to have episcopalian ordination of ministers and episcopalian confirmation of Church members made into a sort of new circumcision within the limits of which alone is there full and valid and regular operation of God's grace.'[16] We decline therefore not the form but the principle. We decline it because we know that our experience of God's grace through ministry and sacrament has not been in any way deficient. We decline it because we know our witness to the faith and our service to Christ has been faithful to the Apostolic witness. We decline it because God is sovereign and free and we know that from all time God had some friends in the world who were not part of the commonwealth of Israel. The sovereignty and freedom of God's grace is one part of catholic truth about which the Reformed tradition is not prepared to be vulnerable.

Notes

1. Both remarks are cited in Alan Sell's *A Reformed, Evangelical, Catholic Theology: The Contribution of the World Alliance of Reformed Churches 1875–1982* (Grand Rapids, MI: Eerdmans, 1991), p. 123. Sell was for a period the theological secretary of WARC and this article is much indebted to the overview of the ecumenical activity of WARC that he provides.

2. Philip Schaff, cited ibid., p. 112.

3. For a full list of Reformed participation in the formation of United Churches and the churches involved see J. J. Bauswein and L. Vischer (eds), *The Reformed Family Worldwide* (Grand Rapids, MI: Eerdmans, 1999), p. 710.

4. URC Basis of Union – the Manual.

5. J. T. Cox (ed.), *Practice and Procedure in the Church of Scotland* (Edinburgh: Church of Scotland, 1976), p. 391.

6. J. Calvin, 'Letter to Cranmer', cited in Sell, op. cit., p. 114.

7. Lovell Cock, cited ibid., p. 111.

8. *Called to Witness to the Gospel Today* (Geneva: WARC, 1982), p. 24

9. J. Calvin, *Institutes of the Christian Religion*, ed. J. T. McNeill (Philadelphia, PA: Westminster Press, 1960), 4.1.12, p. 1025.

10. Lukas Vischer, 'The Church – Mother of Believers', in D. Willis and M. Welker (eds), *Toward the Future of Reformed Theology* (Grand Rapids, MI: Eerdmans, 1999), p. 273.

11. Janos Pasztor, 'The Catholicity of Reformed Theology', in Willis and Welker, op. cit., pp. 25–6.

12. Martin Cressey, 'The Invisible Church Revisited', unpublished article, p. 2.

13. A. Sell, 'The Reformed Family Today', in D. McKim (ed.), *Major Themes in the Reformed Tradition* (Grand Rapids, MI: Eerdmans, 1992), p. 435.

14. D. Willis, 'The Ecumenical Future of Reformed Theology', in Willis and Welker (eds), op. cit., pp. 178–9. Although I agree with the central thrust of his point here, Willis overstates

the case in relation to the four ecumenical councils. Surely, in faithfulness to the *sola scriptura* principle, Reformed acceptance of these councils is because of their accord with scripture and that this is the ultimate standard for all subsequent confessions.

15. Lest this seem unduly negative I am not arguing against the acceptance of any form of episcopal oversight by Reformed churches. This is perfectly possible and has been advocated as such by figures as different as Tom Torrance and Martin Cressey. However, episcopacy here would, as Cressey has argued, have to be an understanding of the '...apostolic succession, in terms of a corporate succession of the whole church, expressed and focused, but neither guaranteed nor exhausted by the succession in the episcopal sees.' 'Three Games in a Long Ecumenical Set: Leuenberg, Meissen and Porvoo on Ministry and *Episkopé*' in P. C. Bouteneff and A. D. Falconer (eds), *Episkopé and Episcopacy and the Quest for Visible Unity* (Geneva: WCC 1999), p.124. With this in mind it is very helpful to read Bishop Stephen Sykes commenting in the same volume that 'It is also not a part of any historic formularies of Anglicanism to insist that episcopacy belongs to the *esse* of the Church.' 'Episkopé and Episcopacy in some recent Bilateral Dialogues', Bouteneff and Falconer ibid., p. 100. Sykes also notes accurately that there are no explicit condemnations of episcopacy in the Reformed confessions. His general thrust, that there can be a positive exercise of episcopal office in accordance with the gospel but that the development of episcopacy cannot be regarded as a supra-historical phenomenon (and is therefore provisional and requires to be subjected to criticism and reformation in the light of the gospel), would find glad acceptance in the Reformed tradition.

16. Bernard Lord Manning, cited in Sell, *Reformed, Evangelical, Catholic Theology*, p. 165.

5

The Unity We Seek:
Prospects for the Local Church

Jeremy Morris

It is a safe assumption that those engaged in the official, bilateral and multilateral ecumenical dialogues are themselves members of 'local' churches. To say this is to say something fairly obvious. It would be as absurd to claim to be a member of the Christian Church and not to have any sense of belonging to a particular Christian community as it would to claim to belong to the human family and yet disavow any place within a particular family, however small and attenuated. Belonging to the worldwide Church entails belonging to a particular local church; vice versa, belonging to a local church thereby involves membership of the universal Church. Of course I can say all that only at the cost of gliding over the problematic issue of definitions. What is the 'Church'? What constitutes membership of it? How do you define what 'local' means? In even the most innocuous-seeming of statements about Christian belonging, enormously controversial issues lurk under the surface. Even so, the basic inseparability of actual human communities and 'Church' is – at least at the theoretical level – surely not contentious.

And yet there is a paradox about the term 'local' in the ecumenical movement today. However one defines it – and Lesslie Newbigin long ago demonstrated how slippery a term it was[1] – it expresses an essential reality of ecclesial life, namely its rootedness in particular human communities, in particular places, at particular moments of history.

91

Newbigin developed his concept of 'local' church according to a reading of 'place', which was then subjected to Christological and missiological pressure:

> we must say that a local church will be a congregation in which everyone who belongs to that place will be able to recognize the call of Christ addressed to him or her in words, deeds and patterns of life and worship which he can understand and receive as being truly the call of his own Maker, Saviour and Friend.[2]

The Gospel is universal, yet it addresses actual, 'placed' human beings – indeed it can only be universal in so far as it is also particular.[3] The explicit theme of the local church in the official dialogues and reports is something apparently new, which has crept up on us almost unnoticed, and which only now demands to be received and examined with due attention. Partly this may be because of the well-known disillusionment with 'grand' schemes of organic unity.[4] Partly, too, it may be because of subtle and yet profound shifts in denominational identities: the growing ecumenical sensitivity of denominations themselves may have had a paradoxical effect locally, with a declining conviction that there really are matters of fundamental difference between churches, and consequently a declining interest in national and international schemes for unity.

The difference can be detected, for example, in a comparison of the two major documents on ecumenical ecclesiology produced by the Faith and Order Commission of the World Council of Churches. One could hardly say that *Baptism, Eucharist and Ministry* (*BEM*) was actually insensitive to the local church – to suggest as much would be to misunderstand its purpose. Particular, 'placed' churches are touched on again and again at various points in the document. Unity 'among the local churches', for example, was cited as one of the 'permanent characteristics' of the Church of the apostles, and hence of the continuity of the Apostolic tradition.[5] Particular church practices (and especially differences between them) also featured again and again in the paragraphs of commentary. And yet the claim of some responding churches that what was lacking in *BEM* was explicit attention to fundamental ecclesiology arguably found support in the absence of an underpinning discussion of catholicity and locality.[6] By contrast, *The Nature and Purpose of the Church* (*NPC*), in its reflections on the meaning and significance of *koinonia*, not only attends directly to the communion of local churches (in paragraphs 65 and 66) but emphasizes this by treating it as the third of three interlinked dimensions of the communion of the Church, following the communion 'real but not fully realized' and the existence of diversity in unity.[7] It could not be more emphatic on the interpenetration of specificity and catholicity: 'The communion of the Church is expressed in the communion between local churches in each of which the fullness of the Church resides.'[8]

Exactly why reflection on local churches should have begun to feature more prominently in major reports in recent years is a question for historical analysis lying well beyond the aim of this chapter. Two things are pertinent here. One is that it is at least arguable that this new-found attention to issues of locality raises continuing questions about the nature of church division in a much sharper and potentially more fruitful way than is likely to be the case at the level of national and international church relations. Though this is a far from definitive list, at least three main areas of challenge might be identified: the problematic way in which ecumenical relations assume a common Christian tradition, yet are forced to acknowledge different interpretations of that tradition, and different practices accordingly; the distinctiveness of particular histories, constructed from the interplay of culture, history and theology, and all too often coloured by mutual prejudice and persecution; and the strikingly different ways in which the exercise of authority and responsibility is structured in different Christian communities. These three areas represent a sort of agenda for local ecumenism which I shall explore in what follows.

The second pertinent reflection is that issues concerning the ecclesiology of the local church have become pressing precisely at the point at which local ecumenical experience has itself begun to raise new challenges for the churches. In some cases, what appear to be genuinely new issues of order and practice have raised in an unexpected way fundamental questions about Christian identity and belonging. In other cases, well-known, long-established issues of ecclesiological difference have been highlighted and then called into question by the willingness of local churches to set them to one side.

This chapter is written out of the experience of teaching ecumenism in an ecumenical federation of theological colleges and courses, and draws particularly on the British context. British ecumenism is a remarkably rich and diverse phenomenon, which itself would merit sustained analysis. The existence in Britain of nearly 1,000 Local Ecumenical Partnerships, of hundreds of church-sharing arrangements, of thousands more ecumenically run church agencies, as well as the highly developed pattern of local ecumenical councils, drawing on the doubly pluralistic character of British society (its history of denominational competition and its ethnic diversity) provides a laboratory of local ecumenical experiment possibly unrivalled in Western Europe.[9] But little of the breadth of British ecumenism can be reflected accurately in this chapter. Its aim is rather, I hope, a modest one, not seeking either to survey the richness of contemporary British ecumenical experience at the local level, nor to propose a comprehensive vision for local ecumenism, but simply to test each of the three areas of challenge noted above, putting down, in effect, 'plumb-lines' into some aspects of the contemporary British experience. At the end, I hope to draw some specific conclusions, approving (with qualification) the relevance of *koinonia* theology to the production of a 'grammar' of local ecclesiological reflection, and the need for a more complex and untidy understanding of conciliarity than the critics of many local ecumenical arrangements have desired.

Tradition and Traditions

The very fact that the divisions of the Church constitute a problem indicates how central to its existence is the gathering together of the community of Christians in one place. Rather than turning to the Johannine corpus – as we could very well – with its endorsement of the unity of the believers in God, we might profitably consider the Pauline preoccupation with asserting the unified nature of the Apostolic tradition, that which Paul 'received from the Lord' and which 'I also handed on to you' (1 Cor. 11:23). Paul's appeal to the Corinthian Christians is premised on an essential unity of belief and witness: 'Has Christ been divided? Was Paul crucified for you?' (1 Cor. 1:13). It is, of course, to a local church that Paul here is writing, though it is a local church which he considers to be bound to the whole Church through Christ: 'To the church of God that is in Corinth . . . together with all those who in every place call on the name of our Lord Jesus Christ' (1 Cor. 1:2). This unity in locality undergirds Paul's address throughout the letter to his 'brothers and sisters', just as it does his carrying of greetings from other churches of Asia Minor and the church 'in the house' of Aquila and Prisca (1 Cor. 16:19). We find, of course, the same concern for the unity of the local church in Paul's letter to the Galatians: 'not that there is another gospel, but there are some who are confusing you' (Gal. 1:6).

There is, admittedly, a sinister way of reading this emphasis on unity of belief and witness secured through the identity of local churches with the faith of the whole Church. As the Church grew, its increasing preoccupation with the matter of regulation, which originally served merely to support and resource the freedom of local churches to follow the Gospel, subtly and almost imperceptibly became transformed into preoccupation with jurisdiction, discipline, sanction and excommunication. The relative fluidity of common faith and practice gave way to a concern for *correct* belief and *correct* practice, secured through a universal hierarchy with executive power.[10] But even acknowledging the abuses of power to which this development could lead (abuses which surely lie behind the fears of some in the ecumenical movement that unity could lead to loss of diversity and to a sterile uniformity), the essential unity of the Apostolic tradition has remained an incontestable feature of the ecclesiological frameworks within which most mainstream churches operate.[11]

And yet the common tradition is configured differently in different churches in history – *that*, we might say, is exactly the ecumenical problem. Different historical configurations of the common tradition themselves constitute the heart of the specific traditions of Christian denominations. When we consider whatever 'local' might mean, in the context of divided history, it is clear that the organization of particular Christian communities at the most basic level inevitably reflects the complex structuring of their 'parent' denominations. At least four patterns can be traced through Christian history, though this is scarcely an exclusive typology.

One model would tend to emphasize the concept of the congregation, or the community of 'gathered believers', as commonly described.
In this case, though the prior emphasis is so often on the association
of likeminded believers, equally important is the gathering *in one
place*. A concept associated closely with the inheritors of the Reformed
tradition of Protestantism, its actual existence – as a concept – is
much more extensive. On the one hand, it can feed into an 'official'
ecclesiology which emphasizes the importance of membership of the
local worshipping congregation as membership of the Church (an
ecclesiology which, in the British context, remains strong in the
Congregational tradition, and in various strands of the United
Reformed Church).[12] On the other hand, it can be present as an 'implicit
ecclesiology' in many denominations, sponsoring an 'associational'
understanding of Christian belonging.[13] A second, distinct type of local
church is that of the parish. Here, the historical origins of parishes in
the early medieval practice of establishing churches for communities
in one place – often founded on lines rather like the Congregational
model – became transmuted, by social and economic growth, into one
in which the significant feature was the concept of spatial extension,
secured through boundaries.[14] Boundaries marked one community off
from another, and one jurisdiction off from another, but they also
served as a way of defining a community's own sense of identity – it
was the community of 'this area'. The existence of parishes permitted
the development of ecclesiastical law around the holding of the office
of local minister, but it also permitted, in time, the emergence of a
concept of a ministry of place which stood in some contrast to that of
the gathered congregation.[15] Needless to say, *this* ecclesiological model
– often misleadingly summarized as 'community church' – can exist
in different denominational contexts, and is dependent very much on
its roots in medieval church history: hence its presence in various forms
in the Reformed Church of Scotland, the Lutheran Baltic and German
churches, and Roman Catholic churches throughout the Mediterranean
world, as well as in the Church of England.

With these two models, we might seem to have exhausted the
possibilities of local ecclesiology at least for the British context. But
that is by no means the case. At least two other examples are available.
A third model is that of the diocese. The canons of the Church of

England offer a sobering corrective to those inclined to see the parish as the fundamental unit of the Church's ministry, for it is there evident that the real focus of local unity is the diocesan bishop, who is 'the chief pastor of all that are within his diocese' and 'the principal minister'.[16] In this instance, spatial extension is also vital, but on a regional basis, and with the residual notion that the diocesan boundaries reflect the potential for gathering together all the worshipping people of one place. This model significantly enhances the role of the bishop, naturally enough, and focuses the exercise of *episkope* in the person of the diocesan bishop.[17] The bishop, then, can be seen as the 'local' minister, exercising responsibility for the local church. A fourth possible model is a further expansion of the notion of spatial extension, and that is the 'national' church. This too is dependent upon the formation of linguistic, cultural and historical identities, which remain remarkably impervious to the growth of globalism, and yet which are in many cases extremely extended geographically. Autonomous 'national' churches are commonly assumed to have been – at least in the West – mainly the product of the Protestant Reformation, but that is a somewhat myopic reading of church history. For British church historians, the example of Catholic France – from the sixteenth through to the eighteenth centuries marked by a vigorous 'Gallican' movement to assert considerable ecclesiastical autonomy – ought to be a reminder that matters are not so straightforward. The eclipse of some versions of 'national' ecclesiology by, on the one hand, the vigorous Catholic Ultramontanism of the nineteenth century, and on the other by the growth of international denominationalism, should not blind us to the fact that 'national' identity remains a powerful if contentious ingredient in describing the nature of religious identity for many people.[18]

There are significant omissions from this typology – they include province, communion and denomination – but it is arguable that each of them fails to do sufficient justice to the concept of place to qualify for inclusion in a consideration of local ecclesiology. More of a case can certainly be made for inclusion of the Methodist understanding of 'connexion', as David Carter argues elsewhere in this volume, though again it is not entirely clear how well such a contention could serve a reading of the 'local' church.[19] Certainly, the major contribution of the modern sociology of religion to the typology of religious community – the concept of denomination, with its associated threefold organizational typology of church, denomination and sect – is of not much more than tangential relevance to modern ecumenical discussion of local ecclesiology.[20] This is perhaps because our attention to social context has made us increasingly aware that, disturbingly, the predominant features of particular Christian communities may not be those held directly in common with other members of the same denomination across vastly different times and situations, but those shared by people living in the same time and place, however broadly defined. White, middle-class Western Christianity may look much the same to African Christians, for example, whether it is Catholic, Anglican, Methodist, Lutheran or Reformed. Conversely, fundamental differences of opinion run right through most Christian denominations, and often counteract the prominence of shared denominational characteristics.

In summary, then, what the diversity of local Christan experience indicates is the inescapable interaction of church organization and particular history. The common tradition of the Church may well be a necessary presupposition of ecumenical relations – I must recognize that I address the other in ecumenical dialogue as a 'thou', that is as someone with a shared history and Christian identity, for the ecumenical project to make any sense at all – but actual local churches conceive their role in the formation of that 'common tradition' in radically different ways. And this makes the task of local ecumenism immeasurably complex.

The British ecumenical scene provides many examples of local arrangements in which there has been a deliberate attempt to honour and preserve contributing traditions, but for contrast's sake it may be worth examining closely one instance of a highly integrated ecumenical partnership. Christ the Cornerstone is a new church in the centre of Milton Keynes, a new city built mainly in the 1960s and 1970s some 50 miles north of London. Milton Keynes is generally prosperous, designed around use of the motor car, with wide dual carriageways running through it, and lacking a pedestrianized, historic centre of the kind found in most British cities and large towns. Christ the Cornerstone is a modern building, completed in 1991. It describes itself as 'the first Ecumenical City Centre Church in the United Kingdom'.[21] Certainly, the extent to which different denominational traditions have been integrated not only into one site – there are many other examples of church-sharing in Britain – but into one congregation is very striking. Five denominations are involved – Roman Catholic, Anglican, Methodist, Baptist and United Reformed – and four of them officially worship together on Sunday morning, with members of the fifth, the Roman Catholic Church, also often joining them, though not officially to receive communion when there is a Eucharist. The shared order of service is from the Church of South India. On Sunday evenings, worship takes place in which members of all five traditions 'share together'.[22] The four 'Protestant' traditions together have consti-tuted an ecumenical parish for the church, and the covenant which lies at the heart of the partnership of the five represents a commitment between the ecumenical parish and the Roman Catholic Pastoral Council of the church. The covenant concedes the existence of plural 'congregations' ('Believing that the unity of the Church is the will of God, we, the members and ministers of the congregations at the Church of Christ the Cornerstone, hereby covenant upon the founda-tion of the recognition that we have one Lord, one Faith, one Baptism'), though so much of the church's life is based on the effective assumption of one worshipping community.[23] It is not entirely clear, in any case, whether the plural 'congregations' refers to the two (that is, Protestant and Catholic) or to the five denominations.

The very high degree of integration achieved at the church – and affirmed constantly to students of mine on a visit to meet ministers and members of the church in June 2001 – has not altogether ironed out the complexities of contrasting 'local' ecclesiologies, however. As an 'ecumenical parish', the church has a defined geographical juris-diction, and takes its place in the network of other local Anglican parishes. Yet evidently this concept of 'parish' does not significantly enhance or alter the understanding of the role of the local church held by other participating denominations. That is, actually, something of a tribute to the arrangement: it is not at all clear that the participating traditions consider the church to have been 'Anglicanized'. Publicity literature for the church tends to highlight the principle of worshipping together, implying that *that* is the fundamental expression of the local church, and so introducing certain aspects of the 'congregational' or 'gathered church' model. Moreover, there are some signs that the sociology of the local church in Milton Keynes is such that the congregation at Christ the Cornerstone is to some degree a self-selecting one, one in which there is a conscious and deliberate affiliation on the part of members to an 'ecumenical' church, with dissenting voices over the years displaced to other local churches in which distinctive denominational traditions can find definite expression. This tension between 'parish' and 'gathered' models of local church is an entirely familiar one in the Anglican context, at least in urban areas, where church-choosing has been common at least since the middle of the nineteenth century.[24] But the situation at churches such as Christ the Cornerstone is further complicated by the relationship of the new, ecumenical congregation to the sponsoring denominations, and by the possibility that what is emerging there is something like a new, 'ecumenical' tradition in its own right, with a style of worship which owes something to all of the participating traditions, but which is particularly influenced by a common 'evangelical' culture, and marked by a particular worshipping style.

The coming together of five churches with a concomitant variety of theological and liturgical traditions, ecclesial structures and patterns of authority is a remarkable achievement. The complexity of the structures through which Christ the Cornerstone is managed is testimony to the commitment and energy required to sustain it. There is a team of five full-time ministers, appointed from across the five participating denominations. Though ministerial teams are a common feature of ministry in all our churches, it is rare for so many to be based at just one church building (other than a cathedral), making Christ the Cornerstone the modern equivalent of a minster or collegiate foundation. Over a hundred volunteers staff the various activities and agencies run at the church throughout the week, including a café, bookshop and reception area. Overseeing the work of the church is the Milton Keynes Christian Council, an intermediate body associated with Churches Together in England and comprising an ecumenical assembly and presidency. Some 64 churches of various denominations in the borough of Milton Keynes are members of the Council (including 23 which are 'ecumenical congregations' in their own right), which has its own full-time Ecumenical Moderator.[25] Indeed, the role of the Ecumenical Moderator is an intriguing and particularly significant one.[26] To have a full-time ecumenical executive officer for a local council of churches is itself unusual, but the position's job description is an extensive one which, in places, suggests a profile for the Moderator somewhat akin to a convergence of models of authority present in different traditions. The title 'Moderator' suggests one such model, but amongst the roles defined for the post are to 'exercise visionary and pastoral ecumenical leadership' and to 'focus and symbolize in a personal way the unity of the Christian community in the Borough of Milton Keynes', descriptions which are also resonant for the notion of episcopacy.[27]

Thus, at Christ the Cornerstone, the presence of hitherto competing Christian traditions in one local ecumenical partnership has been developed to such an extent that it seems as if distinctively new – if somewhat synthesized – ecumenical institutions are coming into being. Many would feel that it was hard to recognize *their* church in this situation.[28] Yet it should be noted that the attempt to embody the one, common Christian tradition in Milton Keynes is precisely dependent on distinct elements offered to the partnership by the participating churches. And that means that, in a spirit of genuine ecumenical partnership, and therefore of equality, the vital means for expressing the Church's unity in that place has been essentially conciliar. That much, of course, can be acknowledged without exploring at this stage in detail what models of conciliarity may or may not be present there.[29]

Particular Histories

Enough has been said already to suggest that what is striking about the diversity of local ecumenical activity in Britain is not so much its 'advanced' quality – though it is at least arguable that churches such as Christ the Cornerstone do indeed represent an extraordinary achievement which may very well blaze a trail for others – as the strong and culturally embedded nature of the contrasting traditions which, time and again, are obliged in ecumenical encounter to work together and to discover the truth about each other. That in turn implies that ecumenical method, whether applied at the local, national or international level, must involve a process of historical retrieval and understanding, a process of *verstehen*, in the term used by Max Weber.[30]

Two major ecclesiological theoreticians in the history of ecumenical thought provide a brief illustration. Frederick Denison Maurice (1805–72), the Anglican theologian who is most often thought of today in connexion with Christian Socialism and his expulsion from his chair at King's College, London for apparently casting doubt on eternal damnation, wrote his most substantial contribution to ecclesiology when comparatively young.[31] *The Kingdom of Christ* (1838; revised 1842) remains something of an Anglican 'classic', tracing the lineaments of the catholicity of the Church in what Maurice called 'hints' of the 'Principles, Constitution, and Ordinances of the Catholic Church'.[32] The centrepiece of the book is a long fourth chapter on the 'Signs of a Spiritual Society', which draws on the Anglican tradition of the 'notes' of the Church and anticipates the Chicago–Lambeth Quadrilateral, tracing six 'signs' in the Scriptures, the creeds, baptism, Eucharist, ministerial order (particularly episcopacy) and a 'fixed liturgy'.[33] But this is preceded by a series of chapters which seek to explore the catholicity of the Church through divided Christian history. Maurice's method was profoundly influenced by S. T. Coleridge, and assumed a dialectical epistemology; the presence of truth in divided Christian traditions could be discerned in the positive affirmations they had made, which in turn had been obscured in history by the development of these affirmations to the exclusion of others.[34] By a historical method, then, retrieving these fragmented affirmations, the survey of separated Christian traditions could enable the recovery of a full vision of the 'spiritual society' Christ had founded.

Maurice's method was admired by Yves Congar (1904–95), whose *Divided Christendom* (ET, 1939) is in many ways a modern Catholic counterpart to Maurice.[35] Congar operated with a fundamentally different set of assumptions about the locus of the fullness of the catholicity of the Church, needless to say: where Maurice seems simply to have assumed the Church of England as his starting-point (in that no fundamental defence of the Anglican position as such was offered in *The Kingdom of Christ*), Congar – admittedly in a much more sophisticated way – correspondingly assumed the inherent truth of the Roman Catholic position. *Divided Christendom* is a much more systematic work, too, more thoroughly grounded in patristic and medieval history than was Maurice's ecclesiology.[36] Congar was not indebted to the Romantic, Platonist tradition of Coleridge; his positive reading of many aspects of the separated communities of the Church has to be placed in the context of Catholic *ressourcement*, reaching back perhaps as far as Johann Adam Moehler, or even further.[37] But like Maurice, Congar's ecumenical sympathies are evident in his assumption that the truth of the Church – a rich and 'comprehensive' truth, to apply the term often used of Maurice – is fully enmeshed in its history, and its expression is shaped historically, so that the grounds of Church division can be understood only through a sensitive and sympathetic appreciation of the histories of separated Christian communities. In this way, Congar was able to countenance the re-reception of Christian truth, including those doctrines which may have been ignored or distorted in the Church's history.[38]

It would be claiming too much to argue that the historical approach pioneered by Maurice and Congar, amongst others, is the only necessary way to enter into ecumenical dialogue. Others have pointed out different approaches. Paul Avis, for example, has contrasted the dialectical method of Coleridge and Maurice with the 'propositional' approach he supposes to be typical of Roman Catholic theology (an identification surely open to question).[39] The 'propositional' approach, even assuming that to be a satisfactory designation, remains central to the process of theological evaluation lying at the heart of ecumenical dialogue, and its imprint is evident for example in the Lutheran–Roman Catholic Joint Declaration on the Doctrine of Justification.[40] But the dialectical approach to divided church history is certainly of evident value no less locally as in the national and international context. It is a method which seeks not to transcend history or to abstract from it but to work with and through it, opening up the possibility of receiving with sympathy the histories of different Christian communities.

Correspondingly, the dialectical method also offers a way through some of the excessive 'contextualizing' arguments currently encountered in many church circles, which, unless challenged or qualified by the evaluation of conviction, can actually hinder the process of understanding the sources of different theological opinions. The impact of contextualizing arguments bears some brief consideration here. Susan Durber's reaction to the ecumenical movement's search for linguistic and conceptual correspondence is a neat illustration of the approach: 'If we are to be contextual theologians, then we cannot have unity on the basis of a struggle for the truth which is above all our contexts and which is somehow universal, original and absolute.'[41] At a superficial level, the view Durber represents seems to serve local communities particularly well, since it affirms their own narrative and apprehension of the truth, and it is an insight central to recent attempts to develop ways of expressing and understanding theology from 'within' particular communities, drawing on the inspiration of liberation, feminist and other 'advocacy' theologies.[42] Contextualization is, suffice it to say, a vital tool for encouraging local communities to have theological confidence, and at the same time it is a way of reading how they give an account of themselves. Yet the possibilities of the contextual approach are not as extensive as its proponents seem to think. There are fundamental questions about the nature of Gospel truth and about epistemology which it scarcely touches satisfactorily. The contextual approach can imply an almost hermetically sealed specificity of local narrative which may presuppose no firm point of contact with competing narratives. It may imply too a polarization of the 'local' and the 'universal', and effectively empty the universal Church of meaning and significance. Furthermore, unless the contextual approach is balanced by attention to questions of truth, it is difficult to understand what the character of local ecumenical discussion might be, other than the rehearsal of particular narratives, implying a series of monologues rather than genuine discussion. Dialogue surely implies a readiness to open up my own narrative to the searching examination of others, and thereby a readiness to admit error, the need for repentance and change. The truth cannot *only* be 'above all our contexts', for sure, but nor can it only be contained within them: its embodiment in particular contexts suggests a universal *and* local presence, and the apprehension of this complex notion of presence is precisely what the dialectical method seeks to achieve.

Thus, far from reinforcing the commonly heard view that ecumenism 'on the ground' simply gets on with things which are made unnecessarily difficult by theologians and church leaders, the dialectical approach to church history offers a way of relating local ecumenical encounter to ecumenical relations at a more general level. Again, the illustration of this can only take us back to specific local instances. I shall offer at this point just one. East Barnwell is a relatively self-contained community of mainly local authority housing on the eastern edge of Cambridge, hemmed in by the railway, the River Cam, the main Newmarket road, and by Cambridge airport. Developed mainly in the 1950s and 1960s, it is home to four mainstream Christian churches, Anglican, Methodist, Roman Catholic and Baptist, with the first two by far the largest. At the beginning of the 1980s, a new Anglican district was carved out of the neighbouring parish of Fen Ditton, but from the early 1990s, when the district was made into a parish in its own right, a new local ecumenical partnership has been in the process of formation. As yet, the four congregations continue to use their own buildings, meeting together at least once a month for joint worship, and otherwise sharing resources and activities as much as possible. In terms of the integration of traditions, then, East Barnwell is not as 'advanced' as Christ the Cornerstone in Milton Keynes. But it is, to that extent, perhaps more typical of ecumenical arrangements in Britain at the local level.

Meeting representatives of the churches in June 2001, it was evident that there is a great deal of enthusiasm for common initiatives, and hope for further ecumenical progress in the area. Yet this is not without an awareness of the need to hold on to authentic traditions, and to understand those of the partner churches. Indeed, the covenant by which Churches Together in East Barnwell was formed makes explicit reference to the importance of understanding and valuing each other's histories: 'We repent of all that is sinful in our past histories and present attitudes. On our pilgrimage together, we celebrate the richness of our own traditions, honour each other's and thank God for the unity we are discovering.'[43] This is, arguably, a richer understanding of the role of distinctive histories than is evident (at least in the literature available) at Christ the Cornerstone. Perhaps Churches Together in East Barnwell is, in that sense, representative of a more positive way forward for local ecumenical arrangements, since its aim is to hold in creative tension the distinctive traditions out of which the four local congregations have emerged with a commitment to an ongoing process of united action and witness. Certainly, their approach is at least a realistic one for the context. One assessment of the attitudes of the Methodist congregation, for example, captures very well the hope of unity and the fear of loss of identity shared by members: 'the feeling of most of the congregation and of the Church Council is that a certain degree of caution should be exercised. There is a natural fear of losing those traditions which are held dear.'[44] In East Barnwell, the four congregations are wrestling with exactly the same issues of unity and diversity which concern the ecumenical movement as a whole.

Structures of Authority

So far, I have drawn attention to two overlapping, problematic issues for local ecumenism – the relationship of separate traditions to the common Gospel tradition, and the question of respecting historic identities whilst engaging in a search for the expression of full and genuine Christian unity. Now I shall turn briefly to my third area, that of the models of authority present in local ecumenical arrangements.

My main concern here is not with the 'classic' discussions of models of ecclesial hierarchy and responsibility, as illustrated for example in recent ecumenical reflection on the relationship of episcopacy and *episkope*. There is a variety of ways in which the formal constitutions of particular churches can be accommodated to each other in specific ecumenical arrangements. We have already seen how, for example, the executive Ecumenical Moderator in Milton Keynes is a figure whose job description reflects a number of different ecclesial traditions; yet even at Christ the Cornerstone, there continue to be formal relations of responsibility and jurisdiction for each of the full-time ministers (with the Anglican licensed by the local diocesan bishop, for example, just like other parochial clergy). Rather, at issue are the implicit patterns of authority and power within local ecumenical arrangements. Conceptually, confusion abounds in this area. I have already pointed out the complex nature of the contrast between 'local' and 'universal', with 'local' itself subject to different ecclesiological interpretations. Naturally, *that* complexity is echoed in the many different ways in which decisions are made and initiatives are taken. If one were to adapt the language conventionally used in relation to political institutions, the pertinent question would be, '*Where* is policy on local ecumenical activity created?' To put it that way is to invite a plural answer, taking into account local personnel and institutions, intermediate and regional bodies, and finally national, denominational and international bodies: *all* of these contribute to a process of policy formation which affects what happens on the ground.

Yet this complexity is scarcely reflected in much of the language used about the structure and exercise of authority in local ecumenism. To the false polarity of 'local' and 'universal', others could be added: 'vertical' and 'horizontal', 'centre' and 'periphery', 'hierarchy' and 'universal priesthood'. Of course, terminology such as this can help to construct varieties of heuristic device, useful to clarify thinking about the exercise of authority in ecclesial contexts. But they are useful only so far as they do not oversimplify and so falsify the description of the reality they seek to express. In practice, all too often they are deployed in arguments which seek to locate legitimation exclusively in one area of ecclesial activity. To accent the local, horizontal authority embodied in the 'universal priesthood', for example, could lead to a determination to prioritize the role of local church members over and against that of intermediate and national or denominational representatives, unsettling the delicate balance between all these levels of church polity that a truly integrated ecclesial life requires. To overemphasize, on the other hand, the hierarchical constitution of the Church might lead to an equal and opposite inattention to the place of local church members (the 'whole people of God', in the language popularized by *Lumen Gentium*) in all that has a bearing on the life and mission of the Church. There are some conceptual similarities in all this to the limitations of the language of 'base' and 'superstructure' deployed in Marxist discourse: the distinction was designed to clarify the relationship of culture to modes of production, with the implication that the latter represented the 'real' driver of historical change, but the over-simplifications to which it could lend itself (and which were arguably never true to Marx's own understanding of human agency) undermined its usefulness.[45]

All this suggests that theologians have much to learn from sociologists of power, who in turn have had to come to terms with the metaphorical character of the descriptions of reality they offer. The application of conventional terminology to describe the patterns of authority latent in ecclesiastical arrangements requires a sophisticated sociological and cultural analysis, which in turn requires theological evaluation, in the light of a hermeneutic. Any one local ecumenical partnership or arrangement, analysed this way, will bring to light multiple, overlapping and sometimes competing situations present in all formal 'models' of ecclesial authority. My final concrete example is not a local ecclesial community as such, but an ecumenical federation of institutions in theological education – the Cambridge Theological Federation, in which I taught for five and a half years. The Federation first came into being in the early 1970s, when four colleges – two Anglican, one Methodist and one United Reformed Church – came together to form a combined teaching arrangement, with a commitment to frequent common worship together. More recently, the Federation has expanded rapidly, with the inclusion as full members of an ecumenical part-time training course, a Roman Catholic theological institute for lay women, and an institute for Orthodox studies, and – as associate members – of two further institutes, a Centre for Jewish–Christian Relations and a mission studies institute.[46] The Cambridge Theological Federation thereby represents a remarkably diverse organization, with its 'core activity' still the training of students for ordained ministry, but with a significant number of non-ordinands amongst its students, and with a great diversity of backgrounds, ages and confessional traditions. The federal system combines joint ecumenical teaching across the whole range of subjects in theological education with primary formation in the particular traditions from which students have been sponsored.

Where and how is authority exercised in the Federation? As with ecumenical arrangements involving local congregations, it is possible to perceive the operation of the dominant ecclesial systems of each confessional tradition. This, it should be said, is complex enough. For the Anglicans, for example, ordained members of teaching staff are licensed by the Bishop of Ely, and the chapels of the two Anglican colleges are under the bishop's jurisdiction. Any significant innovation, such as the recent introduction of the reserved sacrament into one of the chapels, requires episcopal approval. The two colleges are also in a strong sense under the authority of the House of Bishops in particular, and more generally the General Synod of the Church of England. They receive income from the payment of fees which are set centrally; they are subject to regular inspection by teams accountable to the House of Bishops; and their teaching and curricula are 'moderated' and validated through the central Ministry Division, which is in turn a branch of the new Archbishops' Council. Already, then, one can see several different models of authority at work, including episcopal direction, the 'representative' principle of synodical government, and bureaucratic regulation. Actually, the two colleges are technically independent institutions, with their own charters of foundation, their own governing bodies, and their own powers to regulate their affairs – more complexity still. Similar complexities exist for all the other non-Anglican institutions.

Yet it is as a collection of partners in an ecumenical enterprise that the Cambridge Theological Federation concerns us here. What has to be given up, or compromised, or mediated and negotiated, for the Federation to work? Perhaps the closest comparison is to local ecumenical partnerships which are not fully integrated on one site, unlike Christ the Cornerstone at Milton Keynes, or even at Bar Hill, a small ecumenical parish just west of Cambridge. As discrete institutions, the particular pattern of authority distinctive of each tradition remains largely in place, to a considerable extent unaffected by the development of the Federation. Yet the Federation is now a powerful institution in its own right, with its own budget, its own governing structures, its own executive officers, and its own ability to consider and adopt 'policy'. It has, over the three decades of its own existence, correspondingly developed its own traditions and its own 'life'. At the time of writing, its governing structures and constitution are undergoing a thorough overhaul, but until very recently its sovereign body was its governing Federation Council, constituted on a representative basis: teaching and administrative staff of all member institutions were automatically members, and students nominated representatives. This council has been served by an executive committee, an elected president, and various subcommittees. Teaching and worship are largely matters in which the Federation has autonomy, but the mixed, representative nature of the Federation Council has meant that competing Christian voices have been heard on specific issues of controversy. Majority voting theoretically has been the order of the day, but there has been an unwritten convention that a proposal would not be pursued if very strong opposition was encountered from one particular member institution, even if in a minority. Yet where has real power lain in the Federation? Not, finally, with the Council, but with the informal meeting of college principals, each of whom has been able to exercise effectively a veto over any policy proposal mooted in the Federation.[47]

In this particular 'local ecumenical project', then, authority has been structured in complex and often undefined ways, and power likewise has been exercised as much through invisible and informal media as through the formal mechanisms of Federation and member institution government. But this complexity and invisibility has often been the saving of the Federation. The understandable reaction of some participants – staff and students alike – that the whole system has lacked clarity might, beyond a certain point, itself lack a certain realism. For the remarkable feature of the Federation is precisely the coming together of no less than six different denominational and faith traditions, each with its own different history, culture and polity. In such a situation, short of finding a clear and streamlined mode of government that would be likely to exacerbate tensions between the Federation and particular sponsoring churches, the very pliability of the Federation's *modus operandi* has enabled significant ecumenical progress to be made despite fundamental disagreement on major issues of theological (and especially ecclesiological) principle. The very diffuse structuring of authority I have outlined has created generous space for exploring common activity and common commitments, without requiring that member institutions resolve all the outstanding areas of ecclesiological difference remaining between them.

The Goal of Unity and the Local Church

In three ways, then – the relationship of specific traditions to the common tradition, the need for mutual understanding of each others' histories, and the complex ways in which authority is often exercised in local ecumenical situations – local ecumenism has both anticipated and reflected the same sets of issues which have faced churches at the pan-denominational level. Far from reinforcing the common perception that local ecumenism 'gets on with simply doing it' rather than 'just talking about it', these considerations suggest that the ecumenical challenge is essentially the same, whatever the nature of the enterprise in question. At the local level, just as much as in the ecumenical dialogues, the question of what kind of unity is desirable, and what kind of diversity is possible within this unity, is a very pressing one. And yet local ecumenism in practice reminds us that we cannot have a 'context-free' unity, but have to deal with real differences of history, culture and identity, which must in some sense be transcended by the pursuit of unity, but also fulfilled through it.

Looking at the three related sets of issues above, I have – perhaps implicitly – traced a trajectory from the pragmatic to the paradigmatic. I have described three local ecumenical situations which 'work' more or less successfully, and yet each of which is the outcome as much of practical pressures as of theoretical commitments. In all three cases it would be possible, though blinkered or reductive, to allege that anxieties over shortage of resources – in a general context of continued Church decline – has been as much of an influence as ecumenical idealism.[48] But, in sketching the way in which these local situations have developed, I have also begun to hint at a quasi-theoretical position that I would see as undergirding most local ecumenical partnerships and projects. At the risk of oversimplifying the issues somewhat, in what remains I shall draw out key features of this, albeit briefly.

First, then, is the observation that the very untidiness of these local ecumenical arrangements in most cases is a strength rather than a weakness. Tidy arrangements suggest the taking of short-cuts, the cutting off or tidying away of uncomfortable or awkward practices and the imposition of unwelcome imperatives. No ecumenical project – particularly where strong but contrasting identities are concerned – can afford to treat any of its participants with arrogance. Ecumenism is an end as well as a means, if by an 'end' we mean the achievement of a situation of unity in which full respect is accorded to fellow Christians. Untidiness can, of course, be obstructive and inefficient;

but it also seems an inevitable product of a situation that seeks to take multiply contrasting church traditions and practices seriously. Untidy institutions, paradoxically, are likely to be those which adapt well to change, and which can be flexible enough to contain serious disagreement.[49]

Clearly, though, some clarity of goals and commitments is necessary for any local ecumenical arrangement to come into being at all. And that in turn suggests that there is always a place for formal agreements, even if their terms are not precise. In most local ecumenical partnerships in Britain today, at the heart of the arrangement lies a document invariably called a 'covenant'. A common criticism of these documents is that they are vague. But, if the suggestion above is correct, their very vagueness is likely to be a strength. Their commitments are usually stated simply enough, and locate the particular project in the mainstream of trinitarian Christianity. The opening paragraphs of the East Barnwell covenant are a good example:

> We Christians [of the churches in Barnwell], continuing our response to God's call to be one in Christ, rejoice in our common inheritance of the Scriptures and historic creeds.
>
> We affirm our faith in one God, Father Creator, his Son Jesus Christ our Lord and Saviour and the Holy Spirit who continues God's work in the world today.[50]

The East Barnwell covenant does not address specific, contentious issues such as baptismal policy, but by leaving them out it allows space for continuing discussion and development in this *within* (and this is vital) a common recognition of each church's location in the stream of Christian community and mission. The clarity as such, then, lies in the articulation of fundamental, shared theological truth, rather than in the settling of controversial ecclesiological issues.

But then there is a further implication of this need both for untidiness in institutions and clarity about basic goals, and that is that there must be a mechanism by which member churches and traditions can participate in the evolution of the partnership, and inevitably that raises the question of conciliar models. That ecumenical arrangements at the local level require conciliarity in some shape or form seems inescapable. Without prejudging arguments about desirable models of conciliarity, what is noteworthy in the English context is the way in which the development of networks of local and then intermediate or regional councils of churches has proceeded largely in a piecemeal way, without the imposition of one dominant pattern.[51] This, following my defence of untidiness, suggests again that the diversity of context may very well demand a plurality of institutional forms, at least in a provisional sense.

Untidiness, covenant and conciliarity can work as governing features of local ecumenical partnerships above all because they are held in place by the tangible recognition of common Christian identity and discipleship, and that is particularly well expressed in the language of communion, or *koinonia*. It is not that *koinonia* theology can really take the place of a systematic explication of fundamental Christian principles.[52] Rather, it can provide a grammar for apprehending how Christians are bound together in particular situations, and yet how their actual unity may still fall well short of the unity to which they are called.[53] But it is, again, an untidy and often deliberately vague grammar. Degrees of communion can be traced in actual situations, and yet there is no textbook definition of what perfect communion would be like; all there is, in summary, is a way of committing ourselves to shared discipleship with fellow Christians, wherever it leads.

But 'communion' as a working concept is not enough. One of its weaknesses, possibly, is that it can all too easily become a static concept, confirming existing relationships but not sufficiently outlining how they may develop for the better. A further feature of local ecumenical relations, in terms of sketching their future, is a principle of dynamism, and that requires recognition that actual local arrangements are invariably provisional, and yet committed to a process of convergence.[54] In this way, local ecumenism can acknowledge its achievements as well as its shortcomings, and look forward to further development of the unity it has already presupposed as its living heart.

Notes

1. L. Newbigin, 'What is a "Local Church Truly United?"', paper delivered to the Nairobi Assembly of the World Council of Churches, 1976; an abbreviated text appears in M. Kinnamon and B. E. Cope (eds), *The Ecumenical Movement. An Anthology of Key Texts and Voices* (Geneva: WCC, 1997), pp. 114–21.
   2. Ibid., p. 115.

3. The incarnationalism of Tillard touches directly on this: 'Unity and catholicity are part and parcel of the *very flesh* of the Church': J.-M. R. Tillard, *Church of Churches. The Ecclesiology of Communion* (Collegeville, MN: Liturgical Press, 1992), p. 9 (my italics).

4. For a striking note of scepticism about the unifying methodology of the ecumenical movement, see for example S. Durber, 'One or Many Languages?', in *Returning Pilgrims. Insights from British and Irish Participants in the Fifth World Faith and Order Conference, Santiago de Compostela* (London: CCBI, 1993), pp. 46–9.

5. *Baptism, Eucharist and Ministry* (Geneva: WCC, 1982), 'Ministry', para. 34, p. 28.

6. See, for example, the Church of England's response, which urged further consideration of the ecclesiological insights of the Lima text: Max Thurian (ed.), *Churches Respond to BEM*, Vol. 3 (Geneva: WCC, 1987), p. 65.

7. *The Nature and Purpose of the Church* (Geneva: WCC, 1998), p. 24.

8. Ibid., para. 66, p. 32.

9. Some recent surveys include: Churches Together in England, *Called to be One*, ch. 5, 'Experience of Unity' (1996), pp. 31–44; M. Reardon, 'Ecumenism in England', in C. Podmore (ed.), *Community–Unity–Communion. Essays in Honour of Mary Tanner* (London: Church House Publishing, 1998).

10. Hans Küng has recently recycled this pessimistic view of Christian history in his *The Catholic Church. A Short History* (London: Weidenfeld & Nicolson, 2001).

11. I am using 'Apostolic tradition' here in the sense which ARCIC II, referring back to the Montreal conference Faith and Order in 1963, has applied to the capitalized 'Tradition', 'the Gospel itself, transmitted from generation to generation in and by the Church': ARCIC II, *The Gift of Authority* (London: Church House Publishing/Catholic Truth Society, 1999), p. 16, n. 1.

12. See, for example, the brief contrast drawn between Anglican and Reformed under-standings of church 'membership' in the report of the Anglican–Reformed International Commission, *God's Reign and Our Unity* (London: SPCK, 1984), p. 36.

13. For a contrast of the 'associational' church with 'community' church, see G. Ecclestone (ed.), *The Parish Church?*, especially ch. 1, 'Discussion Paper: What is a Parish Church?' (Oxford: Mowbrays, 1988), pp. 3–21; the associational model provides the basic framework for a sensitive reading of local church history in S. J. D. Green, *Religion in the Age of Decline. Organisation and Experience in Industrial Yorkshire 1870–1920* (Cambridge: Cambridge University Press, 1996).

14. See the recent account by N. K. G. Pounds, *A History of the English Parish. The Culture of Religion from Augustine to Victoria* (Cambridge: Cambridge University Press, 2000).

15. In Anglican discussion, the 'classic' text to which reference so often is made is George Herbert's *A Priest to the Temple*, but it is as well to heed the warning Mark Pryce has made about treating this text too naively as a manifesto for pastoral practice today: M. Pryce, 'The Parson is a Woman: Rereading George Herbert', in J. Morris (ed.), *Third Millennium*, Vol. 1, *Sex and the Christian Tradition* (London: Affirming Catholicism, 1999).

16. Canon C18, 'Of Diocesan Bishops', *The Canons of the Church of England*.

17. Significant Anglican documents on this include, most recently, The Cameron Report, General Synod (GS) paper 944, *Episcopal Ministry* (London: Church House Publishing, 1990) and the House of Bishops' Occasional Paper, GS Miscellaneous 432, *Apostolicity and Succession* (London: Church House Publishing, 1994).

18. This is particularly so for many of the Orthodox churches; see, for example, D. C. Lewis, *After Atheism: Religion and Ethnicity in Russia and Central Asia* (New York: St Martin's Press, 2000).

19. See David Carter's essay in this volume, pp. 65–6.

20. The *loci classici* of this discussion are the works of Ernest Troeltsch, *The Social Teaching of the Christian Churches* (London: Allen & Unwin, 1931) and H. Richard Niebuhr, *The Social Sources of Denominationalism* (New York: Meridian, 1929), but there is a clear outline in M. Hill, *The Sociology of Religion* (London: Heinemann, 1973), pp. 43–70.

21. *Christ the Cornerstone. Mini Tour Guide* (n.d.), p. 1.

22. *Join us Here at Christ the Cornerstone* (pamphlet, n.d.).

23. *Covenant of Christ the Cornerstone* (n.d.).

24. The phenomenon was fuelled by the tripartite division of the Church of England in the mid-nineteenth century, with, for example, 'Church Tourist' guides produced for Anglo-Catholics who wished to find a church of their liturgical and doctrinal preference in an unfamiliar town.

25. *Milton Keynes Christian Council* (pamphlet, n.d.).

26. 'Milton Keynes has gone further in this regard than anywhere else in England (or the world) in appointing an Ecumenical Moderator to whom the leaders of the local denominations . . . have delegated certain elements of their normal denominational oversight of the town': Reardon, Churches Together in England, *Called to be One*, p. 38.

27. Milton Keynes 'Ecumenical Moderator Job Description', 6 April 1995.

28. That was the reaction of many of my students, themselves a mixed group composed of Roman Catholics, Anglicans, Methodists and United Reformed

29. See, for example, Alan Falconer's discussion of the four models of councils of churches identified by the WCC Office for Church and Ecumenical Relations, 'An ecclesiological understanding of Councils of Churches', in Podmore, *Community–Unity–Communion*, pp. 104–17.

30. H. H. Gerth and C. Wright Mills, *From Max Weber. Essays in Sociology* (London: Routledge & Kegan Paul, 1970), p. 56.

31. Still by far the best short introduction to Maurice's work is A. Vidler, *The Theology of F. D. Maurice* (London: SCM Press, 1948); there is a succinct and positive appreciation of him in P. D. Avis, *Anglicanism and the Christian Church* (Edinburgh: T&T Clark, 1989), pp. 260–70.

32. F. D. Maurice, *The Kingdom of Christ*, 2 vols, 4th edn (London, 1891), title page. The 1842 revision remained the basis of all subsequent editions and has been used much more widely than the first edition, for which the print run was small.

33. See M. Woodhouse-Hawkins, 'Maurice, Huntington, and the Quadrilateral: an Exploration in Historical Theology', in J. Robert Wright (ed.), *Quadrilateral at One Hundred* (Oxford: Mowbray, 1988).

34. I have explored the historical presuppositions of Maurice's argument in 'Newman and Maurice on the Via Media of the Anglican Church: Contrasts and Affinities' (*Anglican Theological Review*, forthcoming).

35. Y. M. J. Congar, *Divided Christendom: A Catholic Study of the Problem of Reunion* (London: Geoffrey Bles, 1939).

36. Though I am not aware of any direct scholarly comparison of the two men, it is interesting, for example, that B. C. Butler, himself an admirer of Maurice, in his ecclesiological work *The Idea of the Church* (London: Darton, Longman & Todd, 1962), turns approvingly to Congar for a description of medieval ecclesiology: ibid., pp. 6–7.

37. See, for example, Congar's own tribute to Moehler, in *Diversity and Communion* (London: SCM Press, 1984), pp. 149–52.

38. On 're-reception', see ibid., pp. 171–2.

39. P. D. Avis, *Ecumenical Theology and the Elusiveness of Doctrine* (London: SPCK, 1986), pp. 7–11. In drawing such a contrast, Avis is clearly influenced by John Coulson's description of 'fiduciary' language and its contrast with 'analyical' language in *Newman and the Common*

Tradition. A Study in the Language of Church and Society (Oxford: Oxford University Press, 1970), pp. 4–8. But the identification of Roman Catholic theological method as 'propositional' is surely much too sweeping, and leaves little space for the mystical and participative interpretations of Catholic theology and doctrine traced, for example, in D. Turner, *The Darkness of God: Negativity in Christian Mysticism* (Cambridge: Cambridge University Press, 1995), and in J. Milbank and C. Pickstock, *Truth in Aquinas* (London: Routledge, 2001) .

40. I mean that, of course, simply in the sense that the joint declaration amounts to a systematic, comparative explication of Lutheran and Roman Catholic approaches to justification.

41. Durber, 'One or Many Languages?', p. 48.

42. Important recent instances include L. Green, *Let's Do Theology* (London: Mowbrays, 1990), and J. Reader, *Local Theology: Church and Community in Dialogue* (London: SPCK, 1994).

43. 'A Covenanted Partnership of the Churches in East Barnwell, Cambridge', signed on Good Friday, 2 April 1999.

44. 'Meadowlands Methodist Church – Church Profile', *c*.2000.

45. I have in mind here Raymond Williams' influential essay in the *New Left Review* in 1973, 'Base and Superstructure in Marxist Cultural Theory', reprinted in J. Higgins (ed.), *The Raymond Williams Reader* (Oxford: Blackwell, 2001), pp. 158–78.

46. So far no account of the formation and history of the Cambridge Theological Federation has been published; some relevant information is included in the Common Validation Document submitted for the validation of the Federation's academic programmes in 1996, privately printed and circulated.

47. It is only fair to note that this governing structure, though unwieldy and unnecessarily time-consuming, has generally operated well, ensuring that the principle of consensus remained at the heart of ecumenical relationships across the Federation.

48. I am well aware that I am skating over a complex, interlocking debate within the sociology of religion both about the real nature and extent of secularization in Britain, and about the relationship of church decline to the ecumenical movement. The classic *topoi* of the discussion include B. R. Wilson, *Religion in Secular Society* (London: Watts, 1966); R. Currie, *Methodism Divided* (London: Faber, 1968); and A. D. Gilbert, *Religion and Society in Industrial England* (Harlow: Longman, 1976). More recently, C. G. Brown has transformed our understanding of secularization in *The Death of Christian Britain. Understanding Secularisation 1800–2000* (London: Routledge, 2001).

49. I am making no specific commitment here to an organic, 'Burkean' notion of gradualism, though it would be interesting and perhaps illuminating to pursue that particular line of reflection further in the context of local ecumenism.

50. 'A Covenanted Partnership of the Churches in East Barnwell, Cambridge'.

51. Though Reardon, *Called to be One*, does suggest that there are signs of ecumenical convergence in different denominational models of decision-making: pp. 27–8.

52. For an incisive survey of the place of the concept of *koinonia* in contemporary ecumenical dialogue, see N. Sagovsky, *Ecumenism, Christian Origins and the Practice of Communion* (Cambridge: Cambridge University Press, 2000), pp. 18–47; for a challenging examination of competing readings of *koinonia*, see T. P. Looney, 'Koinonia Ecclesiology: How Solid a Foundation?', in *One in Christ*, 36 (2000), pp. 145–66. Looney concludes that *koinonia*, 'like all ecclesial images, requires complementary theological images to help manifest its deeper significance': ibid., p. 165.

53. One perhaps rather ambiguous development that illustrates this is the deployment of the language of 'impaired communion' within Anglicanism itself, over issues such as the ordination of women and the ordination of practising homosexuals.

54. As Professor Sagovsky points out, Duquoc's embracing of the concept of provisionality and communion, in C. Duquoc, *Provisional Churches* (London: SCM Press, 1986), itself raises further questions about the limits of possible diversity and integrity within the goal of a reunited Church: Sagovsky, *Ecumenism*, p. 202.

6

The Future of Ecumenism in Europe

Keith Clements

The future of ecumenism in Europe, and the future of Europe, are two sides of the same question. This may sound an outlandish assertion. It may seem incredible to those of a secular, Western cast of mind who see the future of Europe only in terms of economic development, creation of common institutions, generally agreed norms of citizenship, human rights and so forth, and who see 'religion' only as a subdivision of that aspect of human affairs known as 'culture': a purely marginal concern of individuals in their private lives without any bearing on the public sphere where hard bargains are made and policies implemented. It may sound equally strange to some of those passionate advocates of the cause of visible Christian unity who see ecumenism in terms only of a narrowly focused ecclesiological agenda, of seeking agreement on authority, ministry and sacraments, an agenda which is not to get mixed up with that distracting and dangerous sociopolitical shopping list of race, ecology, sustainable development, women's rights and so on.

But it is not such an outrageous suggestion when you listen to some of the voices around Europe at the moment. A senior Austrian politician was recently reported to have said that Europe ends where Orthodoxy begins: a statement with which I profoundly disagree but which is at least a recognition of certain realities, ecclesial realities, which cannot be ignored. More hopeful in some ways I find our British Prime Minister's statement in a recent interview that the German he most admired was Dietrich Bonhoeffer.[1] More disturbing were the sort of comments which came out of Yugoslavia during the NATO bombing campaign, that what was taking place was – thanks to President Clinton's religious affiliation – a 'Baptist' war on Orthodoxy. What is striking, is that all over Europe, religious and confessional perspectives are becoming more accepted as the frame of reference within which social and political questions, national and international, are being viewed. The ideological glaciers and icefields of the Cold War having melted and retreated, the still more basic, underlying features of the geology of Europe are becoming exposed: above all, the ancient fault-line between Byzantine East and Latin West, formalized in the great medieval schism but unwittingly grounded centuries earlier, in the division of the Roman empire by Theodosius IV. That historic geographical and cultural boundary today runs right through Bosnia-Hercegovina.

What is Europe?

The fundamental European question today is, 'What *is* Europe?' or, 'Is there really one Europe?' During the promising days of glasnost and perestroika, Mikhail Gorbachov spoke of 'a common European house'. Pope John Paul II echoed and amplified that call. But Europe today seems to be at a moment of loss of nerve as to whether it really is a distinct identity in its own right, or whether there are two or more Europes contending for the same title. Here we have to look closely at the process of 'European integration'. In fact there are several processes making for the integration of European society. For many people in the West, 'Europe' is a short-hand term for the European Union and its fifteen member-states. The EU is indeed a remarkable and formidable phenomenon: it is not just an arrangement between governments, not just an intergovernmental organization, but government on a European level. But amid all the arguments about its policies and the behaviour of its commission in Brussels, the churches above all should not forget that its origin after World War II in the European Coal and Steel Federation was motivated by a profoundly Chrisian idealism. Its parents, Jean Monnet and Robert

Schuman, were remarkable Christian visionaries and at the same time deeply practical realists who wanted to build an economic inter-dependency which would ensure that war, above all war between France and Germany which had three times in 70 years brought devastation, would not only become undesirable but impossible.[2] The EU today is a mighty motor for change, democratization and economic development – its total economic capacity already exceeds that of the USA.

Poland, Hungary and the Czech Republic – members of the former Soviet bloc – are in line for membership.[3] But underlying this dynamic of integration lurks the question of how far will this eastward march continue. Is the EU to be the means of pan-European integration, or is it destined to be yet another repetition of the age-old story of a basically Western, non-Orthodox (with the notable exception of Greece) unity? Perhaps the treatment of Romania will be a crucial test-case. The same is equally true of the efforts of NATO to transform itself from a Western defence alliance into an instrument of wider interests – or are they in fact still primarily Western interests but operating on a wider scale? To be put alongside these questions is the grim scenario of economic degradation and social disintegration in countries of the former Eastern bloc, and especially those of the former Soviet Union itself, as detailed with stark clarity in the latest United Nations Development Programme report. Add to this that if one is talking about Eastern and Western Europe 'united by mutual economic interests' the most widespread European trading system at the moment is the horrific trafficking of women and even young girls, mainly from the economically deprived regions of the East to the lucrative red-light districts of the West.

Of course, as well as the EU there are the genuinely pan-European institutions of the Council of Europe and the Organization for Security and Cooperation in Europe (OSCE). It also has to be said that the more pan-European the institution, the less well known it is in the public mind and the less highly regarded it is by politicians. When in 1999, after the Kosovo conflict, the British Defence Secretary George Robertson was appointed to be the chief of NATO he revealingly described his new post as the greatest job in the world.

I have not said much so far, it may be thought, about ecumenism in Europe. But what I have been talking about is the context in which European ecumenism is inevitably caught up, and with which it must grapple if it is really to be a sign of hope for the *oikumene*, the whole inhabited earth which is the object of God's love made known in Christ. And, far from being divorced from the practicalities of ecumenical life, these matters bear closely and very practically upon it. For example, for straightforwardly financial reasons it is often now far more difficult for church representatives from Eastern Europe to participate in ecumenical gatherings in the West, or for such meetings to be hosted in the East, than it was during the Cold War. In a speech in 1997 Patriarch Alexei of Moscow warned of an economic 'silver curtain' now dividing Europe in place of the iron curtain – and therewith in danger of separating its churches too. (Incidentally, for similar reasons the teaching of Russian in British schools has markedly declined in the past decade: so few Russian schools can now afford exchanges of pupils with the West.) Added to this is the fact that, especially since the Kosovo crisis, popular anti-Western feeling is stronger in Russia now than during the Cold War.

The Churches: a New European Awareness

I have given a somewhat sombre account of the European context of ecumenism today. There is another side, however, which deserves equal emphasis. I believe a basic sea change has also come about in recent years in the attitude of the European churches to their European home. When the World Council of Churches was inaugurated at Amsterdam in 1948, the context, the ambience and the whole perception of the gathering was inevitably Northern, if not actually European, shaped by World War II and the devastation it had wrought largely upon Europe itself. By the time of the fourth Assembly at Uppsala in 1968, even though that Assembly was held in Europe, there was a massive change. The emphasis now was upon the South, upon the issues of racism and economic injustice at the end of the colonial era. European Christians, with the exceptions of those interested in helping the bureaucrats in Brussels and the gallant peaceniks concerned for East–West relations, understandably felt that their attention should be elsewhere, in sorting out the problems caused by European exploitation of the rest of the world. The Conference of European Churches (CEC) had been founded in 1959 to be a bridge-builder between the churches of Eastern and Western Europe but was regarded as essentially an amiable side-show to the real dramas being played out in southern Africa and Latin America and Asia. A new heresy was discovered and anathematized: eurocentrism. Now, 30 years after Uppsala, ten years after the collapse of the Berlin Wall, it is OK for European Christians and churches to be concerned about Europe again – to be concerned, not as an alternative to concern for the wider world, but out of a recognition that some of the major problems of the world have been caused by the transmission of peculiarly European infections which need to be dealt with at home no less than abroad.

CEC, in its 40th anniversary year (1999), could justly claim in its present membership, life and work, to be both reflecting and fortifying this new mood among the European churches.[4] It now has 125 churches in membership, from all parts of Europe and from all the major confessions except Roman Catholic: Anglican, Baptist, Lutheran, Methodist, Old Catholic, Orthodox, Pentecostal and Reformed. Over 30 bodies, including women's and peace groups, national councils of churches, mission and diaconal agencies and youth organizations, are 'associated organizations'. While the Roman Catholic Church is not a member, there is close cooperation with that church at a number of levels, most especially with the Council of Catholic Episcopal Conferences in Europe (CCEE). There is a joint CEC–CCEE committee which meets each year and acts as a steering group for CEC–CCEE collaboration, and there is close and continual contact between our CEC office in Geneva and the CCEE secretariat in St Gallen, also in Switzerland. Here, it is appropriate to record a profound debt of gratitude to the late Cardinal Hume who was inspired by a tremendous vision for Europe and who, not least in the 'ecumenical encounters' sponsored jointly by CEC and CCEE, gave vital leadership to ecumenical progress at a number of critical points.

A major sign and instrument of the new European awareness by Christians and churches was the first European Ecumenical Assembly held at Basle in 1989 under the title 'Peace with Justice', sponsored jointly by CEC and CCEE.[5] It was significant that it took place in the early summer of that year, as the first tremors of change shivered across Eastern Europe. The people who gathered in Basle realized that they had concrete challenges to work for and that changes were coming, worthy of celebrating even then. And it was significant that that Basle Assembly, more than any other ecumenical gathering in the world, was able to give such a clear and cogent affirmation of the interconnectedness of justice, peace and the integrity of creation – more so, many would argue, than the world conference on the same theme at Seoul the following year, or the next WCC Assembly in Canberra 1991. Through its own conciliar process, European ecumenism was rediscovering itself.

The second European Ecumenical Assembly took place in Graz, Austria, in 1997.[6] In some ways it was a more sober gathering than Basle 1989. But it was a further stage in the maturation of European ecumenism. Basle had declared that there were no situations in Europe which could justify their solution by violence. To Graz, however, came people from the former Yugoslavia, from Croatia and Sarajevo bearing the inner and outer scars of violence – as they did also from Northern Ireland and Albania. The theme was 'Reconciliation – Gift of God and Source of New Life'. It was a recognition of the *need* for healing – and of *hope* for that healing. It was noteworthy for being the most genuinely ecumenical gathering in Europe, ever. For to it came Eastern Europeans in their thousands – a thousand from Romania alone – who were able to speak for themselves rather than be talked about, however compassionately, by Westerners. Moreover, it was a gathering in which Europeans felt no embarrassment in seeking the help of the wider world. One of my own most cherished memories of Graz is that of bumping into an old friend, a black South African on the staff of the Truth and Reconciliation Commission with Desmond Tutu. Asked 'What on earth are you doing here?' he replied: 'I've come to talk to *you* guys about reconciliation.'

A great and positive fact of our time, then, is that the churches of Europe are increasingly aware that Europe itself is a proper concern, for themselves and the wider family of the worldwide Church. That is healthy and liberating.

The European Churches in this Context, and their Ecumenical Commitment

The question of the European churches' commitment to ecumenism tody is closely bound up with the question of their own place in societies and cultures which can variously be described as secular, post-Christian or postmodern. Nearly all Christian traditions in Europe show signs of acute anxiety about their future and their role in society. That is as true of the Western as of the Eastern churches. And it is right that they should be concerned. If they are not asking questions, there will be no answers. Or, in terms of the Gospel sayings, if they are not asking, seeking and knocking, they are unlikely to receive, find or move through opening doors. The issue is whether their quest is serious and honest enough. There is of course much intense bilateral and multilateral activity. But let me ask a question about some of this activity. There is no doubt of the importance of the Meissen and Porvoo agreements, which the Anglican communion has, respectively, concluded with the Evangelical Church of Germany and a number of the Lutheran churches of the Nordic region and elsewhere. But, if I may for a moment take off the polite diplomatic hat which I wear in Geneva, and sport my English dissenter's forage cap, let me ask my dear Anglican friends: was it really necessary to go all the way to Meissen or Porvoo to enter into such agreements with churches which do not have the same doctrine of ministry as you do? Why not start nearer at home? Do not misunderstand me. I am only asking the question. In these processes, how significant is the fact that such agreements are largely between churches which claim to be *national* churches? And how much, therefore, is the underlying agenda one of seeking to maintain the concept of a national church? And what are the implications of that agenda for the future of a Europe where the concepts of nationality and ethnicity, and their religious labelling, is now so fraught? I am sure that I do not need to expand on the point that the interplay between religion and national or ethnic identity must now be top of the European ecumenical agenda. For the churches, if they are really committed to ecumenism – which means being committed to the *una sancta*, the universal Church of Jesus Christ

125

found in and transcending all national boundaries – it is crucial that they face the theological challenge of this, and not seek theological justifications for the status quo in the divisions of the human family – in Europe or anywhere else.

It is easy to find soft targets in the situation in Eastern Europe and the Balkans, in the shape of identification of religion and national identity and confessional privilege. But there is need also for much more self-awareness and self-criticism in the West. Since taking up office in CEC, I have heard, for example, a bishop of the Lutheran Church of Denmark stating that since Denmark is essentially a Lutheran nation, one must beware that ecumenism does not lead to syncretism and thus undermine the national culture. And why is it that in Germany it took two years of hard bargaining with the Protestant Church authorities before a Free Church theologian was allowed to take up his chair in ecumenics – yes, ecumenics! – in the University of Bochum?

On the pan-European level, all the main confessional families are going through a difficult time as they seek to reorientate themselves in the context of a society which is being driven inexorably towards pluralism at every level, and massively so since the tremendous changes that swept across Eastern and Central Europe with the ending of Soviet-style communism ten years ago. Just after most of those changes were completed, during 1991–92 three important confessional gatherings took place. There was in 1991 the first Synod of European Catholic Bishops in Rome, where the theme of the 're-evangelization of Europe' was dominant. Some observers saw this as 'triumphalism': the Church, having withstood the atheist tyranny for 40 years or more, was now in a strategic and morally justified position to reclaim its authority over European life. Rather different in tone was the Protestant Synod which met in Budapest. Here the tone was more modest: the question was how a Christianity in many ways marginal to the public life of Europe could offer a meaningful word to Europeans seeking a reconstructed, genuinely human society. The Reformation message of justification by grace through faith still has something to say. But it was essentially a reactive stance. Then there was the Synod of Orthodox bishops in Constantinople. Here again there was talk of a 'Christian Europe' -- but a Christian Europe somewhat under siege, in need of preservation against the twin threats of secularism from the West and of militant Islam from the East. No one of these three stances by itself is adequate to the mission of the Church in Europe – which makes the ecumenical task all the more important.

I have spoken of three main confessional families. But to be truly ecumenical means also recognizing another family or movement in Europe: the vibrant and growing evangelical and Pentecostal movement, a number of whose branches, significantly, wish to be part of what we like to call 'mainstream' ecumenism. It is significant that in CEC we are receiving a series of applications for membership from these smaller evangelical and Pentecostal churches. Within this stream is one tributary into the European church scene which certainly cannot be ignored. For there is taking place here in Cambridge, at the same time as this conference, another conference of ecumenical significance: on the African diaspora in Europe. Migration from the South into Europe is bringing with it a vibrant African Christianity determined to be at least as missionary as was the European migration into Africa. In the south of Italy there are Protestant congregations (Waldensian, Baptist, Methodist) where the majority are now African. Or not only African. In the Rome area alone there are now upwards of 6,000 Protestant Chinese, worshipping in or alongside the established historic Protestant communities.

But having said all this, there is no doubt of the overarching ecumenical challenge in Europe at the moment: that of the relations between the Orthodox East and the Latin (Catholic and Protestant) West. Not only are the tensions just now so great as to threaten a rupture in the ecumenical fellowship painstakingly developed over the last 40 years, but they bode ill for the future of Europe as such, bringing as they do the possibility of a new division – far more emotionally entrenched than the ideological division of the Cold War – between East and West Europe as such. In some circles in the East, especially in Russia, 'ecumenism' has become an almost unusable word. There are powerful fundamentalisms at work, which have rushed to fill the ideological vacuum left by the demise of Stalinist-Leninism, and allied to a new nationalism which regards ecumenism as *ipso facto* a betrayal of Orthodoxy. Outside Russia, this has taken the Orthodox churches of Georgia and Bulgaria out of membership of both the WCC and CEC. Those committed to ecumenical life within the Russian church itself are having a hard time of it. Vladimir Fedorov of St Petersburg, addressing the Graz Ecumenical Assembly, graphically put this anti-ecumenical and anti-internationalist mood in its context:

> People who have lived their whole lives under a totalitarian ideology and who were brought up with the conviction that they were surrounded by enemies and needed constantly to be vigilant and unmask them are lost without any ideological support in the new conditions. Many have chosen Orthodoxy . . . not out of personal conviction but as a new ideological system. The temptation is understandable, since from outside many see Orthodoxy as a harsh system of rules and regulations, a doctrinal system which believes itself to be the only true one, a system which binds together people who not only do not share a complete set of values but differ in all kinds of ways in their outward appearance. This kind of understanding of Orthodoxy has meant that those who maintain the spirit of Bolshevism have easily been able to find support in Orthodox circles. In a microclimate of 'party control' like this it is impossible to imagine openness towards non-Orthodoxy or ecumenism; these will immediately be interpreted as making a deal with the CIA, Zionism, masonry or other enemies.[7]

It is important to recognize that such views as Fedorov describes are not those of the official leadership of the Russian church. But they do indicate the immense pressures under which that leadership is having to operate in trying to maintain the unity of the church, and it is this internal agenda which is having a consequent effect on ecumenical relationships. Added to which are all the well-known controversial issues of alleged proselytism from the West, both Catholic and Protestant.

Ecumenism in Europe is facing both the worst of times and the best of times. The features of the worst of times I have described adequately already, I hope. The best features are recognizable in what I believe is an underlying current, a gut-feeling, especially among the people of God at large, that there really can be no going back from where we have got to, and the only way is forward, whatever the difficulties. That was sensed at Graz, which really was a people's assembly: an assembly which after all the platform tensions and disagreements culminated in a huge outdoor celebration, carefully scripted for the television cameras but deeply joyful, and which moreover after the final benediction burst into an spontaneous riot of singing and dancing hand-in-hand – Franciscan monks and Swedish women pastors, Orthodox bishops and black Pentecostals, and everyone else. As at

Amsterdam in 1948, people from all confessions and all parts of Europe were saying '*We* intend to stay together.'

But spirit needs to take form. Heavenly vision needs to be realized in deeds on earth. Goals need agendas if they are not to be vain dreams. I can only speak here for what CEC sees as the lines of action for the immediate and medium-term future. I would like to use three words for what I see as our agenda: *encounter*, *engagement* and *envisioning*.

Encounter

'Not by might, nor by power, but by my spirit, says the Lord of hosts' (Zech. 4:6). None of us became ecumenically committed because we were told to be, but because we actually experienced the spirit of unity through meeting, through entering new situations where minds were opened and new awareness was sparked within us, whether of another person's spirituality and understanding of Christ, or another church's life and story, or another country and its churches, or a common task to be shared. The future of ecumenism in Europe depends upon our capacity and willingness to provide such encounters and the means of dialogue.

Sometimes this need emerges in situations of crisis and actual conflict, as has happened over the past few years in the former Yugoslavia and, especially, with the conflict in Kosovo. At such a time the stance and response of churches in that situation becomes of major concern to the wider ecumenical community – especially, in this case, the role of the Serbian Orthodox Church. Where the stance of such a church appears ambiguous or only partially known, it is tempting to opt for two approaches, each of which I would call (echoing Bonhoeffer's phrase about 'cheap grace'), 'cheap ecumenism'. One is to fire off criticisms, like cruise missiles, from the safe distance of our offices in the West or in Geneva. The other is to cosy up to that church and uncritically endorse all that it is saying and doing – or not doing. Both approaches are cheap ecumenism; they cost us little. It is quite another thing to go and sit with that church in Belgrade as the air-raid sirens go off and the lights go out in the patriarchate, and *there* talk and listen and put the awkward questions about our different perceptions of what is going on in Kosovo; personally to challenge and be challenged, and learn how things actually are with them, and in turn communicate that to the wider ecumenical family. That is the way of costly ecumenism. It is not a way which easily delivers results. More often it draws criticisms about fudge and compromise. But one of the hardest experiences of genuine dialogue is the realization that the truth *is* more complex and messy than appears from any one context.

In CEC we are deeply aware that our role as a bridge-building fellowship is no less critical today than in the time of the Cold War. In our Commission on Churches in Dialogue we are undertaking a programme of meetings between, for example, majority and minority churches in both East and West; of joint meetings on the missionary task in Europe; and, particularly important, of providing encounters between younger theologians who are, or wish to be involved in, the teaching of ecumenics. And with our Roman Catholic partners in CCEE we are working on issues facing Christians and Muslims in Europe, and wishing to move towards dialogue with Muslims on common problems in Europe. We want there to be dialogue not just in the exchange of views and established positions, but in real encounter where people are exposed to each other, challenged and enriched by each others' differences. We have got to get beyond the mutual stereotyping which is in danger of corrupting our relationships. To hear some voices from the West at the moment, one would imagine that Orthodoxy is a wholly and inherently autocratic and uniform system allowing no room for individual expression of piety or thought, whereas in fact Orthodoxy abounds in the most splendid examples of personal spiritual genius. To hear some contemporary voices from the East, the impression is given that Western Christianity has wholly given way to post-Enlightenment individualism, whereas in fact much of the most creative theology and practice in the West in the twentieth century, both Protestant and Catholic, has emphasized the *communal* nature of humanity, both in society and in the Church. Such stereotyping, and the self-righteousness which it breeds, can only be countered through actual meeting, however slow and risky a process that may appear to be. But such encounter needs to go further. Bishop Rowan Williams has recently stated quite admirably the difference between the theological horse-trading that much ecumenical discussion involves, and the deepest kind of ecumenism which recognizes 'not just a need to understand each other and to be able politely to work and even worship alongside each other, but a need to *understand God together*' and he calls for the discovery of a 'shared passion', based on the wonder of our incorporation into the triune life of God through Jesus Christ.[8] That of course needs to happen at every level, beginning at the local. But it must also happen at the international level, if we really believe there is one God in Christ for the one Europe. Just after Easter 2001, when with the coincidence of the Western and Eastern calendars Easter was celebrated on the same Sunday by all churches, the Ecumenical Encounter held by CEC and CCEE took place, when the CEC Central Committee and the Presidents of the Catholic Bishops' Conferences in Europe met with an equal number of young people to share together their faith and vision of Jesus Christ for Europe at the start of the new millennium. That encounter at least began to live up to its name in Rowan Williams' sense.

Engagement

The public life and future of Europe is being decisively shaped by institutions as never before: the EU, the Council of Europe, the OSCE in particular. If we are serious about Christianity as public truth, to use Lesslie Newbigin's phrase, we must have the willingness and capacity to engage supportively and critically with these governmental and intergovernmental bodies on the European level, as much as we do with the political powers at national level. Over the past 30 years or so there developed in Brussels and Strasbourg the Ecumenical Commission for Church and Society (EECCS). Supported largely by a number of Western churches, EECCS developed considerable experience and expertise in maintaining close dialogue with the European Commission and the Council of Europe, conveying to these bodies the concerns of the churches on policies ranging from those on unemployment and social welfare to environment and bioethics, and in turn relaying to the churches where the critical issues lay. From 1 January 1999 EECCS has been integrated with CEC in the formation of our new Commission on Church and Society. This is more than an ecumenical tidying-up operation. It is the creation of a new instrument of potentially enormous significance, since it now brings into the debate about European integration not just the churches of the EU countries, nor even just those of the applicant countries, but those of the whole of Europe including the former Soviet Union. It is a prime ecumenical task, as I said earlier, to ensure that when 'Europe' is spoken about, we really do mean the whole of Europe, from the Azores to Vladivostock, from the Barents Sea to the Aegean. This we can now do more effectively – if with difficulty – because it also means the attempt to create a common European ecumenical approach to social ethics, embracing the rather different approaches of Eastern Orthodoxy and Western Protestantism. But the challenge has to be taken up. And in all this, the ecumenical calling is to ensure that no voices are left out, least of all those of the marginalized, the uprooted, the refugees and asylum-seekers who are knocking on the ever more firmly bolted doors of Western Europe.

Envisioning

I said that visions need agendas. But part of our ecumenical agenda is continually to generate new visions, or at least map new directions for the way ahead. Europe is overloaded with its past, a past still sending spasms of unhealed pain from past conflicts and atrocities where religion has played its part. There is need for the healing of memories, the reconciliation of histories. This has to go hand-in-hand with new hopes, hopes for a new way of living together. In face of all the revived suspicions of churches towards each other, there has to be revived hope for new partnerships. I conclude with one such sign of hope, small at the moment, but one to which CEC and CCEE are deeply committed, arising out of the Second European Ecumenical Assembly at Graz. This is the Charta Oecumenica. At Graz there was proposed the formulation of a set of guidelines for good ecumenical practice in Europe: a statement of what the churches of Europe, of all traditions, are willing to commit themselves to, in their relations to one another and to Europe as a whole – what Metropolitan Daniel of the Romanian Orthodox Church has called 'a set of ecumenical beatitudes for today'.

The draft of this was issued, on behalf of CEC and CCEE, to all CEC member churches and to all Catholic bishops' conferences in Europe, for discussion and comment. The revised and final text was signed by Metropolitan Jérémie, representative of the Ecumenical Patriarchate in Paris and President of CEC, and Cardinal Vlk of Prague, President of CCEE, at that Ecumenical Encounter in Easter week 2001, and presented to the European churches for their adoption, and, more important, their action.

The Charta, first drafted in 1999 and agreed in final form in April 2001, is not a long document, just five pages in length.[8] It states very basic things. But they have never before been said by all the churches of Europe together. And in saying them they will take a risk: of adopting a yardstick by which they will not only measure their own behaviour, but which will allow them to be measured by others – and by society at large. Perhaps to say it is taking a risk is too negative. It is making an act of trust and commitment. It is not a blueprint. It is sketching the vision. If in the midst of all the present tensions this can be said together, it will merit the closing words of the Charta, the prayer taken from St Paul's letter to the Romans, and there will be hope for ecumenism in Europe, and hope for Europe: 'May the God of hope fill us with all joy and peace in believing, so that we may abound in hope by the power of the Holy Spirit' (Rom. 15:13).

Notes

1. Interview for German–British Forum website (press release, 7 September 1999).

2. See David L. Edwards, *Christians in a New Europe* (London: Collins, 1990).

3. Since this paper was delivered, the EU enlargement process has developed to the extent of a total of ten countries, mainly from the former Soviet bloc, now being candidates for admission.

4. See R. Gurney (ed.), *CEC at 40*, Conference of European Churches (Geneva, 1999).

5. See *Peace with Justice. The Official Documents of the European Ecumenical Assembly, Basel, Switzerland, 15–21 May, 1989*, Conference of European Churches (Geneva, 1989).

6. See *Reconciliation – Gift of God and Source of New Life. Documents from the Second European Ecumenical Assembly*, Council of European Bishops' Conferences and Conference of European Churches (Geneva, 1998).

7. Vladimir Fedorov, 'Barriers to Ecumenism: an Orthodox View from Russia', *Religion, State & Society*, 26(2) (1998), p. 133.

8. Rowan Williams, 'Thanks, Uncle Sidney', *The Baptist Ministers' Journal* (January 1998), p. 24.

9. *Charta Oecumenica for the Cooperation of Churches in Europe*, CEC, Geneva and CCEE, St Gallen, July 1999: see Appendix this volume.

7

Between Christ and Caesar: the Politics of Mission and Ecumenism Encountering African Myths and Realities

Valentin Dedji

The main purpose of this chapter is to present and discuss the politics of Christian mission and ecumenism in the context of sub-Saharan Africa. My argument will echo Nicholas Sagovsky's warning that we must be concerned 'to prevent the term *koinonia* being used in a slovenly and over-general fashion to paper over ecumenical cracks'.[1] We will see that, as it emerged from recent theological debates in Africa, ecumenism appears as an ardent option to make the Church the centre of existence from which African Christians may derive the fulfilment of their life's aspiration whether in time of need or in time of feasting, and where they may experience a communal life which has a vaster scope and meaning than tribal life without Christ could ever provide.[2] This will be highlighted in my section on the 'moratorium issue' within the circle of the All Africa Conference of Churches. The major issues at stake here are those of identity, leadership, representation, division of resources and justice.

Having thus come to terms with the fact that 'politics and *koinonia* are interwoven',[3] I will draw the conclusion that in our discussions about Christian mission, politics and ecumenism in any human community we need increasingly to realize that the separate histories of our churches and societies find their full meaning only if seen in the perspective of God's dealings with his whole people.

African Realities Uncovered

For many in the West, Africa is still a vast geographical area that is little known, essentially backward and rather mysterious. This is surprising, because it has been explored and studied for a long time. The Phoenicians had already circumnavigated the continent in the sixth century BC. Vasco da Gama and Bartholomew Dias explored it as a route to India 400 years ago, and the Dutch had begun to settle its southern regions by the mid-seventeenth century. Yet Africa does need to be rediscovered. As G. Balandier has written, Africans are now challenging the West, trying 'to gain recognition as subjects of history', and, paradoxically, demanding 'the attention of a world which has become more curious about their destiny'.[4]

Africa is the second largest of the world's continents. Its estimated population in 1990 was 642 million, scattered over 53 countries in an area of 11,700,000 square miles. Altogether, its peoples speak four European languages (English, French, Portuguese and Spanish) and more than 700 African languages and dialects. Human societies in Africa exhibit a wide range of social and political organizations. Some are vast kingdoms with millions of subjects, thus belying the term small-scale. Nigeria and the former Zaïre are good examples of such a society. Others are small groups of families wandering in the hot sands of the Kalahari Desert. Some Africans from the earliest times developed town life, for example, the Yoruba of West Africa. Other Africans, such as the Zulu of South Africa, have lived for centuries in small villages. Social changes have been so abrupt that many Africans have 'progressed' from carrying loads on their heads to shifting these by jet-planes without ever having seen a wheelbarrow. The coherence of Africa's historical reality is distorted and falsified if it is reduced exclusively to a single dimension – say, the cultural dimension or the political dimension alone. To be sure, there are differences in the social, economic and political structures and ideological presuppositions between African countries. These differences could even be extended to include cultural, linguistic and ethnic diversity. For instance, as pointed out by John Pobee,[5] within West Africa and even within one country, such as Ghana, there are remarkable differences based on tribal background. Furthermore, as Adrian Hastings has pointed out, 'within every ethnicity are sub-ethnicities . . . just as a spoken language varies across quite short distances of place, class and profession', and in ordinary daily life 'the inner differences of ethnicity might often seem to matter more than the outer ones'.[6]

Thus, the issue of ethnic pluralism cannot be ignored by African theologians and by ecumenical organizations operating in Africa. The different manifestations – both positive and negative – in the phenomenon of ethnicity must be explored and those that provide a nurturing African humanity must be identified and promoted. In this perspective, the case of Tanzania is worth mentioning. There, the religious divide does not correspond at all closely with an ethnic divide, and Swahili (the national language spoken everywhere by every ordinary citizen), despite its Islamic cradle, is now as much a Christian as a Muslim language. According to Adrian Hastings, 'it was the Christian adoption of Swahili – despite some early missionary misgivings – which may well have been crucial for the successful construction of Tanzanian national identity'.[7] This, in Hastings' view, began with Bishop Steere's Swahili Bible in the nineteenth century, but the deciding moment was probably the 1960s when, in the wake of the Second Vatican Council, the Catholic bishops agreed that mass should normally be celebrated everywhere in Swahili and not – as in virtually every other African country – in a multitude of different local languages. Seemingly, 'the Catholic Church's self-imposed Swahilisation stands at the heart of Tanzanian nation-formation', however much the social analysts have managed to overlook it.[8] It does, of course, closely cohere with the aspirations of Julius Nyerere, himself a devout Catholic, the 'King Alfred' of twentieth-century Africa, with his Swahili translations of *Julius Caesar* and *The Merchant of Venice*.

In much of this, Tanzania resembles the otherwise very different society of Yorubaland, comparably divided between Christians and Muslims. However, while Tanzania is recognized as a nation-state, Yorubaland is not. Therefore, 'if a religion does not necessarily undermine national unity, a religious community does not necessarily ensure it'.[9] A common Catholicism has had strangely little effect on merging Tutsi and Hutu in Burundi or Rwanda. The reality of ethnic clashes in Burundi, Rwanda, Sudan or Kenya can be observed and interpreted from the standpoint of political and economic history as well as from church history. Even their cultural undertones can no longer be ignored.

However, for all these divergences, there is an overriding common denominator that binds the whole African continent together. It is from this unyielding commonality that a common theological perspective or a synthetic theological interpretation may become possible. In their efforts to come to terms with this common reality in their different environments, African theologians and church leaders, gathered in national, regional and continental ecumenical bodies, have adopted hermeneutic concepts such as 'Africanization', 'liberation' and recently 'reconstruction'. In an effort of rehabilitation, African historical reality must be viewed as a unity, a combined presence of traditional African and the influence of Euro-Christian and Arabic-Islamic elements. The different dimensions of this coherent reality open themselves to the theological investigator who approaches them with the right questions concerning human existence, its relation to the Supreme Being and to the rest of the world.

Perhaps it is here that we might take an invaluable insight from African thinkers whose works stress the importance of Africa's triple religious heritage and therefore provide an opportunity for reflection on the challenging implications of Africa's religiocultural pluralism for an alternative ecumenical enterprise.

Interfaith Encounter in an African Setting

As rightly pointed out by Jehu Hanciles,[10] motives for religious conversion in Africa are complex, but it cannot be emphasized too strongly that for many Africans conversion to Christianity became a way of coping with innumerable crises and dilemmas, a means of adapting to rapid change. In truth, potential converts were confronted with two obvious choices, Christianity or Islam, two religions linked into a wider universe and able to provide 'keys to meaning and a means to adjustment when a people's traditional lore is no longer able to do so'.[11]

In his essay 'Africa's Place in Christian History', Andrew Walls highlights the origins of Christianity in Africa. He points out that Origen, the first systematician who helped lay the foundations of Western theology, was an African, as were Tertullian, Cyprian and Augustine. The North African church pioneered the vernacular use of Latin. Walls even sees the African Donatists as the 'first liberation theologians'.[12] In Walls' work there is also mention of early Christianity in Africa taking root on the eastern shores of Axum, off the Horn of Africa. This unique brand of Christianity found an ancient connexion with Israel through Solomon, and the term 'Ethiopian' became symbolic for something that is authentically African:

> Ethiopian stands for Africa indigenously Christian, Africa predominantly Christian; for a Christianity that was established in Africa not only before the white men came, but before Islam came . . . African Christians today can assert their right to the whole history of Christianity in Africa, stretching back almost to the apostolic age . . . If Christianity is indigenous to Africa . . . then African Christian thought belongs in the Christian mainstream; and African theology should not be satisfied with a place that reduces it to resolving local difficulties.[13]

The South African theologian Anthony Balcomb is accurate in commenting that these are 'truly significant words when seen in the light of the contemporary search for African identity'.[14] Kwame Bediako has also sought to make connexions between the earliest periods of African Christianity and its more modern manifestations. In this perspective, it is John Mbiti's thought that has had the most 'original' impact on Bediako: for Mbiti, historically 'Christianity is very much an African religion.'[15] Bediako points out that 'no other major African theologian uses the expression "Christian Africa" as freely as Mbiti'.[16]

The major thrust of Christian mission activity in Africa was, however, to coincide with the hunger for empires, the termination of slavery and the 'scramble for Africa' following the discovery of precious metals and other natural resources. Throughout this period the churches in Africa were the outposts of churches in Europe, the USA and elsewhere.

But Africa is also a fertile ground for Islam. In his *West African Christianity*, Lamin Sanneh rightly points out misleading historical presuppositions about the relations between Christianity and Islam in Africa.[17] Missionary Christianity, he says, has encouraged the view that the overtaking of Islam is an overriding consideration: thus 'the myth has been perpetuated that Christianity is locked in a bitter rivalry with it, with Africa serving as the arena and the prize'.[18] In the prime setting of African nationalism and the sentiments of reaction that preceded it, this misleading view has ignited into a full-blown ideological device which brings Christianity within the same firing range as the colonialism it seeks to demolish, with Islam now serving the role of favoured bystander. Thus the mental outlook inherited from the Crusades is allowed to impose itself in a situation where every reasonable circumstance militates against it. In this regard we cannot help but agree with Sanneh that if historical reality diverges so clearly from cherished myth, then to dispel myth we need to allow the details of historical contact to shape our formulations and determine our view.

The historical evidence in fact reveals a rather surprising picture, including the fact that African religions played an important role in moulding the two 'missionary' religions. Both Christianity and Islam have been confronted with the decisive issue of indigenization. The African response to Christianity and Islam constituted an independent religious phenomenon; what emerged from the process of Africanization revealed as much about Africa's ancient religious heritage as about the separate opportunities of the two 'missionary' faiths. Perhaps no post-independent African theorist has emphasized so forcefully the need to combine the presence of traditional Africa, Islamic Africa and Euro-Christian Africa as Kwame Nkrumah in his ideological statement, *Philosophical Conscientism*.[19] Like other Africa analysts, Nkrumah did not deny the traditional African egalitarian concepts of humanity and society. However, he also believed that such an old egalitarian society no longer existed, because of the influences of Islam and Euro-Christianity. Therefore, if there was to be genuine growth and development in contemporary Africa, Nkrumah insisted, there was the need to forge a new harmony 'that will allow the combined presence of traditional Africa, Islamic Africa and Euro-Christian Africa, so that this presence is in tune with the original humanist principles underlying African society'.[20] But unlike the nineteenth-century ordained Christian minister and statesman Edward Blyden who, in his *Christianity, Islam and the Negro Race* demonstrated his admiration and sympathy for Islam, Nkrumah's bias rather leaned toward traditional Africa, for 'in the new African renaissance, we place great emphasis on the presentation of history'.[21] He added that African history must be written as the history of African society and any other outside contact 'must find its place in this history only as an African experience, even if as a crucial one'.[22]

The contribution of both Islam and traditional religion to the shaping of the Church–society relationship is indeed a 'crucial reality' of which African churches are aware. For example, at its Second General Assembly in Abidjan in 1969, the All Africa Conference of Churches (AACC) gave special attention to Islam in Africa and the contribution that it could make toward African theological expression. Giving reasons why Islam is attractive to most Africans and enjoys incontestable prestige, the AACC resolved to intensify its 'Islam in Africa Project', which, among other things, should pay attention 'to the promotion of a true dialogue and a movement towards African theological expression'.[23]

The Church in Africa and the Need for a Continent-wide Ecumenical Body

Although in the early twentieth century foreign Christian missions in Africa became churches, with the formation of national church councils in Ghana in 1929, South Africa in 1936, Kenya in 1942, and what was northern Rhodesia in 1944, continent-wide consultation among those councils was almost non-existent. The identity of the African churches was provided by foreign missionaries, while what the South African church leader Donald M'Timkulu calls the 'quiet intrusions of African culture, nibbling away at the new institutions of change', was always a feature of the African church.[24]

One can understand, therefore, why the African church has always been both divided and united. Its division is a reflection of the divided Church which sent missionaries to Africa. Its unity is grounded in 'the social ties binding the African Christians to their extended family and clan [which] have always been stronger than the forces of separation that arise from membership in different denominations . . . a unity that [has] roots in the traditional past'.[25] It is this division and unity which have influenced Church–state relations in Africa over the years and which have been manifested, from the time of its inception, in the hopes and fears of the AACC regarding the prophetic role of the Church in relation to African nationalism.

When the International Missionary Council (IMC) met in Jerusalem in 1928, only five African countries were represented. At the IMC Tambaram Conference in 1938, priority was given to the participation of 'people from the younger churches', and although seventeen African countries were represented by seventeen African delegates, there were also eighteen white missionaries in the African delegation.[26] One can therefore understand why the first International Africa Christian Conference convened in Ibadan (Nigeria) in 1958 was viewed as a historic event. It was the first Christian conference to be held on a continental scale which sought specifically to bring together the churches working in Africa, and it was so planned that the majority of the delegates would be African church leaders rather than missionaries. Representatives from all the major Protestant churches from 25 countries were present, and 96 of the 144 delegates were African.[27] As the Assembly's official report pointed out, 'Here for the first time the Church in Africa found its voice.'[28]

This experience of unity was so rich and deep that it naturally led to a penitent acknowledgement of 'our many divisions which have prevented us from witnessing to our unity in Him'.[29] The conference appointed a provisional committee to create an African regional ecumenical body. As it was later said, 'The days of Christianity by proxy for Africa were over.'[30] At the same time the political 'winds of change' were being experienced in every capital, and pan-Africanism was being affirmed as an ideology to counter imperialism.

In April 1963 at Makerere University in Kampala, Uganda, the All Africa Conference of Churches was created 'as a fellowship of consultation and cooperation within the wider fellowship of the universal church'.[31] The basis of its membership was confession of the 'Lord Jesus Christ as God and only Saviour according to the Scriptures'.

About 350 representatives of Orthodox churches, Protestant confessions and Roman Catholic churches of Africa, from 42 countries
were present.[32] Seeing denominationalism as 'the cancerous destroyer
of genuine Christianity', the pioneers of the AACC saw its birth as an
'oasis of significance'.[33] Such an 'ecumenical mind' was informed by
the strong conviction that 'the things we have in common are much
more important than our divisions'; and that it is only by returning to
the heart of the miracle of the grace of God in Christ, to the all-
embracing love of our Saviour, that 'we can truly become a Holy,
Catholic and Apostolic Church'. Moreover, at Kampala there was a
feeling that 'Western Christianity has perhaps overemphasized
theological thinking at the expense of the true brotherhood of those
redeemed by Christ.'[34]

Thus Africa came of age in the ecumenical movement under the
grip of a revolution aimed at shrugging off denominationalism as
incompatible with true Christianity, and colonialism as a denial of
human freedom and being. What someone like Kwame Nkrumah
identified as hateful and oppressive, many a church leader had experienced within the Church. 'African Christians', warned M'Timkulu,
'. . . are growing impatient with the so-called non-participation in
politics or political neutrality of Protestant churches and missions . . .
Freedom from colonialism thus means the freedom and obligation of
all nationals to participate in the nation's political life.'[35] Indeed, this
'obligation' has not always been easy for African churches: sometimes they have become trapped in political intrigue.[36] It must suffice
to cite only two of the better-known events of Church–state confron-
tation in Africa: Kwame Nkrumah's claim to be Saviour, in appro-
priating the term *Osajefu*, was rejected as outright heresy, while Idi
Amin was confronted with a team of churchmen who went 'to speak
the prophetic truth of God' to him.[37] The AACC has also been involved
in negotiations to end the Nigerian–Biafran civil war, in pre- and post-
independent Zimbabwe, in the Horn of Africa, in Sudan, Angola and
recently in Rwanda and Burundi. In ecumenical circles the AACC
voiced the problems and dilemmas not only of the churches but the
new states of Africa. The organization of the AACC and the role it
played 'within the fellowship of the universal Church' helped to
sensitize Christendom to the problems of interstate relationships, and

to make the World Council of Churches a 'conscience to the nations'. Soon 'Third World' problems began to dominate the agenda of the WCC.

Of primary concern whenever Christian Africans met during the first two decades of the AACC was the question of how Africa interpreted and appropriated to itself the Christian Gospel brought by the missionaries. The question was raised at a consultation of African theologians held at Enugu, Nigeria, in 1965.[38] It produced a theological enterprise which Andrew Walls has termed making 'Christianity at home in the life of the people'.[39] After this, thanks largely to the work of Bolaji Idowu and much later John Mbiti, African perspectives on Christian faith began to be taken seriously, taught in universities and researched in church circles around the world. It is at this level that 'African ecumenism has been openly inclusive and has crossed sacred barriers'.[40] The Association of African Theologians is a comprehensive organization in membership, drawing its members from all Christian denominations on the African continent: Protestant, Roman Catholic and independent churches. It is essential to emphasize that the Negritude (Blackness) movement and the Ecumenical Association of Third World Theologians (EATWOT) have also contributed substantially to the expansion of an authentically African theology.[41] The impact of the 'African revolution' on the emergence and development of contextual theologies was indeed tremendous in francophone Africa, as it impressed upon the African church and its leaders the need to relate their gospel faith to 'the African search for a fuller human life in new societies'.[42]

Ecumenical Visions in Africa and the Threat of Denominations' Chess Games

At its second General Assembly in September 1969 in Abidjan, Ivory Coast, the AACC envisioned unity among Christians as a demonstration of African uniqueness and responsibility. Drawing lessons from unitive trends among churches, the AACC demonstrated a 'real desire for unity on the part of a great majority of churches'.[43] For example, in both Kenya and Tanzania, cooperating churches have managed to formulate a common liturgy and catechism. In southern Africa, the Malawian churches were able to produce common pedagogical tools to train both 'teaching' (clergy) and 'serving' (laity) elders. Similarly, the Zambian churches were cooperating in various educational and social services, despite diverging creeds. Continentally, the gulf between Roman and non-Roman churches was beginning to narrow as a result of increased pulpit exchanges.[44]

On the other side of the ledger, the AACC's 1969 review revealed the danger of unbridled optimism and hasty union plans. An unavoidable example came from Nigeria, a country which was becoming a pet peeve for some and a source of pride and envy for others. In 1965 its celebrated union negotiations had collapsed, when party politics and economic considerations overshadowed other variables.[45] Later, this monumental setback sent shock-waves beyond the Nigerian borders, prompting some Ghanaian Protestants to postpone their own plan for union from 1969 to 1971, a postponement that led to *de jure* cancellation. If unionists had at any time taken anything for granted, including submission of tribal sentiment to ecumenical spirit, they quickly learned from these failures that authentic unity 'will be a long task; [and that] it is necessary to accustom the grass roots' level' to the idea of unity before embarking on any grandiose union plan.[46] Because some negotiations easily turned into a chess game of numbers (with larger denominations using their numerical strength, not to mention their wealth, to coerce smaller denominations), the AACC in Abidjan reminded the 'rich' and 'powerful' churches of the ethics of the Kingdom, particularly the exponential responsibility of those to whom much is given. Efiong Utuk is right in commenting that 'at stake was the churches' authentic mission in the world rather than who gains more politically'.[47]

Another result of the review was the approval of interconfessional communion services, when organized under strict supervision, as a sign of past Christian achievements and a prayer for more 'intimate and realistic unity'.[48]

One of the major decisions of the AACC's second General Assembly was to make joint involvement in missions a litmus test for church unity in Africa, noting that 'God is moving us . . . to seek unity . . . to search for renewal of the church structures and life for the realisation of her God-given task in the world.'[49] Seen from the standpoint of the theme 'With Christ at Work Today in Africa', this unitive view was both theologically and pragmatically sound. From this perspective, old ecclesial labels, produced and used more out of ignorance than fact, were seen as 'inadequate' and in need of 'redefinition'. Specially, this meant a new way of relating the AACC to African independent churches (AICs), to African conservative evangelicals and to African Roman Catholics.

(i) African Independent Churches

Historically treated as a group of misfits both within and outside the Protestant community, AICs received both direct and indirect commendation from the Abidjan Assembly in a manner reminiscent of Edinburgh 1910.[50] Going beyond Kampala's largely 'we-can-do-without-you' attitude, Abidjan saw what the missionary conferences were unable to see, namely that these indigenous churches were dramatically transforming many aspects of African Christianity, and that the conciliar churches' ability to process an authentic message was becoming increasingly dependent on coming to terms with the AICs. Whereas, as children of mixed parentage (African and European cultures), the AACC and its constituency were still betwixt and between, a statement praised the AICs for their pioneer authenticity work. These AICs, the statement said, have shown that the road to the authenticity of African Christianity is not only exciting but also constructive.

From 1969 to date, the presence of the AICs has become more remarkable on the ecumenical scene in Africa. They are now active members not only of the AACC but also of National Christian Councils in many African countries.

(ii) African Conservative Evangelicals

As an ecumenical body, the AACC's watchword is 'doctrine divides, service unites'. This explains its strong social orientation. With this ecumenical spirit, the AACC's member churches are considered liberals by evangelicals because of their concern also for the material well-being of the human condition. In contrast to this, evangelicals stress evangelism and personal religious experience, biblical inerrancy and authority, human sinfulness and the necessity of a new birth. Their *raison d'être* has remained fellowship in the Gospel.

Despite such different approaches to the concept of mission, the AACC has opted for a conciliatory attitude as the way to break past impasses. In that perspective, since Abidjan 1969, evangelicals have had the right hand of fellowship extended to them, and they have been courted to join the continental effort for peace and reconciliation. A four-point programme, 'cutting across the whole range of relations', aimed at opening new vistas.[51] These ranged from contacting indigenous conservative leaders to winning the minds and souls of young conservatives with the message of unity. This resolution has been given special attention during the double mandate (1987–97) of Archbishop Desmond Tutu as President of the AACC; consultations have begun between the AACC and evangelical churches. For instance, in November 1994, the AACC and the 'Association of Evangelicals of Africa and Madagascar' (AEAM) jointly convened the second Pan-African Christian Leadership Assembly (PACLA). At that Assembly, the 'evangelicals' were challenged to appreciate the necessity of ecumenical openness, while the 'ecumenicals' were challenged to appreciate the necessity of evangelical witness. The challenge now for both parties is to prove that they are all prepared to move from conservatism to pluralism.

(iii) African Roman Catholics

Caught by the radically changing situation in relationships since its Kampala Assembly and the Second Vatican Council, the AACC voted in Abidjan for *rapprochement* with African brothers and sisters who for one reason or other became Roman Catholics. If it was unprecedented to seek closer ties with the Roman Catholic Church, this decision was a bombshell to some delegates who did not think this day would come in their lifetime. To those who could not imagine African Protestants and African Roman Catholics sharing the same platform, it was a bold and giant leap towards an African affirmation of the necessity of mature ecumenical structures. However, for many African countries with a history of Protestant–Roman Catholic rivalry, this day came too late. Thus, while many saw the hidden hand of God at work, weaving disparate groups together, some settled for applauding the Roman Catholic observers at the meeting, reasoning that their physical presence spoke louder than words.[52]

Since that historic event, there have been many examples of the way in which churches have acted as mediators and reconcilers throughout Africa, and some instances where Protestant and Catholic action has been usefully complementary, as in Mozambique where their combined endeavours led to negotiations between the Frelimo government and Renamo.[53] As such, churches are in daily touch with people; they often have a larger and more committed membership than political parties and, in many instances, their understanding of the situation on the ground is better than that of politicians. While the witness of the Church to central government is obviously critical, it is at the local community level that the Church is often stronger and able to make the greatest difference in democratic transition. A notable example is the emergence of popular democratic movements in Benin (West Africa) and in Uganda, where constitutionalism has developed from grass–roots level largely through churches. As well observed by John De Gruchy, 'rural areas are of particular importance in this regard, for it is there that democratic structures will have to be adapted to local traditions, and in turn be shaped by them'.[54]

Institutional Dialogue with Muslims

Initiated in 1969 in Abidjan, the AACC's project on dialogue with 'Muslim co–religionists' was considered a matter of urgency during the sixth General Assembly in 1992 in Harare, Zimbabwe. At issue was the nature of such dialogue. The AACC made it clear that it was incumbent on churches in Africa to 'initiate conversation and interaction with Muslims . . . at a variety of levels and in a variety of forums', even though there was some perception that Christian overtures are not always reciprocated by the Muslim community.[55] The civil war which has been opposing Muslims and Christians in Sudan for more than two decades now and the recent violence between Muslims and Christians in the northern states of Nigeria are serious challenges to institutional dialogue with Muslims in Africa.[56] However, there are both Christian and Muslim leaders who, in the interests of justice, human rights and national reconciliation, have been able to transcend the divide which has traditionally separated the two faith communities. For example recently, the Prelate of the Methodist Church in Nigeria, Dr Sunday Mbang and his fellow co-chair of the Nigeria Inter-Religious Council (NIRC), the Muslim Sultan of Sokoto, Alhaji Muhammadu Maccido, have been given a trouble-shooting role by the nation's head of state, President Obasanjo – a Baptist and a former military leader – to try to bring peace to areas of conflict in Nigeria.[57]

The AACC's Proposal for a New Paradigm in the Theology of Mission: the 'Moratorium' Issue

In addition to these patterns of relationship, the AACC sought mature relations with the churches in Western Europe and North America. It urged them to encourage indigenous African evangelical initiatives, instead of sabotaging them. Building on Kampala's unobtrusive plea for devolution, it also encouraged foreign missionary societies to make devolution a quick reality, without a showdown or shouting match. Unfortunately, as the 1974 Assembly in Zambia would show with its Moratorium Statement, some missionaries did not quite get this message or simply dismissed it as another African bluff.

In 1974, a decade after the creation of the AACC and the call for the formulation of an authentic African theology, African churches found that though leadership was given to Africans at independence, the 'newly' established institutions were still evolving within an anachronistic structure. At issue were the paternalistic structures through which the decisions concerning the needs of the mission church were made.[58] According to Robert Dayton, the number of American and Canadian missionaries sent to the Third World grew from 27,039 in 1960 to 35,458 in 1976.[59] In the light of these figures, one wonders what chances and choices African churches could have of raising up missionary agencies that could participate effectively in the global missionary work of the Catholic Church. How could the institutional power-gap, the wealth-gap, the numerical strength-gap, the global geopolitical-gap enhance 'partnership in obedience', 'mutuality in mission', 'internationalizing mission', 'ecumenical sharing of personnel' – concepts that are formulated in missionary conferences? How could the glaring inequalities in the socioeconomic world order be prophetically confronted by these missiological formulations? In view of these dilemmas, we will have to consider the moratorium call by the AACC as part of a contemporary African response to the ideological and institutional tendencies of Western missiological initiatives which preserve the traditional relationship between the centre and the periphery.

The concern was expressed by the third Assembly of AACC at Lusaka, Zambia, in 1974:

> To enable the African Church to achieve the power of becoming a true instrument of liberating and reconciling the African people, as well as finding solutions to economic and social dependency, our option as a matter of policy has to be a 'moratorium' on external assistance in money and personnel. We recommend this option as the only potent means of becoming truly and authentically ourselves while remaining a respected and responsible part of the Universal Church.[60]

The initiator of that statement was Canon Burgess Carr, a charismatic Liberian church leader, then the General Secretary of the AACC. He summoned the delegates to reappraise foreign influence on the continent, particularly David Livingstone's missionary legacy in the region, and to make 'a fresh commitment to radically renew the form and content' of African Christianity, leading it to 'cultural authenticity and integration, human development, dignity, justice and peace'.[61]

Noticing 'a deliberate Christocentric thread' that locked the first two AACC General Assemblies into 'this earnest [liberation] commitment', Carr, appropriately, beckoned the 1974 Lusaka General Assembly to be ready for hard reflection on the necessity to revisit the 'theology of mission' in Africa.[62]

The high level of the debate roused by the call for a moratorium gave an opportunity for its proponents to advance some arguments which could constitute the basis of a contextual ecclesiology. For John Gatu, a Presbyterian church leader from Kenya, the moratorium was a means for transforming mission from being the mission of the West to the Third World into mission as mission of God: 'The need is commitment and a decision to go forward in faith. For Africa has money and personnel . . . Let mission be the mission of God in the world, but not of the West to the Third World.'[63]

The WCC was the first international ecumenical body to recognize the moratorium question as a crucial issue in contemporary missionary strategy. In July 1972 at Choully, Switzerland, the task force of the WCC on Ecumenical Sharing of Personnel (ESP) was confronted with the moratorium proposal by African members. The Africans spelled out the case for moratorium thus:

In this document the word moratorium is used to mean:

(1) withdrawal of present and discontinuation of future personnel sent into the service of receiving churches by foreign Church agencies;

(2) discontinuation of money given to support churches and their institutions by the same sources;

(3) provision of a reasonable length of time to allow for review, reflection and reassessment regarding the best use of money and personnel in response to the mission of God in our day and the searching for selfhood of the church in mission;

(4) seeing anew the living Lord incarnated in the local situations and expressing that Lordship without foreign domination.[64]

The purposes of the moratorium, according to the African proposers, were:

A. To allow the receiving churches a time for critical questioning of the inherited structures and programmes which may be cherished by some and yet are only relevant to a different age, and therefore remain a constant and unnecessary burden to the church.

B. To seek and struggle for the maturity which comes from the understanding of selfhood and self reliance without which ecumenism becomes an illusion and not a reality;

C. To give the sending churches the opportunity to question seriously the relevance of the expansionist missionary psychology which characterised the past and which still persists today, impoverishing the church by neglecting 'witness in Jerusalem';

D. To encourage the churches in powerful nations to look objectively at the exploitative practices in which their countries are involved through trade, investment and aid in the two-thirds world;

E. To give opportunity to receiving churches to prophetically challenge their governments, Christian councils and other institutions on the evils of over-dependence on foreign resources which hinder the necessary total liberation of man.[65]

The AACC's ambition was to innovate in the field of missiology by proposing a 'theology of moratorium' which would be the counterpart of the Western theology of mission. In Carr's words, for the search for unity in the Church in Africa to remain faithful to Christ, committed Christians must ask themselves the following disturbing question: 'Why is it possible for us to unite in programmes of "good works" towards those whom we call "poor", but remain fiercely divided at the level of the common faith which we profess?'[66]

As in many such passionate intellectual confrontations, the subtleties in the debate are not easy to disentangle. Gwinyai Muzorewa discerned four theological issues related to the moratorium. These have to do with the meaning of 'catholicity', 'fellowship', 'liberation' and 'authenticity'.[67] Regarding catholicity, Muzorewa pointed out that the commonest view held by the opponents of the call for a moratorium was that without a white missionary presence, the Church in Africa would lose its universality. Implicit in this statement was the thinking that the African church, without white missionaries, would lose the essence of Christianity. There are some African Christians and white missionaries who could not conceive of a genuine Christian Church in Africa without some white missionaries in it. This view was challenged by Burgess Carr, who posed the question: 'Is it really true that the catholicity of the Church is linked to the presence of missionary personnel?'[68] For most African theologians, the answer was negative. Rather, it was the presence of the Holy Spirit that authenticated the community of believers, whether in Europe, America, Asia or Africa. To require the presence of white Christians as a condition for the Holy Spirit was to affirm and confirm the allegation that Christianity was a white people's religion. Muzorewa was right in asserting that 'catholicity is not invoked by a multiplicity of races, but is ensured by the presence of the same Christ, the Lord, in every land'.[69]

The AACC was charged with being divisive along racial lines, as well as isolationist, rejecting and contradicting the spirit of fellowship that ought to characterize the Church of Jesus Christ everywhere. In response, Burgess Carr asked:

> Who brought Christianity to Africa in its denominational compartments? Who sends money to Africa tied with strings that say 'for United Methodists only' or 'for Presbyterian High School lab expenses only'? Can a United Methodist-

supported medical doctor serve in an indigenous African Christian Church in Zaïre?

For Burgess Carr, isolationism 'is maintained and perpetuated by those same financial and personnel policies, agenda setting and decision-making processes that have given rise to a call for moratorium'.[70] There is no doubt that the theological ramifications of denominationalism are devastating for Africa. For the AACC, the denomination has definitely lost its image as 'the Body of Christ', expressing isolationism rather than universality and fellowship. More importantly, the proponents of the moratorium advocated a deeper commitment to Christ and the mission of the Church. True fellowship can exist, they asserted, only among liberated people who share the faith from the point of view of equality, not inferiority versus superiority. Indeed, one of the stated goals of the moratorium was to produce African churches 'whose relationships with other churches are based upon equality under the lordship of Jesus'.[71] As one would expect, there was an immediate reaction to the AACC's resolution on moratorium, not only in Africa itself but all over the Christian world.[72]

The theological arguments that underpin the AACC's call for moratorium were regarded as disturbing because of their innovative and 'revolutionary-like' strategy. Yet, those arguments were compelling, having regard to the legitimate ambition of African churches to find their ways towards identity and selfhood. The African indigenous churches were not surprised by the moratorium debate. They had never been supported from outside, and had, therefore, evolved structures by which they were able to support themselves. In these churches, from the village fellowship to the church headquarters, the church was self-reliant and self-ministering. Ordinary men and women led the church in its worship as well as in ecclesiology and theology.[73] Zabulon Nthamburi is right in quoting the Kimbanguist church as a good example here. Not only has that church built its own institutions of higher learning that train some of the most educated pastors in Zaïre and Congo, but the Kimbanguist church is a missionary church that has spread to the neighbouring countries.

Ecumenicals' and Evangelicals' Responses to the Moratorium Call

For a closer enquiry into the ecumenical responses, let us examine the views of Ruben Lores and Paul Hopkins, whose ideas on the subject of moratorium could be said to represent the ecumenical position.

Lores is a thoughtful missionary and former Rector of Seminario Biblico Latinamericano, San José, Costa Rica. He sees the call for moratorium more as a symptom than a disease. Hence he speaks of it as the quest for identity and selfhood for which the missionary presence is a hindrance and from which freedom is sought. It is a search for a new image of the Church, and an insistence to let the Church be the symbol of the universality of the Gospel and not the missionary. It is a plea against any acts of dehumanization of the weak by the strong.[74]

Lores considers the call to apply to both the evangelicals and the ecumenical missionary agencies regardless of their style of relationship. He calls for a total revision of the theological and ideological conceptions that have undergirded the missionary movement since its inception. He protests that the presence of missionaries is an onerous blessing from which deliverance was expected. In effect Lores says 'We should call for an end to the foreign missionary enterprise much in the same way as colonialism.' He is sceptical about the effectiveness of the present structures which he calls 'Christian corporations' with all their vestiges of the colonial era, their aggressive mentality and their spirit of capitalism; they are 'quite remarkable for their lack of a theology of poverty'.[75]

Paul Hopkins, in his response, indicates a good grasp of the moratorium issue. He writes from personal knowledge and long involvement in the missionary effort in Africa. His book *What Next in Mission?* bears directly on the issues of moratorium.[76] Unlike other North American and European missiologists, he perceives the problem in mission through the lenses of Third World church leaders. He understands the issues to be basically conflicting motives (affluence versus poverty) and conflicting objectives (imperialism versus self-determination): 'We have failed our membership. We talk about partnership, yet we try to hold on to the strings. We have been told for years that this continuing colonial attitude is no longer acceptable and yet we do nothing about it.'[77]

In the light of these perspectives, Hopkins rightly diagnoses Gatu's call as 'the cry of a man who is desperate: "If you can't hear us, get out!" This isn't a rational statement, it is a cry of despair engendered by our refusal to listen.'[78] What then is the moratorium all about? According to Hopkins:

> It is that the overseas church tends to see us as attempting to hold on to an outdated system of missionary endeavour, of trying to maintain control of their lives through our people and dollars, of refusing to assist them in developing their selfhood because we want to keep them dependent on us. It is the need to change totally our missionary system . . . because evangelisation belongs to every church in every nation not just to the church in the West.[79]

In sum, Hopkins calls not only for changes in attitude and strategy and paradigm, but also for a look beyond the religious frontier to the economic and actual living conditions of people in the Third World. He quotes the ESP committee meeting report that 'Moratorium [should be] understood to be a process of liberation from active relationship.'[80] The cry of these people is that of a powerless and oppressed group, demanding a hearing from their masters. It is a product of their historical and cultural experience as those who have been unequally yoked to more powerful and more aggressive partners.

Given Lores' and Hopkins' views, we could say that the ecumenicals' response to the moratorium call has been favourable. Nonetheless, in practice some have interpreted moratorium as a retreat in mission rather than a renewal and reconciliation in mission. This misinterpretation seems to underscore the need for a theoretical framework to enable some of the ecumenicals to understand the full implications and dynamics of the moratorium. One pointer in this direction is the understanding of the moratorium call as characteristic of utopian mentality, with its tendency to have grossly inadequate means for the achievement of desired ends. This is clearly seen by the fact that while the AACC was agitating for a moratorium it was at the same time seeking a $500,000 grant from the US mission boards to help construct a new headquarters.[81]

Having looked at two representative views of the ecumenicals' responses to the moratorium, let us now look at the evangelical Christian responses. The Lausanne gathering of the International Congress on World Evangelization in July 1974 can be seen as the first place where evangelical Christians publicly confronted the issue of moratorium. Billy Graham, who delivered the opening address, said unequivocally that a moratorium on the sending of missionaries should be rejected by evangelicals. Until then, evangelicals had paid no serious attention to the early calls for moratorium.

Many evangelicals at Lausanne considered the issue a conciliar concern and none of their business. Nonetheless, John Gatu, who figured on the list of 'convenors' of the Lausanne Congress, kept the discussion alive, especially with his East African colleagues. Eventually the drafters of the 'Lausanne Covenant' broke the evangelical silence in the section on 'The Urgency of the Evangelistic Task'. Although the term 'moratorium' was not used, the congress approved a 'covenant' statement that declares:

> A reduction of foreign missionaries and money in an evangelized country may sometimes be necessary to facilitate the national church's growth in self-reliance and to release resources for unevangelized areas. Missionaries should flow even more freely and to all six continents in a spirit of humble service.[82]

With this lead from Lausanne, evangelicals began to participate in the moratorium debate and their voices began to be heard in theological and church journals. Their initial responses were basically negative, especially in North America. Later they were more positive. We shall consider the views of Peter C. Wagner, an influential missionary scholar, as typical of the Western evangelical stance on the moratorium.

As Wagner admits, 'I myself shouted a hasty "no" along with many others' when the call for a 'moratorium of missionaries' went up from some Christian leaders from such platforms as the WCC Assembly in Bangkok.[83] Later, he responded with 'yes and no'. In general, he raised typical evangelical concerns about the crucial theological and missiological issues about the ultimate, unique and universal significance of the Lordship of Jesus Christ and the question of the unevangelized parts of the world. He was critical of 'a churchman such as Burgess Carr', who, while advocating the crumbling of the missionary-sending agencies and a ban on Western missionaries, was at the same time asking for funds from the Western mission churches. This posture, according to Wagner, suggested that the proponents of moratorium were saying, 'we need your Dollars and Marks and Pounds, but not your people'.[84] Wagner was the first evangelical to spell out the occasions in which there was a need for a moratorium on missionary work. In this connexion he recognized the cultural, theological, ecclesiastical and missiological pitfalls in Western missionary enterprise. His arguments in this connexion sounded like those of the advocates of the moratorium, but differed radically from theirs in that he applied them only with reference to the Great Commission. In sum, we could say that Wagner advocated a type of selective moratorium, not a total moratorium. As he puts it:

> The moratorium issue has surfaced at an opportune moment in history . . . it is time to prune the dead and fruitless branches from the missionary enterprise and graft in new vital branches through which the power of Jesus Christ will flow unimpeded producing abundant fruit for life eternal.[85]

A Preferential Option for a New Ecumenism

In November 1991 the AACC convened a symposium in Mombasa, Kenya (9–16 November 1991), on the 'Problems and Promises of the Church in Africa in the 1990s and Beyond'. The convening of that symposium was considered as timely and as 'an opportunity for exchanging ideas, as a process of self-criticism was urgently required if churches in Africa are to survive'.[86] The survival of African churches was really at stake in regard to the far-reaching changes taking place in today's world, and especially in Africa. Such a situation made it necessary to adopt new strategies in regard not only to the life but also to the work of the churches in a changing society. In other words, the time had come to re-evaluate African values and learn from the past. It was during that symposium that the theme of 'Theology of Reconstruction' was launched. This was an appropriate opportunity for distinguished African theologians, church leaders and guest speakers to tackle different aspects of the promising theme of the Church and nation-building.

J. N. K. Mugambi was invited to reflect on the 'Future of the Church and the Church of the Future in Africa'. In his paper, he discussed the 'theological imagery [that] would be appropriate for Africa' after the political liberation of most African countries had been achieved.[87] Mugambi proposed that in the context of the new world order, the African church needed 'to shift paradigms from the Post-Exodus to Post-Exilic imagery, with reconstruction as the resultant theological axiom'.[88] Mugambi's paper pointed out that the 1990s were a decade of reconstruction in many ways, with calls for national conventions, constitutional reforms and economic revitalization. Mugambi strongly expressed his conviction that 'the 21st century should be a century of reconstruction in Africa, building on old foundations which, though strong, may have to be renovated'.[89]

The metaphor of crossroads surfaced repeatedly at the symposium, signalling the need to take courageous decisions. As Klauspeter Blaser, a guest theologian from Switzerland, argued:

> The Church is always 'at the crossroads'. It is true today that African churches are going through a special period which is reminiscent of the time when the primitive Church was at the crossroads. This situation is not unique to African churches. This is the very nature of the Christian faith. Faith is always and at all times 'at the crossroads', faced by the choice between life or death; between the Cross and resurrection; between hope and despair.[90]

The launching of the 'theology of reconstruction' at the Mombasa symposium was of paramount importance. It was a landmark, signifying a paradigm shift in theological discourse in Africa. According to Mugambi, the key terms in African Christian theology for the twenty-first century should be 'reconstruction' and 'social transformation'.

During the 1960s and 70s, African theology had emphasized 'liberation' which was then necessary for extrication from colonial servitude, but the Church had been relatively silent on the need for social transformation and reconstruction. Reconstruction was now applied not only to African countries and cultures ravished by colonization, but also to churches embedded in 'inappropriate' socioecclesial structures and 'inadequate' theological thinking. 'Reconstruction' was therefore seen as a necessity for all African societies and churches.

High on the AACC's agenda for the 'reconstruction' paradigm are alternative biblical motifs such as 'repentance', 'forgiveness' and 'reconciliation'.[91] For instance, for Mugambi, reconciliation is embedded in his concept of the reconstruction of African Christianity. In making a strong case for the promotion of cooperation and collaboration that includes Catholicism within ecumenism, Mugambi's vision is to bring about the healing of old suspicion and antagonism. Consequently, he proposed the following diagram as an illustration of his foreseen sharp demarcation between the conflicting past and the promising future.

The New Ecumenism and the Old Antagonism[92]

Catholicism–Ecumenism	Catholicism–Protestantism
Other-centred	Self-centred
Constructive	Destructive
Inclusive	Exclusive
Collaborative	Competitive
Amiable	Combative
Attractive	Repulsive
Appreciative	Deprecating
Progressive	Retrogressive
Sensitive	Insensitive

Some fundamental observations need to be mentioned here. In his position as the then head of the theology department of the AACC, Mugambi's proposal is an echo of the AACC's view on ecclesial reconstruction in Africa. Quite remarkable here is the option for an ecumenical configuration characterized by inclusivity, collaboration, amiability, appreciation and sensitivity. Such an unequivocal option for an unconditional ecumenical dialogue reflects Mugambi and the AACC's critical responses towards ecclesial fragmentation and other multidimensional crises in Africa.

Kä Mana shares Mugambi's views on the necessity of a new ecumenism in Africa. In regard to the present ecclesial configuration in Africa he wonders: 'Why is it that ecclesiastical boundaries are so strong in Africa despite the vaunted African people's strong sense of community life?'[93] Here he proposes what he calls 'une fraternité au-delà de l'ethnie' (a fraternity that goes beyond ethnicity) that will re-establish African communities and churches as spaces of 'true life' open to the realization of the human.[94]

Concluding Remarks

I have attempted here to explore very briefly the intricacies of theo-logical debates in Africa about the subtle politics related to an ecumeni-cal conception of an adequate Christian mission in a pluralistic society.

The whole discussion about the 'moratorium issue' raised within the circle of the AACC may seem complex or even inconsistent with the Africans' aspiration for communitarian life. The substance of the debate, however, consisted in revisiting the missionary calling of the Church with the conviction that mission is not an activity originating in some specific churches for some categories of peoples, but is in the first place God's action. This conviction should be fundamentally grounded in the principles of justice, partnership, interdependency, mutual support and respect for the other. Viewed from this perspec-tive, it is only correct to speak of ecumenism when what is under consideration is the unity of the Church and mission to the world.[95] This has been the noble intention of Sagovsky who, in his study on ecumenism, has sought to 'contribute towards a theory and practice of *koinonia* in the strength of which the Christian churches will be able to draw closer together, despite the tensions they experience as they seek to do so', since '[only] if churches can deepen their *koinonia* in the midst of the tensions that threaten to pull them apart can they truly exercise their ministry of reconciliation in a divided world'.[96] Mugambi and Kä Mana's idea of a 'new ecumenism' as opposed to the 'old antagonism' is indeed very inspiring here.

While African Christians are attracted by the assurance of abundant life in Christ, churches must be concerned about the abundance of Africans' problems. Only a lucid ecumenical engagement translated into practical actions can lead the way to a better future for African churches and communities. In a continent where wars, drought, famine, land-mines and other pernicious effects of political instability affect indiscriminately men, women and children, reconstruction cannot be achieved in isolation. For without the cooperative efforts of believers and non-believers, Christians and non-Christians, it will be impossible to surmount the problems faced by African societies today.[97] Above all, what is dramatically new in ecumenism and interfaith dialogue is the recognition, esteem and love for the other. In the new ecumenism Roman Catholics, Orthodox and Protestants need each other. In interfaith dialogue Christians need Muslims, Hindus and others in the search for truth and community.

Notes

1. N. Sagovsky, *Ecumenism, Christian Origins and the Practice of Communion* (Cambridge: Cambridge University Press, 2000), pp. 3–5.

2. See John Mbiti, 'The Ways and Means of Communicating the Gospel', in C. G. Baëta (ed.), *Christianity in Tropical Africa* (London: Oxford University Press, 1968), pp. 329–50.

3. Sagovsky, op. cit., p. 7.

4. G. Balandier, *Afrique ambiguë* (Paris: Plon, 1957).

5. John Pobee, *Towards an African Theology* (Nashville, TN: Abingdon, 1979), p. 29.

6. Adrian Hastings, *The Construction of Nationhood: Ethnicity, Religion and Nationalism* (Cambridge: Cambridge University Press, 1997), p. 167.

7. Ibid., p. 165.

8. Ibid.

9. Ibid., p. 166.

10. Cf. Jehu Hanciles, 'Conversion and Social Change: A Review of the Unfinished Task in West Africa' (unpublished paper presented during a consultation organized by Currents in World Christianity, Oxford: St Catherine's College, 14–17 July 1999), p. 7.

11. Andrew Walls, *The Missionary Movement in Christian History* (New York: Orbis Books, 1996), p. 132.

12. Andrew Walls, 'Towards an Understanding of Africa's Place in Christian History', in J. S. Pobee (ed.), *Religion in Pluralistic Society* (Leiden: E. J. Brill, 1976), p. 14.

13. Walls, op. cit., p. 6.

14. A. Balcomb, 'Faith or Suspicion? Theological Dialogue North and South of the Limpopo with Special Reference to the Theologies of Kwame Bediako and Andrew Walls', *Journal of Theology for Southern Africa*, 100 (March 1988), pp. 10–11.

15. K. Bediako, *Theology and Identity* (Oxford: Regnum Books, 1992), p. 332.

16. Here, Bediako emphasizes the uses of that expression by Mbiti in many of his articles. Cf. J. Mbiti, 'Church and State: a Neglected Element of Christianity in contemporary Africa', in *African Theological Journal*, 5, December, 1972, pp. 31–45; see also Mbiti, 'The Protestant Contribution to the Cultural Expression of the African Personality', in *Colloque sur les religions: Abidjan, 5–12 Avril, 1961* (Paris: Présence africaine, 1962), pp. 137–45.

17. See Lamin Sanneh, *West African Christianity* (New York: Orbis Books, 1983), pp. 210–41.

18. Ibid., p. 210.

19. See Kwame Nkrumah, *Conscientism: Philosophy and Ideology for Decolonisation* (New York: Monthly Review Press, 1970), especially, ch. 3.

20. Ibid., p. 70.

21. See E. W. Blyden, *Christianity, Islam and the Negro Race*, new edition (London: Edinburgh University Press, 1967).

22. Nkrumah, op. cit., p. 63.

23. AACC, *Engagement: Abidjan 1969* (Nairobi: AACC, 1970), p. 117.

24. Donald M'Timkulu, *Beyond Independence* (New York: Friendship Press, 1971), p. 23.

25. Ibid., p. 22.

26. *Drumbeats from Kampala. Report of the First Assembly of the AACC* (London: Lutterworth, 1963), p. 5.

27. T. A. Beetham, *Christianity and the New Africa* (London: Pall Mall Press, 1967), pp. 171–2.

28. *Drumbeats from Kampala*, p. 5.

29. Quoted by L. B. Greaves, 'The All Africa Church Conference: Ibadan, Nigeria: 10th to 20th January, 1958', in *The International Review of Missions*, XLVII (1958), p. 260.

30. Gabriel Setiloane, 'The Ecumenical Movement in Africa', in Charles Villa-Vicencio and John De Gruchy (eds), *Resistance and Hope* (Grand Rapids, MI: Eerdmans, 1985), p. 140.

31. Preamble to the constitution of the AACC. See *Drumbeats from Kampala*, p. 5.

32. To date, the Roman Catholic Church remains an observer within the AACC. See Efiong Utuk, *Visions of Authenticity: The Assemblies of the All Africa Conference of Churches, 1963–1992* (Nairobi: AACC, 1997).

33. This was specifically stressed by the Nigerian church leader Z. K. Matthews in his inaugural speech at Kampala. See *Drumbeats from Kampala*, p. 10.

34. Setiloane, op. cit., p. 142.

35. D. M'Timkulu, *Africa in Transition: The Challenge and Christian Response* (Geneva: AACC and WCC, 1962), pp. 15–27.

36. See Adrian Hastings, *A History of African Christianity: 1950–1975* (Cambridge: Cambridge University Press, 1979), pp. 86–107, 131–8.

37. Setiloane, op. cit., p. 143.

38. P. Ellingworth and K. Dickson (eds), *Biblical Revelation and African Faiths* (London: Lutterworth, 1969).

39. Walls, op. cit., p. 188.

40. Setiloane, op. cit., p. 142.

41. See Engelbert Mveng, 'African Liberation Theology', in L. Boff and V. Elizondo (eds), *Concilium 199: Theologies of the Third World. Convergences and Differences* (Edinburgh: T&T Clark, 1988), p. 20.

42. Emmanuel Martey, *African Theology. Inculturation and Liberation* (New York: Orbis Books, 1995), p. 7.

43. *Engagement: The Second AACC Assembly* (Nairobi: AACC, 1970), p. 120.

44. Efiong Utuk, *Visions of Authenticity*, p. 92.

45. Ogbu Kalu, *Divided People of God: Church Union Movement in Nigeria: 1875–1966* (New York: York, 1978), pp. 66–78.

46. *Engagement*, p. 121.

47. Utuk, op. cit., p. 92.

48. *Engagement*, p. 121.

49. Ibid., p. 120.

50. Edinburgh 1910 was quick to realize that powerful evangelical role of these indigenous churches, even though it underestimated independency as a religious phenomenon. For more details, see the discussion in E. Utuk, *From New York to Ibadan: The Impact of African Questions on the Making of Ecumenical Mission Mandates, 1900–1958* (New York: P. Lang. 1991), pp. 42–4.

51. *Engagement*, p. 123.

52. Efiong Utuk, *Visions of Authenticity*, p. 94.

53. See John De Gruchy, *Christianity and Democracy* (Cambridge: Cambridge University Press, 1995), p. 187.

54. Ibid., p. 187.

55. *Abundant Life in Christ. Report of the 6th AACC General Assembly* (Nairobi: AACC, 1992), p. 5.

56. The adoption of the Shari'a law by Islamic authorities in some of the federal states of Nigeria has been the major cause of the upsurge of violence between Muslims and Christians.

57. See *Methodist Recorder*, 7416, 10 February 2000, p. 1.

58. See Mahaniah Kimpianga, 'Toward a Self-supporting African Church', in Masamba ma Mpolo *et al.* (eds), *An African Call for Life* (Geneva: WCC, 1983), p. 56. The author argues that church structures inherited by African church leaders were anachronistic and could not be supported from the meagre African resources.

59. Robert E. Dayton (ed.), *Mission Handbook: North American Protestant Ministries Overseas*, 11th edn (Monrovia, CA: MARC, 1977).

60. AACC, Third Assembly, Lusaka, Zambia, May 1974. During the Assembly, there were 112 member churches represented, including mainstream Protestant denominations, Orthodox Churches, African indigenous churches as well as official Roman observers.

61. *The Struggle Continues: official report: Third Assembly of the All Africa Conference of Churches, Lusaka, Zambia, 12–24 May, 1974* (Nairobi: AACC, 1975), p. 72; hereafter cited as *Lusaka 1974*.

62. The first Assembly took place in April 1963 in Kampala on the theme 'Freedom and Unity in Christ'. The second Assembly was held in September 1969 in Abidjan on the theme: 'With Christ at Work in Africa Today'. For more details on those Assemblies see, *Drumbeats from Kampala: Reports of the First Assembly of the All Africa Conference of Churches* (London: Lutterworth, 1963); *Engagement: The Second AACC Assembly* (Nairobi: AACC, 1970); Efiong Utuk, *Visions of Authenticity*.

63. Gatu, 'Missionary Go Home'. *IDOC 9: The Future of the Missionary Enterprise* (1974), pp. 71–2.

64. 'ESP Committee Meeting, Choully, July 1972, Proposal on Moratorium', see *IDOC 9: The Future of the Missionary Enterprise* (1974), pp. 44–5.

65. 'ESP Committee Meeting, Choully, July 1972, Proposal on Moratorium'.

66. *Lusaka 1974*.

67. G. Muzorewa, *The Origins and Development of African Theology* (Maryknoll, NY: Orbis Books, 1987), p. 66.

68. Burgess Carr, 'The Mission of the Moratorium', in *AACC Bulletin*, 8 (1975), pp. 21–4.

69. Muzorewa, op. cit., p. 68.

70. Carr, op. cit., p. 24.

71. *AACC Bulletin*, 1975, p. 28.

72. The proceedings and conclusions of the AACC 1974 Assembly were covered by influential Catholic journals, like the *African Ecclesiastical Review* (AFRER), 16 (1974), pp. 329–34. In his annual report of November 1975, the Secretary-General of the Pontifical Works, the Roman department directly responsible for aid to Catholic mission churches all over the World, made an extensive allusion to the whole moratorium issue. Cf. P. A. Kalilombe, 'Self-Reliance of the African Church: A Catholic Perspective', in Kofi Appiah-Kubi and Sergio Torres, *African Theology en Route* (New York: Orbis Books, 1975), pp. 37–58.

73. Cf. Z. Nthamburi, *The African Church at the Crossroads: A Strategy for Indigenization* (Nairobi: Uzima, 1991), p. 73. Cf. also K. Bediako, *Christianity in Africa: The Renewal of a Non-Western Religion* (Edinburgh: Edinburgh University Press, 1995), pp. 63–73.

74. Ruben Lores, 'The Moratorium Issue and the Future of Mission', *IDOC 9: In Search of Missions* (1974), pp. 53–7.

75. Ibid., p. 56.

76. Paul Hopkins, *What Next in Mission?* (Philadelphia, PA: Westminster Press, 1977).

77. Paul Hopkins, 'A Conciliar Protestant Mission Board Perspective', *IDOC* 9, pp. 18–19.

78. Ibid., p. 18.

79. Paul Hopkins, 'What is the Call to Moratorium and How Should We Respond?,' *Concern* (November 1974), pp. 13–14.

80. Ibid., p. 14.

81. Cited by Peter Wagner, 'Colour the Moratorium Gray', *International Review of Mission* (April 1975), p. 167.

82. Susumu Uda, 'Biblical Authority and Evangelism', in J. D. Douglas (ed.), *Let the Earth Hear His Voice* (Minnesota, MN: World-wide Publications, 1975), p. 6.

83. Wagner, op. cit., p. 167.

84. Ibid., p. 176.

85. Ibid.

86. See the proceedings of the Symposium published under the title, *Problems and Promises of Africa: Towards and Beyond Year 2000* (Nairobi: AACC, 1992), p. 7.

87. J. N. K. Mugambi, *From Liberation to Reconstruction* (Nairobi: East African Educational Publishers, 1995), p. 5.

88. Cf. J. N. K. Mugambi, 'The Future of the Church and the Church of the Future', in J. P. Chipenda *et al.*, *The Church of Africa: Towards a Theology of Reconstruction* (Nairobi: AACC, 1991).

89. Mugambi, op. cit., p. 47.

90. AACC, *Problems and Promises*, pp. 17–18.

91. For more details, see Valentin Dedji, 'Paradigm Shifts in African Theological Debates: From Liberation to Reconstruction', PhD Dissertation (University of Cambridge: 1999).

92. Mugambi, *From Liberation to Reconstruction*, p. 204.

93. Ibid., p. 205.

94. This expression has first been used by Jacob Agossou, a Catholic priest from Benin in his book: *Christianisme africain: une fraternité au-delà de l'ethnie* (Paris: Karthala, 1987).

95. See Konrad Raiser, *Ecumenism in Transition: A Paradigm Shift in the Ecumenical Movement?* (Geneva: WCC Publications, 1991), pp. 33–41.

96. Sagovsky, op. cit., p. 195.

97. See Charles Villa-Vicencio, *A Theology of Reconstruction: Nation-Building and Human Rights* (Cambridge: Cambridge University Press, 1992), p. 4.

Part 2

Prospects for Ecumenism

8

Once More on the Unity We Seek: Testing Ecumenical Models

Michael Root

The major cause of problems is solutions, or so it is said. In recent years, however, the ecumenical complaint has often been that there has been a paucity of solutions, or at least a paucity of solutions the churches were actually willing to accept and act upon. Dialogue followed dialogue, commission followed commission, but nothing happened. In the case of the Lutheran churches, however, the last decade has produced a series of ecumenical actions: the Lutheran World Federation (LWF) and the Vatican have signed the Lutheran–Catholic *Joint Declaration on the Doctrine of Justification*, declaring a consensus on basic truths of the doctrine of justification and the non-applicability of the relevant condemnations in each church's normative documents. After a proposal for full communion between Lutheran and Reformed churches in the US was rejected in the mid-1980s, a new proposal, with strengthened language on the presence of Christ in the Lord's Supper was accepted in 1997. Most notably, a collection of similar Lutheran–Anglican proposals for communion or full communion, including a sharing in episcopal succession, has been accepted: the Porvoo Common Statement involving the British and Irish Anglican churches and most of the Scandinavian and Baltic Lutheran churches; the Concordat of Agreement, now revised as Called to Common Mission, has been accepted in varying forms by both the US Episcopal Church and the Evangelical Lutheran Church in America; and in Canada, preliminary positive votes have already been taken on The Waterloo Declaration between the Anglican Church in Canada and the Evangelical Lutheran Church in Canada.

These are major ecumenical events, especially but not only for Lutherans. The Lutheran–Catholic agreement on justification not only signifies agreement on what the continental Reformers stated to be the central issue of the Reformation, but it is also an affirmation of an ecumenical method oriented toward a carefully and patiently developed, differentiated consensus. The various Lutheran–Anglican agreements represent the fullest response yet to the proposal of *Baptism, Eucharist and Ministry*, §53, on reconciling episcopal and non-episcopal ministries.

But with solutions come new problems, or at least new questions. Anglicans, Lutherans and Reformed in Europe and North America are now all engaged in a complex network of relations of communion. To those already mentioned needs to be added not only the older Leuenberg Church Fellowship of the Lutheran, Reformed and United churches in continental Europe, but also the increasingly important Christian world communions, which add another layer of networks of communion. Whatever the long-term ecumenical future may bring, the immediate ecumenical future will be dominated by such relations of communion that, in contrast to the union and merger talks that dominated much ecumenical discussion in the postwar decades, leave the present church structures intact while the churches seek to live out a common life in visible unity.

With these new relations of communion come new challenges (which the less idealistic might call new problems). Some are simply organizational: what sorts of common commissions will be needed to see that these new relations do not remain merely paper realities? Some problems might be called canonical: what regulations will be needed to govern the mutual availability of clergy among churches? In this paper, however, I want to call attention to the underlying theoretical question these new relations raise: how does communion or full communion as realized in these new relations relate to the unity we are called to seek? Are these new relations in fact *full* communion, true realizations of the ecumenical goal? Are they significant steps toward that goal, but not yet the goal itself? Or are they false steps, misrepresentations of the goal, that lead us astray? In the context of the actions of the last decade, such theoretical questions are not academic in the negative sense, but eminently related to our concrete ecumenical situation.

A full discussion of these questions is obviously impossible within the constraints of a short article. I have presented fuller (or at least more detailed) thoughts on them in my contribution to the Festschrift for Mary Tanner, *Community–Union–Communion*.[1] Here I can only outline what I think is the nature of the question before us and some of the considerations which I think should shape an answer.

The 1960s and 1970s witnessed a significant debate on the goal of ecumenical efforts and models of unity.[2] The New Delhi, Uppsala and Nairobi assemblies of the World Council of Churches (1961, 1968, 1975) made important statements on unity, according to which unity is made visible when 'all in each place who are baptized into Jesus Christ and confess him as Lord and Saviour are brought by the Holy Spirit into one fully committed fellowship' and all such local churches are then united in a 'conciliar fellowship of local churches'.[3] Rightly or wrongly, these statements were widely read as implying that unity required the disappearance of distinct confessional traditions, both in the form of distinct local congregations and in the form of distinct regional, national or international bodies. The assumed ecumenical model seemed to be organic union in the form of united churches.

These WCC statements met criticism within the Christian world communions, especially within the Lutheran World Federation (LWF). The LWF had a history of pressing for a significant role for confessional bodies in the ecumenical movement, for example as members of the WCC. Over against the WCC statements, the LWF and other Christian world communions argued that unity need not imply the complete disappearance of distinct confessional traditions. True communion could be realized between churches which remained identifiably distinct as members of differing traditions. On the one hand, it was argued, the differing traditions had received gifts in their divided histories which unity should not throw out. On the other hand, the ecumenical principle that unity should not require uniformity should allow for the continuing existence of distinct traditions. The phrase used to describe this understanding of the ecumenical goal was 'unity in reconciled diversity'. A typical statement of this outlook was made in the early 1980s by Günther Gassmann and Harding Meyer:

> the principle must be adhered to that at every level – local, regional, and universal – of the ecumenical quest for unity and its realization room must be allowed, in principle at least, for confessionally deter-mined convictions and structures of fellowship, including their indispensable, institutional and structural presuppositions.[4]

The precise relation between the vision put forward in the WCC statements and 'unity in reconciled diversity' was not, however, entirely clear. Unity in reconciled diversity was often put forward as a corrective to the WCC statements, not as an alternative to them. Later WCC statements on unity are open to this corrective, not assuming a united church as the only form unity must take. For example, the Canberra statement on *The Unity of the Church as Koinonia* is neutral on the question whether unity requires the disappearance either of distinct local congregations of different traditions or distinct confessional structures. It states that unity is a *koinonia*, including 'a common confession . . . a common sacramental life . . . celebrated together in one eucharistic fellowship; a common life . . . and a common mission . . . This full communion will be expressed on the local and the universal levels through conciliar forms of life and action.'[5] What is described could be realized without the disappearance of distinct traditions and structures. This openness was noted and criticized by some, such as Lukas Vischer, who saw a retreat from earlier commit-ments to local unity.[6]

Statements such as the Canberra statement were able to avoid the issues under debate in the 1970s by presenting a 'portrait' of unity at a level of sufficient generality that the specific issue earlier debated need not arise. The recent progress in Lutheran–Anglican relations, how-ever, makes the issue harder to avoid. As we make progress toward the ecumenical goal, the need to describe that goal with some precision becomes greater.

Two subtly but significantly different pictures of visible unity can be found among the recent Lutheran–Anglican agreements. On the one hand, in 1983 a report from the International Anglican–Lutheran Joint Working Group (usually referred to as the Cold Ash Report) portrayed the ecumenical goal as 'full communion', defined as 'a relationship between two distinct churches or communions. Each maintains its own autonomy and recognizes the catholicity and apostolicity of the other' (§25). A necessary aspect of communion is 'recognized organs of regular consultation and communication, including episcopal collegiality' (§25d). No explicit mention is made of structures of common decision-making. The churches 'become interdependent while remaining autonomous' (§26). This definition of full communion is 'endorse[d] in principle' by the American proposal 'Called to Common Mission'. The Canadian Waterloo Declaration contains its own definition of full communion, which is a paraphrase of the Cold Ash definition.

The Cold Ash definition was called into question almost immediately, despite its continuing influence in shaping the North American actions. The Anglican–Lutheran International Continuation Committee, organized soon after the Cold Ash meeting, noted the need for continued discussion of the meaning of full communion.[7] The Northern European Porvoo Common Statement is read by some as implying a slightly different understanding of communion (the text significantly avoids the phrase 'full communion'). While Porvoo does not call for common decision-making, it does state a commitment 'to welcome diaspora congregations into the life of the indigenous churches' (§58.b.iv). The significance of this provision was brought out by the report of Section IV of the recent Lambeth Conference:

> [In Porvoo] Where the jurisdictions overlap, expatriate clergy and other congregations are welcomed into the life of the local dioceses. It is intended that episcopal oversight will come to be shared, as a further stage towards the resolution of the anomaly of overlapping jurisdictions.[8]

This comment brings out the difference: the North American proposals give no sign of seeing 'parallel jurisdictions', the continuing existence of two churches on the same territory, as an anomaly, and call a relation that leaves such jurisdictions in place 'full communion'. Porvoo also does not eliminate the relatively minor overlapping jurisdictions among the participating churches, but it does not call the relation full communion and it allows for an interpretation along the lines of that quoted from the Lambeth Conference.

The question this difference raises is fundamental: if the unity we seek ultimately demands the elimination of parallel jurisdictions, then it would seem to demand the disappearance of distinct church structures at the local and regional level (even if they could exist at some more comprehensive level, as groupings of local churches within a single international body).

Is communion between 'distinct churches' the ecumenical goal? On the one hand there are those who argue no. It should be recognized that this argument has tradition behind it. As I argue in the essay in the Festschrift for Mary Tanner already mentioned, not only the patristic and medieval Church, but also most churches up until recent times (including the Lutheran churches) have assumed that unity included local unity, that is, the elimination of parallel jurisdictions. Where parallel jurisdictions were foreseen (as, for example, in the reconciliation processes following various schisms), they were to be a transitional stage leading back to an integrated structure.[9] In addition, the question needs to be asked: will unity be truly visible if a single neighbourhood continues to have distinct Catholic, Anglican, Methodist and Orthodox churches?

On the other hand, there are those who argue that full communion between distinct churches as described in texts such as the Cold Ash Report is adequate or even more than necessary for visible unity. Lutherans tend to appeal to the 7th article of the Augsburg Confession, which states that 'for the true unity [*vera unitas*] of the Church it is enough to agree concerning the teaching of the Gospel and the administration of the sacraments', making no mention of common structures. Here it should be noted that significant differences exist in the ways communion between distinct churches or 'unity in reconciled diversity' is understood. On the one hand, a statement such as that from the Lutheran World Federation on *The Unity We Seek* (1984) describes such communion as realized in 'a committed fellowship, able to make common decisions and to act in common'. Such a communion 'is ordered in all its components in conciliar structures and actions'. Thus, while the statement explicitly affirms diversities not only in relation to 'cultural and ethnic contexts' but also in relation to 'the number of church traditions in which the apostolic faith has been maintained, transmitted, and lived out throughout the centuries', it also affirms a structured and committed fellowship at all levels, capable of common decision and action.[10] On the other hand, some concrete ecumenical proposals and arguments made by individual theologians foresee mutual consultation and an undefined collegiality in the ministry of oversight as adequate. The phrase 'unity in reconciled diversity' does not refer to a single model of church unity, but to a range of models.

How should we think theologically about the adequacy of communion between distinct churches, what I have elsewhere rather negatively referred to as denominational communion?[11] Let me make some suggestions.

First, I believe we need to see this issue in the context of the larger question of the relation between, on the one hand, the unity which is a gift of God's grace and strictly essential to the Church, that unity which one can only leave and never divide, that unity, which if a community falls out of it, it simply is not church, and on the other hand, that unity which is our call to realize, a unity we can lose and regain, a unity always dependent upon and derived from the unity given. These two senses of unity are closely related, but not identical. The point, I am convinced, of the Lutheran confessional insistence on the sufficiency of a common proclamation of the Word and administration of the sacraments for 'true unity' is to focus on the unity given by the means of grace, although this focus should not obscure the importance of the common life and structures that should flow from the unity given. I have elsewhere tried to understand the relation between these two senses of unity in terms of a trajectory of the Holy Spirit, from Word and Sacrament, through the faith that receives Word and Sacrament, and out into a truly common life.[12] In some continental Protestant theology, a tendency exists to cut off this trajectory and see the structured common life we are called to as optional because it is not essential in the strict sense.

Second, I believe we need to see this issue as one of contextual ecclesiology. As noted, the tradition of the Church has been intolerant of parallel jurisdictions, but we need to be sensitive to distinctions between what is truly essential and what is merely historical practice. Much traditional thinking about unity at the local level has assumed a geographical parish system of the sort common within established or formerly established churches in Europe. Thus, the New Delhi WCC statement speaks of 'all in each place'.[13] But does place determine the membership of the contemporary parish or congregation more than does selection among varying styles of liturgy, types of preaching, educational opportunities and so on? Was this already the case in the medieval city, with its variety of churches of different orders alongside parish churches of the secular clergy? Would the preservation of distinct confessional churches be all that different from the ongoing existence in the Church of England of parishes of distinct 'churchmanship'?

The crucial issue lies less with the continuing existence of distinct congregations or parishes and more with the existence of distinct regional church organizations in the same geographical area. Anglo-Catholic and evangelical parishes in the Church of England, for all their differences, are still under the same bishop; Jesuit and Dominican churches are still part of the one Roman Catholic ecclesial structure. Is unity real if distinct Lutheran and Reformed congregations in a city are grouped into distinct and autonomous church structures: dioceses, synods, presbyteries? This question is the decisive one that the recently ratified communion agreements raise.

A theologically and contextually appropriate answer to this question must hold together two fundamental concerns (and, I would add, will need to hold them together for decades, if not longer). On the one hand, the unity of the Church must not only be visible to those who wish to see it, but also evident, even obvious. That there is but one Church must be manifest. In a statement such as that from Canberra, emphasis needs to be laid on the repeated use of the word 'common' – a common confession, common sacramental life, common mission. Conciliar structures at every level are necessary, capable not only of consultation and collegiality in the sense given to that word in the secular world, but also of corporate (and thus binding) decision-making and consequent action. The network of communion agreements now being put into place could degenerate into mere 'status quo ecumenism', an ecumenism that leaves division in place but calls it unity, unless there is the will to realize such a truly common life.

On the other hand, we will not continue to make progress towards our ecumenical goal unless there is significant sensitivity to the way the Church and its unity must be realized within the surrounding social and cultural context. The unity of the late patristic and medieval Church was not unrelated to the unity of the late Roman empire and the complex but real unities of European Christendom. Even the local church unity of the early modern period in continental Europe and Scandinavia was aided by the power of the state enforcing such unity. We live in a different world, in which cultural diversity exists more broadly diffused in more geographically condensed form. In addition, this cultural diversity is often intertwined with already existing church divisions. Many Christians value unity, but they also value the liturgy and typical theology, the customs and habits of their churches, which they are not willing simply to abandon. Any workable and acceptable form of unity will need to find ways of embodying and respecting this diversity. Whatever the ecumenical future may be, it will not be a return to the forms of unity that typified the late patristic and medieval Church.

Complicating the present situation, I believe, is the lack of attractive models for organic union. The twentieth century has seen the rise of the bureaucratically centralized national church, with a large complement of staff and significant budgets to match. At least in the USA – and my sense is also in Europe – such a form of national church institution did not exist previously. (What was the national staff of the Church of England in 1820? Is the question utterly anachronistic?) In many of the union discussions of the postwar period, the model of unity appeared to be the creation of a single, national denomination along these lines. At least in the USA (and, again, my sense is that similar dynamics exist elsewhere) the bureaucratically centralized national denomination is experiencing a thoroughgoing transition. Efforts and funds are more locally and regionally focused, leading to financial crises at the national level in many American churches, even while total funds in the churches continue to rise. The church unions that have occurred have absorbed time, energy and funds for extended periods. The creation of new national denominations along typical twentieth-century lines is not an idea that many find attractive. The path to unity as a series of increasingly large denominational mergers is a prospect few find heartening. But do we have tested models for an organic union that will eliminate parallel jurisdictions other than denominational merger?

The task of our immediate ecumenical future, then, is one of living into new relations of communion in ways that will realize a truly common life and, in the process, discovering within this new common life and structures what unity concretely demands of us. When the Anglican–Lutheran International Continuation Committee called in 1986 for a continuing reflection on the nature of full communion, it added: 'We are persuaded that such reformulation can take place only in the context of our growing common experience with one another.'[14] This statement strikes me as precisely right. We need 'portraits of visible unity' as presented by the Canberra statement, that is, lists of the elements of visible unity with a sense of how those elements fit together, which stop short of becoming detailed models for just how unity is realized. Such statements serve as orienting points that can direct our efforts. But at this point in our journey, we cannot specify the details of the unity we are seeking nor the exact path that will take us from here to there.

We should be prepared for both the path towards and perhaps the details of the unity we are seeking to vary in different ecclesial contexts. The realities of church life that shape ecumenical efforts differ sharply between countries such as Spain or Sweden, where one church takes in the vast majority of the population and is identified with national life and history, countries such as Germany or England, where two or three churches take in most Christians, and countries such as the USA or some African countries, where no church or combination of two or three churches dominates, but Christians are splintered into a multiplicity of denominations. These differing ecclesial situations bring with them different complexities, psychological and sociological, that cannot be ignored.

A final comment before summing up: a crucial test of these new agreements is their openness to new developments. So far, such agreements only have taken place among Western, non-Roman Catholic churches. Is this sort of agreement a workable step at some point in the future also for Catholics and Orthodox? I believe so, but that question is one for another day.

The cause of problems is solutions. In the various communion agreements of the last decade, we have taken some important ecumenical steps. The short- and middle-term ecumenical future seems to lie with these sorts of agreements. With these steps comes the task of testing these arrangements as forms of ecumenical life. Can they overcome ecclesiastical inertia and forge new forms of common life? We cannot know without trying. To change proverbs, the proof of the pudding is in the eating. The grace of the moment is that we have been given the opportunity to test this particular form of life together.

Notes

1. M. Root, ' "Reconciled Diversity" and the Visible Unity of the Church', in C. Podmore (ed.), *Community–Unity–Communion: Essays in Honour of Mary Tanner* (London: Church House Publishing, 1998), pp. 237–51.

2. An excellent history of this can be found in H. Meyer, *That All May Be One: Perceptions and Models of Ecumenicity,* trans. W. G. Rusch (Grand Rapids, MI: Eerdmans, 1999).

3. Cited in G. Gassmann (ed.), *Documentary History of Faith and Order 1963–1993* (Geneva: WCC, 1993), p. 3.

4. G. Gassmann and H. Meyer, 'Requirements and Structure of Church Unity', in Gassmann and Meyer, *The Unity of the Church: Requirements and Structure*, LWF Report, no. 15 (Geneva: Lutheran World Federation, 1983), p. 23.

5. Para 2.1 of the Canberra statement, *The Unity of the Church: Gift and Calling* (1991; text on the Faith and Order Website of the World Council of Churches).

6. L. Vischer, 'Is this Really "The Unity We Seek"?: Comments on the statement on *The Unity of the Church as Koinonia: Gift and Calling.* Adopted by the WCC Assembly in Canberra', *Ecumenical Review* 44 (Geneva: WCC; 1992), pp. 467–78.

7. Anglican–Lutheran International Continuation Committee, *The Niagara Report: Report of the Anglican–Lutheran Consultation on Episcope, Niagara Falls, September 1987* (Cincinnati: Forward Movement Publications, 1988), p. 61.

8. The official report of the Lambeth Conference 1998: *Transformation and Renewal, July 18–August 9 1998, Lambeth Palace; Canterbury, England* (Harrisburg, IL: Morehouse Publishing, 1998), p. 220.

9. Root, op. cit., p. 243.

10. C. H. Mau (ed.), Budapest 1984, 'In Christ – Hope for the World'. Official Proceedings of the Seventh Assembly of the Lutheran World Federation, Budapest Hungary, 22 July–5 August 1984 (Geneva: Lutheran World Federation), p. 175.

11. M. Root, 'A Striking Convergence in American Ecumenism', *Origins* 26 (1996), pp. 60–64.

12. G. Fackre and M. Root, *Affirmations and Admonitions: Lutheran Decisions and Dialogue with Reformed, Episcopal, and Roman Catholic Churches* (Grand Rapids, MI: Eerdmans, 1998).

13. Gassmann (ed.), op. cit., p. 3.

14. *Niagara Report*, p. 61.

9

The Goal of Visible Unity: Yet Again

Mary Tanner

One of the most important questions currently on the ecumenical agenda is the question of the goal of visible unity. What is the goal that motivates the ecumenical movement? Now that separated churches have come out of their isolation, got to know one another and cooperate with one another, what is it that lies beyond this relationship? It is clear, from comparing the results of ecumenical conversations and the various suggestions for moves to closer fellowship, that there are different views of what lies ahead. These views are sometimes expressed explicitly, but more often implied. Harding Meyer, in his recent book *That All May Be One* (1999), traces the discussion of the subject of the goal of visible unity in the last 50 years.[1] He notes in a number of places that 'organic union' was rooted in the Anglican tradition while 'church fellowship' and 'reconciled diversity' were rooted in the tradition of the churches of the Reformation. It is not surprising, then, that the discussion is being carried on between Michael Root, a Lutheran, and myself, an Anglican. Michael wrote an article on the subject in a Festschrift in my honour that many have found thought-provoking and valuable.[2] He raises many of the same themes in the essay in this volume. This essay is intended to carry on the conversation. Before engaging with Michael Root, a few general comments may be made about the subject of visible unity.

First, Lesslie Newbigin was surely right when he said that we cannot simply be committed to unity in some vague, unspecified sense. We have to be able to put some content into that commitment. The same point is made by Meyer: 'A goal-oriented movement . . . must articulate as clearly as possible the aims commonly agreed upon by its adherents.'[3] And in his closing remarks in his essay Root affirms the need to make statements about the unity we seek, for they can serve as 'criteria and orientation points' as we structure and implement the steps now possible.[4]

Second, every ecumenist needs to recognize the tendency to envisage the goal of unity as themselves 'writ large'. The notion of a unity beyond ourselves – 'beyond Anglicanism' (to use the title of a book by Anthony Hanson), 'beyond Lutheranism', 'beyond Methodism' – is threatening for each of us. This is particularly so as for many of us our own identity was formulated over against the identity of the other from whom the separation took place.[5]

Third, in attempts to envisage the goal of visible unity little acknowledgement seems to be given to the fact that each church today is a church in change. The way Anglicans understand their unity and identity as a World Communion has developed as they have spread into the different regions of the world and have had to discern what it is that holds them together in the Anglican Communion. It is no longer enough to refer to the 39 Articles and the Chicago–Lambeth Quadrilateral. Anglicans also have to take account of the developing understanding of their identity that has occurred in this century, as can be illustrated in the reports of Lambeth Conferences, not least of all from the report of the 1998 Lambeth Conference. At the 1998 Lambeth Conference the bishops raised the question of whether a fifth item, describing structures of communion, should be added to the Chicago–Lambeth Quadrilateral. This suggestion came in part from the internal Anglican experience of the struggle to remain together in the face of new and divisive challenges. It came also, in part, from what Anglicans have been learning about the requirements for communion in their discussions with ecumenical partners, not least of all in their discussions with the Roman Catholic Church.

Fourth, it is important to restate the goal of visible unity for the sake of an ecumenical movement which is both increasingly diverse in its membership and also complex in its agenda. The different items on the agenda have come to compete with one another. For example, Faith and Order is often set over against Life and Work; programmes for justice, peace and the integrity of creation are placed at the heart of the ecumenical movement; renewal is set over against unity, and even a plea is made for a paradigm shift which it seems would replace the search for the visible unity of the Church with the search for the unity of all creation. All of this has led, if not to a crisis in the ecumenical movement, then to an unsettled and chaotic ecumenical movement. In this climate the need to restate a common goal becomes more and more important in order to keep the complex ecumenical movement steady and focused, instead of chaotic and 'lost in the fog'. The failure of the Harare Assembly to issue a major statement on the goal of visible unity which built upon earlier assembly statements and integrated the recent ecclesiological insights of Faith and Order, not least of all those from the Fifth World Conference, was a missed opportunity at the end of an ecumenical century. A compelling common statement of visible unity would have helped to give both direction and coherence to a complex ecumenical movement.

Fifth, what is being agreed in bilateral and multilateral theological dialogues about the faith, or sacraments, or ministry needs now to be brought together into a common portrait of the goal of visible unity. Sometimes it seems that partners in dialogue agree things about faith, or sacraments, or ministry, or even authority, without understanding the implications that such agreements have for the sort of visible life that they seek to live together. Surely agreements like those of *The Final Report of ARCIC* on the Eucharist, ministry, and even on authority, describe the sort of united life that Anglicans and Roman Catholics hope one day to live together. These agreements, therefore, are not isolated issues. They should find their place within an overall portrait of visible unity.

To emphasize a need to restate the goal, or portrait of visible unity, is not to deny that unity is God's gift to us – we cannot create it. Nevertheless, while unity is divine gift it is *also* a human task. Root writes that unity is both gift of God's grace and our call to realize it, always dependent upon the unity given. Or, as Meyer puts it, 'the ecumenical indicative gives rise to the ecumenical imperative'.[6] We can never give an exact blueprint of unity but, as we converse together and begin to act together, our understanding of the visible unity we seek becomes clearer.

Root helpfully explains how the multilateral view of visible unity, expressed in the New Delhi, Uppsala and Nairobi Assembly statements, was an organic unity model – 'the all in each place united to the all in every place and in all times', in which distinct confessional bodies would disappear. Meyer and Gassmann, both Lutherans, put forward 'not as an alternative . . . but as a corrective to this', unity in reconciled fellowship, in which the unit which entered into the fellowship was not limited to a local church but might be confessional bodies.[7] The confessional bodies would remain distinct, self–governing entities with possibly parallel jurisdictions. Root explains that the genius of this was that it appropriated much of the earlier understanding of visible unity, but with a 'change in its ontology'. It was possible for both the organic model and the reconciled diversity model to espouse the same fundamental understanding of the Church as *koinonia*. All was well as long as one did not ask what the units of church life were that would come into *koinonia*. Indeed, as he points out, the statement of the Canberra Assembly, *The Unity of the Church as koinonia*, provides a good example of such ambiguity. It is ambiguous precisely because it is not clear what picture of visible unity it is espousing. The statement has been interpreted by some as offering a model of organic unity and by others as offering a model of reconciled diversity. It is most likely that its original authors themselves held different views about the model of unity being offered, but that this was never discussed.

Having helpfully explained the origin of the concept of reconciled diversity, Root goes on honestly to acknowledge its weaknesses. It is not found in the Bible, or in the early tradition, or in the Reformation tradition, nor is there any dogmatic support for it. Root argues rather for what he calls 'structured unity in reconciled diversity'. His argument is based on pragmatic arguments and tests. To quote him: 'the decisive arguments arise out of the concrete ecumenical situations of the Church today'.[8] He points, for example, to the ambiguity of the churches of North and South India, which he calls a 'bureaucratic-oriented model'.[9] He refers in a footnote to a paper given by Bishop

Samuel Joshua at the Fifth World Conference on Faith and Order at Santiago de Compostela. Bishop Samuel stunned those who were anticipating a robust defence of the organic union model by offering a severe critique of it . His critique lamented the weakness of the united churches of the Indian subcontinent and went on to question the wisdom of the aim of organic union.

It is mainly pragmatic arguments such as the above that lead Root in the direction of reconciled diversity. It is no less pragmatic reasons that lead me in another direction in which denominational difference plays a much less significant part in my understanding of visible unity. First, there are concrete examples of church unions, or close cooperations, which do point in the direction of a unity beyond what is usually understood by reconciled diversity: one where unity, rather than diversity, is the dominating and controlling ethos. The experience of the United Reformed Church in England is one example. Secondly, not everyone would agree with Bishop Joshua's assessment of the experience of the churches of North and South India, as was clear from the reactions to his speech from other members of those churches.

Third, evidence of ecumenical life in some places in England also points to a unity in which denominational differences are coming to count for less and less. In some Local Ecumenical Partnerships, particularly those on new housing estates or where churches share a building, the most important fact about identity is being Christians together in that place. Second-generation Christians understand their identity simply as Christian. Many have forgotten their denominational identity, if they ever had one. What becomes a burden in these situations is having to relate to several parallel denominational structures as well as to new ecumenical structures at intermediate and national levels. The duplication of structures of relationship and administration sap energy and divert from the mission of the Church. It was not surprising that in the 'Called to be One' process in England some of the Local Ecumenical Partnerships called for a coming together of denomi-national structures at intermediate, national and even international levels, so that the 'all in one place' would not become isolated. In some places the experience of living together locally calls for the ending of denominational groupings rather than the formation of a relationship of 'full communion understood as a relationship between two distinct churches or communions'.[10] There are, however, other stories from Local Ecumenical Partnerships, which seem to experience a crisis of identity, and where, far from pointing to the ending of denominational differences, those differences seem to be accentuated. However, the establishment of Local Ecumenical Partnerships in England makes little sense without a commitment to a unity beyond reconciled diversity, a commitment to visible unity.

A fourth development that seems to support a goal of visible unity is the relationship established between Anglicans and Lutherans in the Porvoo Communion. Here an interchangeable ministry in the historic succession, regular collegial, primatial and quasi-synodical gatherings are leading towards a unity which is of a closer sort than that implied in reconciled diversity. Allowing for the fact that these churches do not live in the same territories, the life of communion that is emerging bears more resemblance to the old model of organic union than to that of reconciled diversity. In some places diaspora congregations are being welcomed into the life of the indigenous church.

There are, however, other examples where relationships involving Anglicans have been established which appear to be nearer the model of reconciled diversity in structured communion. This is true, for example, of the Bonn Agreement between Anglicans and Old Catholics, and also true of the relationship between Anglicans and the Mar Thoma Church. However, after 50 years, it is being increasingly recognized that these are unsatisfactory as permanent forms of relationship. The bishops at the Lambeth Conference recommended: 'That consideration be given to ways of deepening our communion with the Old Catholic Churches beyond the Bonn Agreement, including means of taking counsel and making decisions together, (and) the anomaly of over-lapping jurisdictions' (Resolution IV: 6.c).[11]

But let me move on from the pragmatic arguments; for my reason for being less willing than Root to emphasize unity in reconciled diversity is, in the end, not a pragmatic one. It has to do with a way of approaching the subject of unity. When Meyer and Gassmann came to propose reconciled diversity as a model it was, at least in part, out of a disillusionment with the slowness of ecumenical progress, a conviction that the denominations would never be persuaded to surrender their separate identities, and a conviction that each tradition had preserved truths at the time of separation that were best preserved through a continuing degree of separate identity. To begin from this perspective is to place the prior and controlling emphasis upon diversity and difference, both the diversity and difference of the present-day situation as well as that of the sixteenth century. Root refers to the hesitation of Jean-Marie Tillard that in reconciled diversity, unity and diversity are being placed on the same level in a way that undercuts unity: 'Thus the temptation arises . . . of understanding unity as an interconfessional adjustment in which diversity is so privileged that unity runs the danger of being fragile, accepted but only to a limited degree.'[12] A rather different approach to unity, however, is to begin by suspending our own particular view of things, born out of separation and out of seeing things over against one another, and to go back together to Scripture and the early tradition in order to restate a common belief about the nature of the Church and what unity requires from that shared perspective. In this way the controlling emphasis is upon unity in which diversity then comes to take its proper place.

But here there is a dilemma. This very ecumenical endeavour in fact seems to lead some to understand unity as unity in one faith, one baptism, one Eucharist, a single ordered ministry, ways of deciding, teaching and acting together, common service and united mission locally, regionally and internationally. In this view, the faith, the sacraments, the ministry and a structure that enables the community to 'walk together on the way' cohere. They belong together in a single web of belonging to the Lord and, in the Lord, to one another. The different elements are part of a single package of life in unity. In this view of things there is a fundamental and integral connexion between the 'Gospel preached with pure understanding of it and the sacraments administered in accordance with the Divine Word' on the one hand, and the ordered ministry which preaches the Word and which, together with the whole body, takes counsel and makes decisions for the life and mission of the Church. This means that in our conversation Root and I are sent back again and again to questions about the place of the ordered ministry and its function within a life of visible unity. This affects our understanding of visible unity. For if the ordered ministry (a single, interchangeable ministry) which has a function not only in preaching the Word and administering the sacraments, but also in the collegial and synodal structures and processes of oversight, is required for visible unity, and is constitutive of the life of the Church, then reconciled diversity, even when structured, is hardly a convincing model of the goal, even if it may be one way towards the goal. The goal of unity must surely be a unity in which communion is nurtured and sustained by 'a single system of communication', by faith, sacraments, ministry and ordered life, for the sake of effective service and mission. It is not surprising that those who espouse reconciled diversity between continuing, recognizably distinct denominations, and those who have no room for continuing denominations, differ in their estimation of the ordered ministry as well as where they place it in the scheme of things. They also differ in the relation they see between the ordered ministry and the conciliar life of the Church. For those who look for an end to distinct denominations, the conciliar life of the Church is not a pragmatic thing concerning structures that would best serve distinct, autonomous churches. Church structures are an ecclesial reality belonging to, nurturing and expressing the inner life of the Church as communion.

This leads to the question of diversity, for some will hear the proposal for the end of recognizable denominations as a plea for monolithic uniformity. Not so. A confident acceptance of all the gracious bonds of faith and order should support a greater and more confident diversity. To echo Martin Cressey's sentiments in his answer to his own question – 'How diverse can a united Church be?' – 'More diverse than we can possibly imagine.'[13] Diversity will be born out of the variety of human temperaments, the different reactions to new challenges to the Gospel, and a diversity that blossoms as the Gospel is lived out in different cultural contexts: 'We don't require a uniformity of expression and formulation at all levels and in all situations but rather a catholic diversity within a unity of communion.'[14] It may be, as Geoffrey Wainwright has suggested, that denominational distinctiveness will be preserved as recognizable traditions, rather like the orders in the Roman Catholic Church.[15] Diversities already exist within each world communion. In a greater unity these diversities will surely blossom in even greater richness. But a graced structure is required in order to sustain diversity and to safeguard against illegitimate diversity that destroys communion. The statement of the Canberra Assembly was right to warn that there are tolerable limits to diversity. At the same time it was very reticent in its statement of what those limits might be. While it is exciting to imagine something of the diversity and dynamic quality of the life of the Church as it faces new challenges, I find it as hard to imagine the need for a permanent protection of distinct denominations as others do to think of their demise. For one thing, the existing diversities go as much across denominational divides as between denominations, as anyone around the ecumenical table knows. I find it hard to imagine that denominations are to be protected because that is the only way in which certain Gospel truths will be preserved. Rather, those Gospel truths that have been protected in the histories of the different denominations need now to be shared within a single, richly diverse communion of unity and truth. As ARCIC II saw, the polarized positions held on the doctrine of justification by faith through grace need now to be brought together in order to restore a balanced understanding which would serve a single communion in faith.

To sum up. There is a difference between the way Root and I estimate the current ecumenical scene and the direction in which it points. There may also be a difference of emphasis in the way we approach the question of visible unity. One of us tends to emphasize the perspective of denominational history and distinctiveness. The other emphasizes the witness of the earliest years of the Church. This leads to a different estimation of the ministry and the structured life of the Church within visible unity. In the end it is perhaps safer not to espouse any particular *model* of unity. The old models, whether of 'organic unity', 'united not absorbed', 'reconciled diversity' and even 'full communion', have become buzz-words, badges of identity that unhelpfully tend to set us over against one another. We think we know what these terms mean. We think we know how our partners in dialogue are using these terms. But it is not long into the conversation before we discover that this is not so. Terminology meant to help the ecumenical cause has tended to confuse us. It is more constructive not to opt for any controlling model of visible unity and instead to go on exploring a portrait of what life in unity might be like. A convincing portrait should challenge churches to renew their own lives now in the light of that portrait, as well as challenge churches in different places, in different partnerships, to move together towards that portrait for the sake of a more effective mission and more authentic worship of the God whose gift is unity.

A portrait of unity needs now to be outlined by the theological dialogues, both bilateral and multilateral. But there are three complementary areas of exploration which have profound implications for the portrait of visible unity that need to be attended to. The first is the need to bring into the faith and order discussion the insights about 'togetherness' which come from those who are already engaging together in moves for justice and peace and the new programme to overcome violence. These active movements have insights to offer about life in unity that should enrich the portrait of visible unity. The Decade of Churches in Solidarity with Women that turned out to be a Decade of Women in Solidarity with Women, for example, had important things to say about the obscenity of violence against women in society and in the churches. But it also had things to say about solidarity that could profoundly enrich the understanding of the visible unity of the Church that Christians are called to live together. The same could be said about what was learnt in the struggles together against apartheid in Southern Africa.

Secondly, it is important to ensure that the community that reflects upon the portrait of unity is an ever more inclusive and diverse one. Those of different ecclesial traditions, women, younger people and marginalized groups, need to be brought within the community of interpretation and reflection. The bringing of more women into the circle of reflection in the 1970s and 1980s has already had an effect upon understanding of the unity to which God calls us. A more inclusive circle of reflection would, moreover, lead to a wider reception of the vision.

Thirdly, thought about the goal of visible unity needs to take much more account of the multifaith, multicultural world in which the Church is called to live out its vocation. This world deserves an example of reconciled life, which testifies to the possibility of diversity being held in unity and which can give united testimony to the faith of the one God, Father, Son and Holy Spirit.

Even if, for some, the goal remains visible unity in which denominations have no place, in the immediate future, as Root suggests, there are likely to be different steps taken, different stages reached in the different regions of the world, as different combinations of traditions learn to act together and bear witness together. The stage of what he calls 'structured communion oriented towards common decision-making' may well make sense as one stage on the way towards a greater degree of visible unity. The different moves to unity currently taking place in the different regions of the world are, however, not without their problems, as Anglicans and Lutherans in Europe and North America are realizing. Roman Catholic commentators are right to express some nervousness about these moves and to raise the question of coherence between them. A common portrait of full, visible unity of the Church, of the sort outlined by the bishops at the last Lambeth Conference, would go some way to maintaining that coherence. And as the Resolution says:

> The process of moving towards full, visible unity may entail temporary anomalies . . . some anomalies may be bearable when there is an agreed goal of visible unity, but there should always be an impetus towards their resolution and, thus towards the removal of the principal anomaly of disunity. (Resolution IV.1)[16]

It is important that this discussion about visible unity continues. The discussion is not about the unity of the Church as an end in itself. It is for the sake of the Lord whose prayer was that we should be one, and because those who have been entrusted with the Gospel of reconciliation are called to be a living and credible sign of reconciliation.

Notes

1. H. Meyer, *That All May be One: Perceptions and Models of Ecumenicity* (Grand Rapids, MI: Eerdmans, 1999).

2. M. Root, '"Reconciled Diversity" and the Visible Unity of the Church', in C. Podmore (ed.), *Community–Unity–Communion: Essays in Honour of Mary Tanner* (London: Church House Publishing, 1998), pp. 237–51.

3. Meyer, *That All May be One*, p. 1.

4. Root, 'Reconciled Diversity', p. 238.

5. A. T. Hanson, *Beyond Anglicanism* (London: Darton, Longman & Todd, 1965).

6. Meyer, *That All May be One*, p. 12.

7. Root, 'Reconciled Diversity', p. 238.

8. Ibid., p. 245.

9. Ibid., p. 246.

10. Report of the Anglican–Lutheran Working Group, Cold Ash, 1983, in J. Gros, H. Meyer and W. Rusch (eds), *Growth in Agreement II*, Faith and Order Paper 187 (Geneva: WCC, 2000), p. 7.

11. *The Official Report of the Lambeth Conference*, 1988 (Harrisburg, IL: Morehouse Publishing, 1999), p. 407.

12. Root, 'Reconciled Diversity', p. 240.

13. M. Cressey, 'How Diverse Could a United Church Be?', in minutes of the meeting of the Faith and Order Standing Commission, 4–11 January 1994, in Faith and Order Paper 167 (Geneva: WCC, 1994), pp. 34ff.

14. *Gift of Authority: Authority in the Church III, An Agreed Statement by the Second Anglican–Roman Catholic International Commission* (London: Catholic Truth Society, 1999), para. 27.

15. G. Wainwright, 'Ecclesial Location and Ecumenical Vocation', in Wainwright, *The Ecumenical Movement. Crisis and Opportunity for the Church* (Grand Rapids, MI: Eerdmans, 1983).

16. *The Official Report of the Lambeth Conference, 1988*, p. 404.

10

Ex Tenebris Lux: Ecumenism Enters a New Phase

Jean-Marie Tillard OP

I

Any serious observer of the ecumenical movement will admit that so-called 'classical or traditional ecumenism' is not a sterile or useless enterprise. Some of the old barriers preventing confessional families from sharing communion with each other have become blurred or have even disappeared. British Anglicans and Nordic–Baltic Lutherans have agreed on episcopacy, opening the way to a reconciled common ministry. Eastern and Oriental Orthodox are ready to clinch a substantial accord. Lutherans and Catholics have finalized an important joint declaration on the burning issue of justification by faith. Anglicans and Catholics have published an important agreed statement on the *Gift of Authority*. Between nearly all the main historical churches, doctrinal consensus is growing.

Fifty years ago such a situation would have been unthinkable. Confessionalism is certainly less triumphant today, or more on the defensive, than during the years preceding the formation of Faith and Order. This is a clear sign of the work of the Holy Spirit through ecumenical institutions, even if these are sometimes misused. Instead of defending themselves, often with great passion and at least a touch of aggression, confessional churches are more and more questioning their own opinion. In so doing, they come to discover that truth is not only on their side and that some of their doctrinal options were too sharp, too stiff, and thus too divisive.

It is evident that these efforts of clarification through interconfessional dialogue have to continue. Theological agreements remain a providential instrument to replace hostility between divided churches by authentic Christian love. In many instances, consensus is the door *sine qua non* to enter the upper room where unity is celebrated in the Eucharist. This consensus may be – and probably must be – a 'differentiated consensus'. Nevertheless, as a matter of reverence or respect for each of the different approaches, churches need to be really sure that the two groups now agree on what was in the past a source of division. For instance, as long as the question of justification by faith – the article by which, according to Lutheran tradition, the Church stands or falls – is not officially and entirely settled through a clear reception of the fruits of dialogue, Lutherans and Catholics will not be able even to envisage a life in communion that is totally sincere, and without reservation.[1] Let me give another example. As long as the problem of the *exousia* (authority) of the Bishop of Rome and its relation to the eastern part of the Church of God is not clearly resolved, Orthodox and Catholic sister churches will not be able to celebrate together the Eucharist, which is for them the seal of full unity. But all these issues, and many others, requiring deep and serious theological and historical knowledge, cannot be clarified outside the doctrinal and theological discussions which constitute the main task of the ecumenical commissions. It is wrong to say (and write) that this task is useless. It would be a huge mistake to suppress it. Committed Christians are shaped by their 'confessional' ethos, and they have to know why some issues are no longer considered divisive.

II

Nevertheless, it is also evident that this kind of theological dialogue is no longer sufficient. It has now to be integrated into a broader type of interchurch relations. An agreement, officially confirmed on both sides and resolving the most crucial confessional doctrinal divisions of the past, is no longer sufficient to allow a true visible unity. From the beginnings of the Faith and Order movement (1927) and the Decree on Ecumenism of the Second Vatican Council (1964) until now, the churches have changed deeply. Consequently, the ecumenical map is no longer exactly the same. The churches – except the Orthodox of the East – are not today, even in their doctrinal positions, exactly what they were in the sixteenth and seventeenth centuries. This seems to be the case even for some Orthodox churches living in the diaspora (the churches of the emigration).

1. New divisive forces – some of them not theological, others essentially doctrinal – are here and now creating walls, polemics and separations not only between the churches but even within the confessional families themselves and their churches. A very important feature of these new causes of division is the fact that they are not confessional and that they can be found nearly everywhere. Nearly all the churches are here and now debating these crucial matters internally.

Yet two very important ecumenical consequences result from this situation. The first of these consequences is the emergence of a strange coalition of all the groups which share a dissatisfaction or a profound anxiety in the face of what they consider the too timid, too liberal or too conservative official position of their own church. For instance, during the eighth Assembly of the World Council of Churches at Harare (December 1998), the meetings of evangelical groups, some of them coming from many denominations. and their unexpected sympathy for Roman Catholic official positions, especially on ethical matters, was a clear sign of this new phenomenon. Surprisingly, many of them approved when I spoke of 'an ecumenical striving for communion in the most basic baptismal requirements of life-in-Christ' (during a padare or discussion), a communion in harmony with some strong affirmations of John Paul II (whose universal primacy was denied!) which members of these groups praised and echoed. Something new, indeed, on the ecumenical scene!

Let me give another example. Just before the Assembly, during the conclusion of the WCC Decade of Churches in Solidarity with Women, Roman Catholic delegates joined the Protestant group of women, eager to challenge the official Roman position, especially on the non-ordination of women to presbyterate and episcopacy. This communion across the borders works in both directions, and the leaders of the churches fear it.

193

The second consequence of these new sources of division is more official. In some countries, the leaders of many churches, including some who did not belong to local councils of churches, because they were more and more aware of the influence of the same divisive causes in nearly all the communities, agreed on the necessity of initiating common study, common teaching and common catechesis on issues at stake. For instance, Canadian Anglican and Catholic bishops, confronted by a fast-growing individualism, decided to examine together the question of the common good. Elsewhere, Protestant and Catholic pastors judged it necessary to consider together the problems around 'the Christian vision of the family'. They were indeed aware that by acting in this way they might create in their own church uneasy feelings, and perhaps make more evident the marginalization of certain groups. But they chose to work together not only for the sake of the *oikumene* (according to the Lund principle) but principally for the sake of their own, confessional Church.[2] This is again a new situation, demonstrating the impact of the last 50 years of ecumenical dialogue, and the sign of a growing consciousness of fraternity. Although the churches are not yet visibly united, they now know that they not only share in God's grace, but also that for the solution of their own, proper, internal problems they may in many cases rely on the help of other churches, even if they continue to stress and to defend their confessional differences. Fifty years ago this would have been unthinkable. The Spirit is there.

2(a). Some of the new divisive forces are cultural, ethical and anthropological. It is useless to explain how, for instance, the thorny question of the ordination of women to episcopacy and presbyterate put an immense obstacle on the road towards the reconciliation of the Anglican and Catholic churches. This happened after the letter of Cardinal Willebrands showing that it was now possible to reverse the verdict of *Apostolicae Curae*. But it also created divisions within Anglican communities. The most recent Lambeth Conference (1998) demonstrated how some other ethical issues – especially those linked with human sexuality – may be divisive within and between churches. For some Orthodox churches, the use of inclusive language to refer to God in liturgy and in the translation of the Bible is stopping any dialogue with Protestant churches and the World Council of churches, but it also creates tension within some Orthodox schools of theology. These are only examples of a growing problem. The more the churches inculturate themselves in the societies where they have to take root, the more new cultural or moral issues may challenge or endanger not only the fruits of long years of ecumenical dialogue but also the internal cohesion of each church, especially when leaders opt for the most liberal positions.

(b). However, many of the new forces which threaten ecumenism and the internal cohesion of the churches are essentially dogmatic or doctrinal. To characterize them I often use the expression 'erosion of the basis';[3] that is, inseparably, the basis of our life in Christ and the basis of the ecumenical movement (of the World Council of Churches). In many circles the credibility of the Bible itself is jeopardized. In all the churches, more and more people are asking, 'In what measure can we rely on what is taught in the Bible?' In some of the churches professing the *scriptura sola*, this situation is already creating chaos. Ecumenically, the question is, 'Where shall we find the common certitudes our communion requires?' The temptation is to base this consensus either on a fundamentalist vision of the Scriptures or on a vague and minimal set of tolerable beliefs. Faith in Christ is here seriously challenged.

Every church agrees that unity must be based on faith in Christ. Every Christian agrees that we have to believe in Christ. But believe what? It is evident that in exegetical and systematic (dogmatic) literature the truth concerning Jesus Christ is now quite often presented as 'the big question'. In the USA, the Jesus Seminar is a manifestation of this radical interrogation embracing the divine origin and the inspired preaching of the Son of Mary. Elsewhere, the following questions are asked, 'Is Christ the only form of God's incarnation, the only saviour, the only mediator? Is not interfaith dialogue the only honest way to deal with God? Is not Christian ecumenism too parochial?' Recently, having returned from Harare, where he represented his church at the Assembly of the WCC, the Moderator of the United Church of Canada, repeating what he had already said the previous year, inflamed his own church and the Canadian churches by his unorthodox affirmations on the divinity of Christ.[4]

3. Even if churches succeed in overcoming their traditional and confessional controversies, visible Christian unity would be only a sandcastle, an empty structure, a canonical skeleton, if they do not take these new issues seriously. Moreover, it is obvious that the reason why they try so hard to remove the confessional obstacles is precisely the necessity of living together the one and undivided Apostolic faith, as authentic witnesses of what the Acts of the Apostles calls 'the Way' (cf. Acts 9:2; 19:9; 19:23; 22:4; 24:14; 24:22). This was the conviction of the Faith and Order Conference in Lausanne (1927). Yet, some of the new divisive issues are certainly more opposed to this unanimity in faith and praxis than the classic confessional differences. Consequently, for the sake of Christian unity, churches need to find together ways to strengthen together, consolidate together, confirm together, clarify together, secure together the common faith of the Church of God, through an authentic search for truth, using the most reliable conclusions of exegetical, theological and historical scholarship. This is not apologetics but the honest quest for truth. It is not restoration but honest search for the revealed *aletheia* (truth). The time has come, and the situation demands, that the churches should act on the basis that what unites them (or is supposed to continue to unite them) is stronger than what divides them. Ecumenism needs this new phase.

This is a very difficult task, but after Harare it is evident to me that it cannot be avoided. Let me say that it is out of their clear consciousness of this necessity that the drafters of the ARCIC II statement the *Gift of Authority* stressed the need of a magisterium.

III

I spoke just now of a new stage. Before tackling this task, if they are convinced of its necessity and understand its goal, the Churches need to recognize how much, for many reasons, they have changed during the last 50 years. The Catholic Church is no longer exactly the church of Pius XII. The Church of England is no longer exactly the church of Westcott or William Temple. And they will never again be what they were in the past. They are historical bodies. Some of these changes are positive; others are to be deplored, but very often positive and negative effects are like two sides of the same coin. In a sane community a negative change may sometimes cause a good reaction. *Ex tenebris lux*.

Let us, for instance, give the example of the Catholic Church. In many parts of the Western world the number of ministers is decreasing dramatically, so that in many parishes weekly Sunday eucharistic worship is no longer possible. The so-called 'dominical assembly in the absence of a priest' – that is a celebration of the Word of God, not always followed by the reception of bread consecrated at a former Eucharist – takes its place, and this happens more and more often. I know a Canadian village where, whilst the Anglicans and Ukrainian Orthodox celebrate the Eucharist every Sunday, the Roman Catholics celebrate a real eucharistic synaxis only once a month. I dared to say that in this village the Catholic community was the low church! This is dreadful and deplorable, a very abnormal situation, but it is quite interesting to note that, through the experience of these Sundays without a Mass, many Catholics have understood better why the liturgies of other churches are not void and empty, even if they do not celebrate the Mass.

At another level, in many local Catholic churches, lay baptized people play a major role in the life of the community. In some parishes, catechesis, visitation of the sick, organization of non-sacramental liturgies, funerals, preparation for baptism and marriage are in their hands. In particular situations, they even preside at baptism. Moreover, canon law itself recognizes that they may, by the bishop's canonical deputation, be actively involved in the pastoral activity of the diocese or parish (canons 228; 230, 3; 517, 2; 861; 1112). It is now clear that – like the Reformed or Free churches – the Catholic Church is not by nature a clerical church. For me, this is a very important observation, even if many of the lay people are not yet ready for the task they are now asked to perform and if this situation may generate certain difficult problems – which it does. *Ex tenebris lux*.

Speaking of new similarities between the Catholic Church and other Christian communities, one has to mention the influence of the Charismatic and similar movements. Reading *Documentation catholique* 95, one sees how long the list of these movements is.[5] From its origins the Catholic charismatic movement has been deeply rooted in the

Pentecostal ethos. Other movements are also typically evangelical in their inspiration and praxis. Indeed, the theology and preaching of these Catholic groups is not always sufficiently balanced, and quite often they propagate fundamentalist points of view. Some probably have too much enthusiasm and not enough discernment. Indeed, all these movements are and want to remain in the Catholic communion. Their members are committed to the renewal of the Catholic Church. Nevertheless, in many places, their teaching, their moral options, their ways of behaving are not easily distinguished from those of Protestant evangelical or Pentecostal groups. Vice versa, many of the evangelical Protestant communities are more at ease with the Catholic movements of renewal than with the words and deeds of their main body or their own church, which they consider too liberal or too far away from the authentic spirit of the Gospel. Strangely enough, because of this evangelical link, even Catholic official teaching on ethics and Christian behaviour is sometimes more echoed on the very Protestant evangelical margins of confessional churches than in their supposedly more Catholic main body.

I said that since Lausanne (1927), Amsterdam (1948) and Vatican II (1962–65), the churches have changed. They are no longer exactly the same. The decisions of official ecumenical gatherings (especially those of Faith and Order) and of the Second Vatican Council played a great role in this evolution. Many classical differences became obsolete even if old confessional walls remain and still have to be pulled down since they continue to make the churches grow separately. Churches are now on many issues nearer to each other. There are many reasons for this drawing together, some of which do not come from ecumenical sources. It comes from their problems. They are questioned in their faith and Christian faithfulness to the Gospel by the same causes. They suffer from the same internal new divisions. They are challenged by the same cultural factors. They suffer from the same difficulty in appealing to younger generations. They have in Africa and elsewhere the same experience of people leaving them to constitute 'national independent churches'. Confronted with such a situation, they begin to understand two things – and the Holy Spirit is not external to this perception – that the future of Christianity is now at stake even within their own confession, and that they cannot continue to work separately.

The Holy Spirit is probably also indicating to some of the churches, through what I have called their 'new similarities' (frequency of the Sunday Eucharist, association of lay persons in ministry, evangelical and charismatic links), how life itself is driving them towards an inevitable decision. They have to work together since life itself makes them more and more similar. Nevertheless, they do their best to be in tune with the convictions of their tradition.

IV

Ecumenism is here and now incited to enter a new phase. Churches that will not accept surrender in the face of the new difficulties, refusing to give up and abandon the struggle for visible Christian unity, have to discover together how, even if they are still divided, they are not discrete units added together nor a collection of fragments of the Church of God. The *una sancta* will not emerge from the sum of these pieces. It is not in pieces. The Church of God on earth is visibly divided, but in its depth it is graced by the indivisible gift of God. Christians are unfaithful; God is faithful. It is evident, indeed, that if one looks at the map of Christianity or reads the *elenchus* (index) of the confessions, the Church of God is visibly divided, even broken into pieces. This is the great scandal. It appears to the eyes of the world as a group of communities unfaithful to the words the Fourth Gospel puts on the lips of Christ as his supreme prayer to the Father: he wants them to be one. Yet, in spite of the disciples' unfaithfulness, God continues to give them faith in the Lord Jesus as God and Saviour, charity and hope, fundamental elements of what we call divine grace. But there is only one faith, one charity, one hope, one foundation of life with God!

The one and only Church of God is already present, though very often in an abnormal way, wherever an authentic baptism is celebrated by a community trying, in good conscience, to be faithful to the Apostolic faith. Sometimes, indeed, one or many of the means of sanctification is either absent or badly understood. We know, for instance, how the Lutherans affirm that the Catholic Church does not correctly comprehend the relation between justification and faith, how the

Orthodox believe that in the churches of the continental Reformation the sacramental life is deficient, how the Catholics think that by refusing the papacy, the Anglican Communion does not adequately keep the hierarchic structure of the Church of God. Sometimes central elements of faith are altered. The Orthodox affirm that the churches of the West do not adequately keep the balance of trinitarian doctrine, the Reformed tradition regards Orthodox and Catholic Marian doctrine as contradicting the place of Christ revealed in the Scriptures. Sometimes important points about Christian behaviour are badly preserved. Catholics consider that the views of some churches on moral issues like abortion, euthanasia and sexual practices are too liberal, and so do many in evangelical circles; some African independent churches think that confessional teaching on marriage is too restrictive. It would be possible to multiply cases demonstrating that all the churches – not only the Orthodox and the Catholic, both convinced that they have kept all the means of salvation and the essential features of the Church of God – are somewhat critical of the way other confessions actualize their Christian identity. Through our bilateral dialogues we have discovered the truth of many of these criticisms. Nevertheless, whether glowing or faded, healthy or wounded, whether with all its capacities or in quite a humble way, the one Church of God is there. It may be veiled, hidden, diminished, decadent, disfigured, *cathedra pestilentiae*, 'more corrupt than any Babylon or Sodom' (as Luther said in his open letter to Pope Leo X). Nevertheless, as Luther himself professed, one cannot cease to believe in the faithfulness of God to all those who put their hope in Christ. God likes to exercise his power *sub specie contraria* ('under the guise of its opposite'). The Spirit never and nowhere erases the Church or the fruits of salvation. *Lumen Gentium*, the Dogmatic Constitution on the Church from the Second Vatican Council, affirms that many elements of sanctification and truth are found outside the visible confines of the Catholic Church. It continues: 'Since these are gifts belonging to the Church of Christ, they are forces impelling towards catholic unity' (*LG* 8). The Decree on Ecumenism is more explicit:

> In this one and only Church of God from its very beginnings there arose certain rifts, which the Apostle strongly censures as damnable. But in subsequent centuries much more serious dissensions appeared and large

communities became separated from full communion with the Catholic Church – for which, often enough, men of both sides were to blame. However, one cannot charge with the sin of the separation those who at present are born into these communities and in them are brought up in the faith of Christ, and the Catholic Church accepts them with respect and affection as brothers. For men who believe in Christ and have been properly baptized are put in some, though imperfect, communion with the Catholic Church. Without doubt, the differences that exist in varying degrees between them and the Catholic Church – whether in doctrine and sometimes in discipline, or concerning the structure of the Church – do indeed create many obstacles, sometimes serious ones, to full ecclesiastical communion. The ecumenical movement is striving to overcome these obstacles. But even in spite of them it remains true that all who have been justified by faith in baptism are incorporated into Christ; they therefore have a right to be called Christians, and with good reason are accepted as brothers by the children of the Catholic Church.

Moreover, some, even very many, of the most significant elements and endowments which together go to build up and give life to the Church itself, can exist outside the visible boundaries of the Catholic Church: the written Word of God; the life of grace; faith, hope and charity, with the other interior gifts of the Holy Spirit, as well as visible elements. All of these, which come from Christ and lead back to him, belong by right to the one Church of Christ. (UR 3)

It is now time for the confessional churches to discern, confirm, consolidate and defend this God-given reality by which they are united, that is the presence of the one Church of God (as such) in each of them, whatever may be the mode of this presence. These elements are those now in danger of being lost. This new phase demands two tasks. The first task is, evidently, for each confessional family to trace in its own confessional life the features, the *elementa* of the Church of God, that is the only One Church present in the world since Pentecost. These basic *elementa* unite each of them to all the Christian confessional churches, in spite of their differences. We know now that it is no longer possible to maintain the ecclesiological pluralism of the Toronto Statement (1950).[6] It became necessary to discover how the map of the Christian world is the emergence – in a lamentable, scandalous, sinful situation – of the one, and only one *una sancta*. It is now time to affirm more clearly and study more deeply the real – even if still very imperfect – communion of all the communities celebrating baptism in the Apostolic faith.

But there is a second task. For, this being done, it will be essential to work together against what I have called the erosion of these basic realities of the Church of God. The goal will be to come to a substantial unanimity concerning their authentic nature and to a common decision to defend them together, always remembering what John XXIII said in the opening address of the Second Vatican Council: 'The substance of the apostolic doctrine of the Deposit of Faith is one thing, the way in which it is expressed or taught is another.' Classic interconfessional dialogue is seized by this dynamic, which today is utterly fundamental. For what is at stake is the inner life of each confessional family, without which unity becomes an empty ideal. No church, no confessional family, is today able to work alone or in isolation for the preservation and growth of its faith. It needs others. This is certainly a 'sign of the times'. An ecumenical sign. *Ex tenebris lux*.

Notes

1. Compare the reaction at the Harare Assembly of the World Council of Churches (1998) of the Northern Irish Presbyterians, who warned the WCC against moving too close to Rome, endangering the principle of 'justification by faith'.

2. In the 'Word to the Churches' from the Lund meeting of the Faith and Order Commission of the World Council of Churches (1952) the delegates put the question, 'Should not our Churches ask themselves . . . whether they should not act together in all matters, except those in which deep differences of conviction compel them to act separately?' This became known as the 'Lund Principle'.

3. See my paper at the Paul Crow Symposium, Indianapolis, November 1998. [Following Fr Tillard's death, this paper remains unpublished.]

4. In answer to the question, 'So was Christ God?', Revd Phipps (*sic*) replied: 'No. I don't believe Christ was God.' When it was put to him, 'He's not part of the Trinity? He's not the Son of God?' he responded, 'I'm no theologian, but the beauty of the Trinity to me is that it recognizes various dimensions to the Christian understanding of God. If Jesus was God, there'd be no need for God in the Trinity.' See *The Ottawa Citizen*, Monday, 24 May 1999 (cf. Sunday, 2 November 1997).

5. See *Documentation catholique* 95 (1998), pp. 620–26.

6. The Toronto Statement of the WCC Central Committee on 'The Church, the Churches and the World Council of Churches' is readily accessible in M. Kinnamon and B. E. Cope (eds), *The Ecumenical Movement, an Anthology of Key Texts and Voices* (Geneva: WCC/Grand Rapids, MI: Eerdmans, 1997), pp. 463–8.

11

Route-Planning the Future Ecumenical Journey

Christopher Hill

> . . . In order to arrive there,
> To arrive where you are, to get from where you are not,
>   You must go by a way wherein there is no ecstasy.
> In order to arrive at what you do not know
>   You must go by a way which is the way of ignorance.
> In order to possess what you do not possess
>   You must go by the way of dispossession.
> In order to arrive at what you are not
>   You must go through the way in which you are not.
> And what you do not know is the only thing you know
> And what you own is what you do not own
> And where you are is where you are not.
>
> 'East Coker', T. S. Eliot

Put prosaically, the trouble about route-planning the future ecumenical journey is that we don't know where we want to go. Or if we do think we know, most other Christians don't seem to. And they certainly don't want to go where we want to go.

Some families have spectacular rows at the beginning of a holiday. Everyone is tired and fractious; there is the temptation to take some work with you on holiday; children don't always want to go where their parents are going, and vice versa; there is more baggage than will conveniently fit in the family car. You will know the story. The Christian family, setting out on its third millennial journey, is already arguing about (a) the necessity for the ecumenical journey at all; (b) whether papal Italy or North American independency or English

Anglicanism is the ultimate destination; or whether (c) an adventure-trek in the direction of the developing World with international debt, peace, justice and environmental issues might not be much more exciting; and/or finally (d) whether a trip to the Middle or Far East and an encounter with other world-faith communities shouldn't be the *ultimate* ecumenical destination. Ecumenical route planning is therefore inherently difficult. Even knowing where we are actually starting from cannot be taken for granted. Where we are on the ecumenical journey is by no means patient of a straightforward answer.

So I suggest that the only place to start from must be where Eliot says the Christian must start, echoing all the spiritual guides who have spoken of the *via negativa* before him. 'Where we are is where we are not.' We begin therefore with ignorance and creaturely confession. We can only advance by daily conversion and renewal. Vatican II eloquently expresses this for all Christians – 'there can be no ecumenism worthy of the name without inner conversion',[1] a theme finely worked by the most recent Groupe des Dombes report.[2]

Approaching the variously disputed ecumenical routes (to recapitulate them: Is your journey really necessary?; Episcopacy, Papacy or Independency; Social Justice Collaboration; Other Faith Community Encounter) from the perspective of our failure and ignorance, from 'where we are not', may well prove to be instructive, even liberating; at least it will be good for puncturing our ecumenical hubris. Starting from our failure and ignorance of the way forward also means we must start with ourselves. For me that means *Anglican* failure and ignorance. We all know how gratifying it is to point out other people's failures and lack of ecumenical achievement: if only the English Free churches and Roman Catholics would be like us episcopally superior Anglicans! It's all so culturally obvious to an English Anglican! I begin, however, with Anglican failure and ignorance rather than others. Christians confess their own sins, not other people's.

So to the first question-mark on the journey: why unity at all? Amongst the churches in the English-speaking world, Anglicans have usually prided themselves on their ecumenical commitment (if not their actual achievement). How well founded is this assumption? Not so long ago in the General Synod a leading evangelical (whom I know and respect) seriously questioned the goal of visible unity in relation to our continuing dialogue with English Methodism. I do not think he is alone in reverting to the concept of a 'spiritual rather than organizational unity'. We are all 'One in Jesus' aren't we? Moreover, the growing Christian communities are the Independent/Charismatic/Pentecostal movements and groups all over the world. Is there not also evidence that a multiplicity of separate neighbourhood churches (as especially in the USA) cater more effectively for different cultural sub-communities in today's fragmented, modular, postmodern society?

The battle for visible, sacramental, organic unity and communion has to be fought over and over again. This will mean paying attention to the history of doctrine and the Reformation discussion about the visible and invisible Church. Anglicans could well look to our links with the Reformed as well as the Catholic tradition here. Much as I love the Lutheran churches, Martin Luther himself and the Lutheran tradition are much less clear than John Calvin and his successors on the necessity of a visible Church. Article 19 speaks of the visible Church but is not so clear as the Westminster Confession on the distinction between the visible and invisible Church.[3] The latter builds on Augustine's distinction between the 'invisible fellowship of love' and the 'mixed communion' of the visible institutional Church, hammered out in his controversy with the Donatists.[4] This takes us back still further to the concrete models, or better, metaphors, of the Church given to us in the New Testament. Try to envisage for a moment the impossibility of an invisible Body, Vine, People, Temple or Bride. And *then* think of communion (not really a model in the same sense in spite of Avery Dulles).[5] With communion there is an invisibility – our relationship with God – but it is made visible in our relationship with each other.[6] Invisible communion with God is logically embodied in visible communion with each other, because as human beings the spiritual is communicated with and through our physical bodies. We also need to explore just how much a stress on the invisibility of the true Church (and thus the invisibility of Christian unity) also reflects a Manichaean denial of creation and incarnation. At the same time we need to recognize the real problem of unfaithful Christians in the Church, as indeed Augustine tried to in his dispute with the Donatists.

Just as the Christian is, according to Luther, *simul justus et peccator* so the Church also is in constant need of renewal and reform. Orthodox reticence in speaking of the Christian Church as sinful – how can the Bride, spotless without wrinkle, be tainted? – will need to be recognized. This reticence is usually respected by Roman Catholic theologians and certainly in 'authoritative' Roman Catholic sources. (There is, however, one interesting example of the present Pope speaking less cautiously of the Pilgrim Church as 'living, holy and sinful'.)[7] All this, I suggest, is part of a theological journey we need to make if we are to get beyond the widespread assumption that visible unity is an unnecessarily high hurdle foisted upon the churches by ecumenists who have forgotten that true unity is merely 'spiritual'.

To the argument that it is the churches least interested in unity which are most successful in growth, we must ungrudgingly acknowledge the partial truth of this socioreligious fact while also highlighting some important questions. Is it not also the case, according to religious sociologists, that with the second or third generation of a new church or religious movement there comes a genuine interest in unity and links with other Christian churches? This has been demonstrated in the life of a number of black-led Pentecostal churches in the UK in the last 30 years. Moreover, where there are no apparent links between Churches, and indeed where there is polarization, there is a real danger of separate churches becoming associated with rival communities or groups. Churches then unwittingly reinforce communal division – as in Northern Ireland or the former Yugoslavia. Instead of the Christian Church being a sign, instrument and foretaste of the Kingdom of God, communally divided churches become precisely the opposite – signs, instruments and articulation of the most bitter human division and hatred.

Caution is also needed before simplistically applying a North American socioreligious analysis to Europe – the more churches there are the better. Such caution is well argued by Dr Grace Davie in her recent study on religion in modern Europe, with evidence presented for the viability, under some circumstances, of a public role for religion in association with the large, historic (sometimes state) churches of Europe.[8] Equally, Robin Gill has persuasively argued that over-provision of churches can be a cause of religious decline.[9]

Now to the second question: what kind of unity? I have characterized the options as between a centralized papacy and congregational Independency or settling complacently for Anglican episcopacy! It's rather more complicated than this of course. And I remind you of 'where we are not'. As an Anglican I am heir to a tradition which, though commending historic episcopacy for quite some time, has not yet (with, of course, the Indian subcontinental great exception) been able actually to deliver the goods of unity and communion with even the English Free churches (although Methodism is on record as accepting episcopacy). The high degree of communion happily achieved with the Nordic and Baltic churches is of course among churches that already have an episcopate, some of them in the historic succession. Large failure and only modest achievement.

We do well to ask why. To start where we are not. One reason may be that Anglicans are obsessed by episcopacy. There may be reasons for this that we Anglicans have not really recognized and exorcized. I have argued elsewhere[10] that the premature raising of the question of Anglican Orders by Lord Halifax and the abbé Portal a century ago, with the consequent Roman negative (almost inevitable granted the state of the theology of ministry and the poor relations between the churches at the time) has skewed ecumenical Anglican conversations ever since. Bishop Bell of Chichester, usually the model of an eirenic ecumenist, once called the Bull 'one of the sharpest and most public rebuffs that the Church of Rome can ever have administered'.[11] An unnoticed consequence of this 'rebuff' was the collapsing of the Anglican ecumenical agenda into the narrow questions of orders and succession.

From 1908 to 1911 the major question before the Anglican–Swedish conversations from the Anglican side was the question of the Swedish episcopal succession. This was not a Swedish preoccupation. The Anglican Report of 1911, presented to the Lambeth Conference of 1920, was largely concerned with the unbroken succession in Sweden and a right conception of the episcopal office. Equally, Anglican conversations with the Old Catholics were dominated by the question of Apostolic succession narrowly conceived in terms of the historical episcopal succession. Though the Bonn agreement in 1931 does not speak explicitly of Anglican Orders, this is because the Old Catholic churches of the Union of Utrecht had *already* recognized Anglican Orders in 1925, after a series of conversations upon the subject. The protocols drawn up for signature by Anglican and Old Catholic bishops sharing in each others' episcopal ordinations after 1931 are impossible to understand without the background of *Apostolicae Curae*. These elaborate Latin protocols are formidable documents and make absolutely explicit the theological intention of both Anglican and Old Catholic co-consecrators – the very subject debated in *Apostolicae Curae*. More surprising is the fact that even the Orthodox were drawn into the Anglican preoccupation with orders. Although the predominant Orthodox ecclesiology would never separate a discussion of ministry from church, the Anglican–Orthodox discussions from 1920 onwards constantly returned to questions of orders and intercommunion.[12] The issue of the reconciliation of ministries has, of course, been at the very centre of all Anglican discussion with the English Free churches and with the Church of Scotland. The necessity or otherwise of bishops for visible unity is also at the centre of the continuing Meissen theological conferences at the present time. How do Anglicans consider this part of the ecumenical agenda at the start of the new century?

Many Anglicans today are embarrassed by any apologia for episcopal ministry in the historic succession which has as its logical consequence the unchurching of Christian groups which do not have such an episcopal ministry. There is, of course, the problem of the historical proof of tactile succession. John Wesley called it 'a fable which no man ever did or could prove'. But I think more important in the demise of such an ecclesiology for many Anglicans has been the entailment of a denial of Word and sacrament in other Christian communities, without which Anglicans are agreed there cannot be Church in the proper sense (cf. Art. XIX). So for our future ecumenical journey I ask whether the only way to understand episcopacy is in terms of sacramental validation of ministry. I suggest we explore rather the role of episcopacy and the *unity* of the Church; the *holiness* of the Church; the *catholicity* of the Church as well as its apostolicity. And I suggest that apostolicity be explored not so much as a lineal history of tactile succession but more as a contemporary 'sending out' by the Spirit (signed by the laying on of hands) invoked by the (prayer of the)

208

whole community of the local church, itself in a doctrinal apostolic succession articulated by and focused in an episcopal presiding, teaching, ministry. I suggest also that Anglicans should look more closely at the existing presiding ministries of non-episcopal churches to see in them perhaps more readily many of the above functions of *episkope.*

Such exploration would not take away a sacramental understanding of episcopacy. It might however seek to locate such a sacramental understanding in terms of an episcopal ministry of unity and holiness through the orderly provision of ministers of word and sacrament, rather than as a pedigree of the Church's apostolicity. Again, a defence of episcopacy in terms of the visible unity and catholicity of the Church could move the debate away from the otherwise almost inevitable suggestion that before episcopacy is restored to a 'non-episcopal' Christian community there is no real church.[13]

But there are consequences if we (and other episcopal churches) try to shift the debate from lineal, historical descent to visible unity and catholicity. We shall necessarily have to take more seriously that difficult question: Where is the local church?

We are all aware of the various ways this term is used. I *write* consistently, as an Anglican, of the diocese as the local church. I *speak* frequently (as a bishop!) to parishes as if they were the local church (which is what every parish really thinks). I listen to the debate in the Methodist Church about episcopacy: and I note the oddity that it is the District Chairman I deal with happily and regularly as an equivalent in *episkope* while historically and theologically it must be the Superintendent's office in Methodism that has continued real *episkope* in Methodism, with Conference itself. I also note the oddity in the Roman Catholic Church of the fullest official theological commitment to the diocese as local church, while Vatican *dicasteries* (departments) continue to supervise in a very detailed way many aspects of every local church. The Pope is surely Bishop of Rome, not Universal Bishop. Nevertheless, many important aspects of *episkope* which ought to be done locally have come to be done centrally by Rome, especially in the last 150 years. There is the equal oddity of congregational and independent congregations coming together in federations, unions, or coalitions and calling themselves churches, when the only use of the word church, according to their polity, ought to be at the congregational level.

Episcopal churches, whether Anglican, Roman Catholic or Orthodox, meanwhile multiply titular bishops, such as the Anglican suffragan or Roman Catholic auxiliary,[14] sometimes giving them a more local delegated jurisdiction. In north Staffordshire who is the bishop? The Bishop of Lichfield or the Area Bishop of Stafford? If the answer is *both*; what of monepiscopacy? Where is the local church? There is in John Zizioulas' fine book *Being as Communion* a theological tirade against titular bishops.[15] Just a year or two after publication the lay professor was ordained as Metropolitan of Pergamon – a titular bishop if ever there was one!

If we are to build up a significantly persuasive argument for a presiding (episcopal) ministry as a sign of the unity of the Church and a sign of catholic communion in the geographical, cultural and historical diversity of the global Church, we do have to work out how such a ministry can be a *real* sign of unity and catholicity. And this means working harder on the meaning of the local church. If the local church is not each single congregation, nor an ultramontane global church under in effect just one bishop, where is the real local church to be found?

To this question, in our largely pluriform, multicultural societies, must be added a further question. Does *local* only mean a spatially localized church? Could we not also affirm cultural locality (as in effect many of the rites of the Oriental churches in communion with Rome and the Orthodox ethnic jurisdictions do)? Do we not already have this as Anglicans in the diocese of Aoteoroa (the Maori-tribal diocese in the Anglican Church of Aoteoroa, New Zealand, and Polynesia)? While we may want to affirm cultural diversity in this way there may be interesting or awkward implications for so doing as English Anglicans (depending on one's 'integrity'). What of locality and culture in terms of particular historical understandings (for example, the non-ordination of women) or ethical development (for example, homosexual practice and ordinations). There are large rocks just below the surface on this part of the journey.

The question of the local church also leads on to our understanding of the universal Church. Unlike the Congregation of the Doctrine of the Faith document *Church as Communion*, but like the ARCIC report of the same name and also like both Vatican II and Anglican divines such as Richard Hooker,[16] the universal Church is best understood as a communion of local churches; the universal Church of Jesus Christ being fully manifested in each local church in communion with the other local churches (through the ministry of bishops in communion).[17] As Vatican II expresses it, 'in and from such individual Churches there comes into being the one unique Catholic Church'.[18] This under-standing of the relationship between local and universal Church has the profound merit of putting bishops and Pope in the same basket. Maintaining communion between the churches is an episcopal ministry. The Bishop of Rome's role, as universal primate, remains still essentially episcopal. It is also worth reminding ourselves that churches which do not have the historic episcopate feel much the same way about it as Anglicans do about the papacy. What seems rational, comfortable and indeed part of God's will for the Church for those who already have episcopal ministry or papacy, looks very different from the point of view of those who do not yet share such forms of ministry. Only, I believe, when we can articulate more effectively the function of both these forms of episcopal ministry in terms of communion and visible unity, local and universal, and clarify somewhat *where* the local church is shall we have some chance of commending them to those who do not already share them. And the commendation of such a 'link' or 'connexional' presiding ministry must probably be distanced from questions of sacramental validation, at least in the absolute forms we have become accustomed to – no bishops, no Church or no Pope, no Church.

Because we must begin where we are, or rather where we are not, I have been giving thought recently, in the context of our continuing discussion with the Meissen churches, of how we move from seeing episcopacy (in its Anglican form) as in some sense necessary for unity even if we have no uniformly agreed Anglican understanding of episcopacy.[19] Dr Geoffrey Wainwright, commenting on recent ecumenical agreements with Anglicans (Meissen, Porvoo and the international Anglican–Methodist Conversations (1996)) poses the awkward question: 'What is the theological and practical significance of *unfaithful* bishops in matters of episcopal succession?'[20] Apart from

211

the observation that all polities and ecclesiologies always assume the ideal rather than the actual (in spite of the actual problems in Corinth, Paul's depiction of the body of Christ in 1 Corinthians is a healthy one!), what are we to say?

I believe it may help Anglicans if we are more honest about our past, or rather more rigorous in our historical analysis of the past. Classical Anglicanism defended episcopacy without denying the presence of Word and sacrament in 'non-episcopal' churches. In the recently published Reuilly Common Statement this is rehearsed in relation to the French Protestant Churches from the sixteenth to the nineteenth centuries.[21] This did not necessarily lead to the inter-changeability of ministries, which is historically more debatable. But very few Anglicans denied such Christian communities were churches or that they had a real ministry of Word and sacrament.

Where does the Anglican apologia for episcopacy therefore lie? I think the answer to this is as an instrument or minister of communion and visible unity in and between local communities of Christians, that is to say local churches. Significantly, the role of bishops came to be emphasized more strongly as the Church of England gradually dis-cerned itself to be at the centre of the network of spiritual communi-cation we now call the Anglican Communion. The Methodist word 'connexionalism' comes to mind. It is a good word. The Tractarian stress on 'Apostolic descent' was originally a protest against the encroachments of the civil power upon the spiritual freedom of the Church; it was not originally an attack on other, non-episcopal churches. The first Lambeth Conference was called to assist the bishops to maintain communion in the face of doctrinal and jurisdictional dispute – the 'Colenso affair'. This is much closer to the patristic understanding of a local church in Apostolic faith embodied in the teaching office or chair of its presiding minister, the bishop, who is himself in communion in faith and sacramental life with other bishops, and thus their local churches.

The more this emerges as an ecumenical consensus, and the more that 'presiding ministry' in 'non-episcopal' churches includes the reality of such an 'episcopal' ministry, the more the question will be: how can the sign of the laying-on of hands be added to these existing ministries *in such a way as to enhance the visibility of that ministry* without the implication that no *episkope* and no reality of ecclesial life existed before the addition of the sign?

And then there are the siren voices of those who would lure us away from the classical ecumenical agenda to collaboration for peace, justice, development and the environment. Dr Konrad Raiser expressed something of this in 1995 during a visit to the Vatican, and described it as 'a much more dynamic understanding of unity – unity as process'.[22] Rather than contrast truth (in some abstract sense) with action, the answer to Konrad Raiser may be in examining the nature of Christian solidarity itself.

While I believe we must not lose heart that the quest for theological truth is still possible in our 'postmodern' age, it is encouraging to study just how much interChristian solidarity there is on certain peace and justice issues and what effect this has had. I would argue that the collapse of Marxism in Eastern Europe is largely due, risking generalization, to the actual collapse of the Marxist economies *and* the continuation of spiritual resistance in the Christian churches, Orthodox, Protestant and Roman Catholic, together with support (largely spiritual) offered by churches in the West. The collapse of apartheid in the Republic of South Africa also owes much to solidarity in Christian resistance from all over the world and to common Christian ground on the need for non-violent resistance. In both cases massive political changes have been achieved without great violence or cost of human life. The current campaign for remission of international debt, now partially successful in the UK, with massive Christian support right across the spectrum of Christian churches globally, is a fascinating contemporary example. But part of this consensus is that certain things are not only wrong morally but also theologically. Liberation theology, in its best exponents and defenders, such as the late Dom Helder Camara, is precisely theology, and not only politics and economics. Bishop Trevor Huddleston argued against apartheid precisely as a heresy contrary to a proper theology of creation, incarnation and redemption. Social collaboration and political protest go together with theological dialogue between churches: they are not alternatives.

It is worth reflecting on the Eastern European and Southern African experience in another way. In the Marxist/Soviet spheres of influence there was often political suspicion of ecumenism. For example, in

Poland the regime gave some limited support to Protestant and Orthodox minority churches over and against the Roman Catholic Church on the old imperial principle of divide and conquer. In South Africa the sharp criticism of apartheid from the Anglican and Roman Catholic churches had little effect on the dominant Afrikaans culture because the churches were divided. It was only when *internal* Dutch Reformed theologians and church leaders began a theological critique of the politics of 'separate development' that Afrikaans' confidence in apartheid as a doctrine began to crumble – alongside increasingly obvious economic and social drawbacks. Christian unity in Southern Africa would have pressed this earlier. Our journey includes both orthodoxy and orthopraxis. Both journeys are necessary – or rather they are *one* related pilgrimage.

The final question-mark leads us to the greater ecumenism of the encounter with other-faith communities. In many ways it is more important and more interesting: and it pertains directly to the Kingdom for the very obvious reason that interfaith rivalry, competition and persecution have been increasingly characteristic of the final years of the twentieth century and the beginning of the twenty-first. Hans Küng has said:

> No peace among the nations
> without peace among the religions.
> No peace among the religions
> without dialogue between the religions.
> No dialogue between the religions
> without investigation of the foundations of the religions.[23]

On this question I must issue a health warning. As a Christian bishop I regularly meet community leaders of other faith communities in North Staffordshire, yet my theological training and experience in dialogue has been largely confined to interChristian discussion. My observations therefore arise from a practical rather than academic encounter. I must also make a caution over the sensitivity of the word dialogue – in spite of Hans Küng. However, although the *objectives* of interfaith encounter usually have to be very clearly distinguished from those of Christian ecumenism, there are some parallels of *methodology* worth emphasizing. These include respect for each others' integrity; letting the other community tell *its* story, history, faith, law, scriptures and understandings, rather than reliance upon the caricatured versions of mutual polemic. This will mean taking the best of another community's history rather than the worst; taking care not to try to fit another community's understanding into an alien conceptual/philosophical/theological social framework. We should also learn from the best of our mutual history, while repenting of the worst. Christian–Muslim relations are characterized today by much suspicion, for example; the long shadow of the Crusades still falls over the Middle East. Yet in some ages past there were wonderful examples of toleration from which we can still learn – classically in medieval Spain where Jews, Muslims and Christians lived in toleration and respect for four centuries until the re-Catholicization of Spain from 1492.

In addition to learning from the lessons of interChristian ecumenism, we can also learn from some of the methodological culs-de-sac of the last century. This is also part of starting from where we are not. One such dead-end is the current preoccupation among fundamentalist Christian groups with Messianic Judaism. It is naïvely thought that if we can ignore the distinct development of Church and Synagogue for 2000 years, the problem of Jewish–Christian relationships will be solved. Yet already in the New Testament we can see the tension between *ecclesia* and synagogue. The words of Jesus in the synoptic gospels and John reflect later tensions or were remembered because of contemporary animosity: 'they shall cast you out of the synagogues'. Only a little later in the history of the Church Christian fast days were deliberately chosen on *different* days from Judaism: 'the hypocrites'. Antique forms of expressing Christian faith in a Semitic/Jewish–Christian context became heretical.[24] After that came the centuries of Christian dominance and persecution. Part of Christian *and* Jewish identity has been formed by our mutual antagonism.[25]

Our response to the recognition of conscious divergence and mutual antagonism is not to try to pretend that this has not taken place, trying to put the clock back, as with the 'Messianic Jews' movement. Rather, the reconciliation of many almost unbearably painful memories, ancient and modern, is required. This does not entail forgetting the past, but that we may forgive each other and be mutually forgiven. This, especially in the case of Jews and Christians, cannot be a cheap or easy exercise and it cannot ignore the holocaust, now part of Jewish identity. We cannot ignore the uncomfortable historical fact that at least some aspects of fundamental Christian doctrines (i.e. christology and the Trinity) were consciously articulated during the crisis of the conflict between Church and Synagogue in such a way that both communities have formed a crucial part of their identity over against each other. Islam, in as much as it is at one with and derives its monotheism from Judaism and Christianity, shares this problem retrospectively. Recent liberal Koranic studies are suggesting that the received versions of the Koran may similarly reflect later and heightened divergence between Islam and Christianity, and that Mohammed may have been more favourable towards both Christianity and Judaism than has hitherto been supposed. The way forward will not, however, be by trying to recreate relationships long since past, or by ignoring cataclysmic events such as the Crusades.

If there have been mistaken practical paths (such as the Messianic Jews' movement), so also there have been theoretical dead-ends in interfaith 'dialogue'. These have been characterized either as *exclusive*, meaning that everything of human existence and meaning is to be found explicity in Jesus; or as *inclusive*, meaning that everything is in Jesus as the eternal Son of God, the Logos; or as *pluralist*, meaning that there are many equally valid ways to find the summation of human existence and meaning. These are equally unsatisfactory: the exclusive view rules out any discussion from the start, since all else but Jesus is error; the inclusive position patronizes other religions, since Jesus is anonymously present in other faith communities; and the pluralist view canonizes either mere coexistence or indifference (both equally 'postmodern', all are true, none are true).[26] We shall need respect and reticence when speaking of Jesus, of incarnation and redemption, if we are not to fall into the traps offered by the first two options, and faithfulness to the Christian story to avoid the pitfall of the third.[27]

Our starting-place should probably be the mystery of the unity, diversity and plurality of the Holy Trinity. (It is not accidental that such a starting-point is also found in fundamental interChristian ecumenism, an ecclesiology of *koinonia* grounded in the mystery of the holy Trinity.) Rowan Williams suggests that we build on the work of Raimundo Panikkar[28] in respect of the Trinity and pluralism.

Williams is not uncritical of Panikkar, but it is worth quoting here what he sees as his most substantial contribution:

> Trinitarian theology becomes not so much an attempt to say the last word about the divine nature as a prohibition against would-be final accounts of divine nature and action. To the extent that the relation of spirit to Logos is still being realized in our history, we cannot ever, while history lasts, say precisely all that is to be said about Logos. What we know, if we claim to be Christians, is as much as anything a set of negations. We know that the divine is not simply a pervasive source and ground, incapable of being imagined, but we know that the historical form of Jesus, in which we see creation turning on its pivot, does not exhaust the divine. We know that the unification of all things through Christ is not a matter of a single explanatory scheme being manifested to us, but of the variousness of human lives being drawn into creative and saving relation to the divine and to each other. We know that the divine is not simply the promptings of 'interiority', religious sensibility, in us, but is called to account by the critical memory and presence of Jesus' human identity. At each point, we are urged *away* from what looks like a straightforward positive affirmation standing alone.[29]

The mystery of the Holy Trinity is not a grand theory in which to place the lesser theories of 'other religions'. It is the testimony of Christian *experience* of God, of Christ Jesus, of the Spirit. Williams speaks of our knowledge as Christians as a set of negations. Paradoxically the *via negativa* allows God positively, creatively, to be God. We cannot absolutize our ideas about him. We return again to Eliot, or rather to the spiritual and theological grammar of reticence he expresses so powerfully.

Our understanding of other faith communities and their identity will inevitably have consequences for mission. On a visit to Malaysia, sensitive church people told me of some current Christian triumphalism and monoculturalism, especially amongst those strongly influenced by the charismatic movement in its American form. For a person of Chinese culture, smashing the household idols on baptism is one thing; a Christian insistence on never going near one's father's pagan grave for fear of ancestor worship is quite another. Or the burning of an antique table because it is decorated with dragons – not a symbol of evil in Chinese mythology.

The history of Christian missions is indeed one of ambivalence to other cultures and faith communities. Early Christian apologetic is largely scathing of popular paganism. That tradition has continued, despite the more positive Lucan speech by Paul in Athens as recorded in Acts 17. When encountering 'philosophy', however, early Christian apologetic tended to be more positive. Yet temples and even libraries – as at Alexandria – were burnt and shrines destroyed. At other times and in other places the shrines or temples became churches, most famously the Pantheon in Rome. Recent studies of the Saxon Church[30] suggest that Anglo-Saxon missionaries may have been more sensitive to pre-Christian beliefs than their Celtic counterparts. In the new millennium Christians need to examine their own history of mission more carefully and discern why there have been such contrasting approaches, and what is most appropriate in the light of the mystery of the Holy Trinity, its unity, diversity and plurality. Or to put it another way: which is the most Christlike, the approach of the seventeenth-century Matteo Ricci who spent years immersing himself in Confucian culture before speaking of Christ – and was later condemned by Rome – or today's fundamentalists with their curiously monistic Jesus or humanity-negating Spirit?

But we need not only reticence, penitence and respect for the mystery of God's creativity and diversity. We also need reverence. Some years ago I visited Mahabilipuram, on the east coast of India, south of Madras. There are intricate carvings of the Hindu pantheon all over the soft sandstone rock cliffs. But on the beach there is a small cave and shore temple of about the seventh century AD. Inside is a wonderful carving of Vishnu as Nara Narayan, Lord of the Primordial Waters in his cosmic rest stretched out on the surface of the ocean. It is at least in part an Indian version of Genesis 1 and 2. I sensed a holy place, a shrine: reverence was the only response. I do not believe that holy place has nothing to do with what I experience of God as Creator, as Word in Jesus, and as Spirit in the Church.

> And what you do not know is the only thing you know
> And what you own is what you do not own
> And where you are is where you are not.

Notes

1. Decree on Ecumenism, 7.
2. Groupe des Dombes, *For the Conversion of the Churches* (Geneva: WCC, 1993).
3. Cf. Westminster Confession ch. 25 and the comparison between the two in Oliver O'Donovan, *On the Thirty Nine Articles: A Conversation with Tudor Christianity* (Exeter: Paternoster Press, 1986).
4. For a starting point for Augustine's ecclesiological insights see the many references cited in J. N. D. Kelly, *Early Christian Doctrine*, 3rd edn (London: A. & C. Black, 1965), especially ch. XV (with its list of Augustinian studies).
5. Avery Dulles SJ, *Models of the Church* (New York: Image Books, Doubleday, 1978).
6. Cf. the teaching of 1 John.
7. Speech at Fatima, 12 May 1982, quoted in Avery Dulles SJ, *The Splendor of Faith: The Theological Vision of Pope John Paul II* (New York: Herder & Herder, 1999), p. 100.
8. Grace Davie, *Religion in Modern Europe: A Memory Mutates* (Oxford: Oxford University Press, 2000).
9. R. Gill, *The Myth of the Empty Church* (London: SPCK, 1993).
10. In R. William Franklin (ed.), *Anglican Orders: Essays on the Centenary of Apostolicae Curae 1896–1996* (London: Mowbrays, 1996).
11. G. K. A. Bell, *Christian Unity: The Anglican Position* (London: Hodder & Stoughton, 1948).
12. Cf. V. T. Istavridis, *Orthodoxy and Anglicanism* (London: SPCK, 1966).
13. Cf. the drift of the argument of *Apostolicity and Succession*, House of Bishops occasional paper (London: Church House Publishing, 1994).
14. The Roman Catholic Church has recently cut back on the appointment of auxiliary bishops, but it has not created smaller dioceses.
15. J. D. Zizioulas, *Being as Communion* (London: Darton, Longman & Todd, 1985).
16. Cf. A. S. McGrade and Brian Vickers (eds), *Richard Hooker, Of the Laws of Ecclesiastical Polity*, Book III.1.14 (London: Sidgwick & Jackson, 1975).
17. *Bishops in Communion: Collegiality in the Service of Koinonia of the Church*, House of Bishops Occasional Paper (London: Church House Publishing, 2000).
18. Vatican II, *Dogmatic Constitution on the Church*, 23.
19. Cf. *Episcopal Ministry: The Report of the Archbishops' Group on the Episcopate* (London: Church House Publishing, 1990), p. 87.
20. In C. Podmore (ed.), *Community–Unity–Communion. Essays in Honour of Mary Tanner* (London: Church House Publishing, 1998).
21. *Called to Witness and Service: The Reuilly Common Statement with Essays on Church, Eucharist and Ministry* (London: Church House Publishing, 1999).
22. Quoted in Dulles, *The Splendor of Faith*, p. 157.
23. H. Küng, *Judaism* (London: SCM Press, 1992).
24. W. H. C. Frend, *The Rise of Christianity* (Philadelphia, PA: Fortress Press, 1984), Chapter. 4, 'The Christian Synagogue 70–135'.
25. R. D. Williams, *On Christian Theology* (Oxford: Basil Blackwell, 2000), pp. 93ff.
26. Gavin d'Costa, *Theology and Religious Pluralism: The Challenge of Other Religions* (Oxford: Basil Blackwell, 1986).
27. See such respect, reticence and faithfulness in Williams, *On Christian Theology*.
28. See his chapter, 'The Jordan, the Tiber and the Ganges', in J. Hick and P. Knitter (eds), *The Myth of Christian Uniqueness* (London: SCM Press, 1988) and his earlier *The Trinity*

and the Religious Experience of Man: Icon–Person–Mystery (London: Darton, Longman & Todd, 1973).

29. Williams, *On Christian Theology*, p. 178.

30. Cf. Benedicta Ward, *High King of Heaven* (London: Mowbrays, 1999) and Paul Cavill, *Anglo-Saxon Christianity* (London: HarperCollins, 1999).

2 Peter and the Third Millennium

Address for the conference Closing Service in
St Michael's Church, Cambridge, September 1999

Nicholas Sagovsky

> With the Lord one day is as a thousand years, and a thousand
> years as one day. The Lord is not slow about his promise as some
> count slowness, but is forbearing towards you . . . According to
> his promise we wait for new heavens and a new earth in which
> righteousness dwells.
>
> (2 Pet. 3:8–13)

Samuel Johnson tells of a young man who had tried 'to be a philo-
sopher', but, as the young man said, 'I don't know how, cheerfulness
was always breaking in.' I have at various points through the last three
days been reminded of this. We met for a theological conference to
launch the Centre for Ecumenical Studies and, I don't know how,
cheerfulness kept breaking in. What I shall take from this conference
is the memory of joy: joy at the number of friends who came together
to give support at the start of this new venture, and joy that it has been
inaugurated in such an atmosphere of friendship. Then, I think to
myself, since joy is a hallmark of the saints, why should I be surprised
that when Christians came together from different traditions and
different lands to share their experience of ecumenism and to celebrate
a new venture 'cheerfulness kept breaking in'? It puts me in mind of
Thomas More, writing to his daughter on the eve of his execution,
'Fare ye well my dear child and pray for me, and I shall for you and all
your friends that we may merrily meet in heaven.'

'That we may merrily meet in heaven.' Small wonder that when Christian friends spend time together on earth there should be merriment, and that this should be for us a touch of heaven, for in heaven the saints do not keep in touch by e-mail but communicate face to face. Yet, when we come to worship on earth, there is bound also to be sadness, precisely because we who have so enjoyed each other's company cannot take bread and wine, and in the simplest way bring them to our Risen Lord for his blessing, and share them with one another and with the thousands who are weary and have nothing to eat. Somehow we sense it's because of sin that we have got into this mess, and it would also be sin to pretend that the problems don't exist, so there is no other road for us to tread but the road of pilgrimage which we call ecumenism.

When there is a long road to tread, it's easy to get tired and to feel that nothing is changing, and maybe we are slipping back. That is part of the reason I chose to take some thoughts for this address from the Second Letter of Peter, for here are Christians who thought God would act more quickly and more decisively than he has, and who are having to learn God's path for them in a history they never expected to face. 'Why hasn't the world ended? Has God gone to sleep?' they are asking. 'When is the promise of Jesus' coming going to be fulfilled?' The Second Letter of Peter (which was one of the last of the New Testament scriptures to be accepted into the canon) shows the early Church grappling with questions Christian teachers have been asked ever since the earliest days. The answer is carefully phrased, and has a lot to teach us in our work for visible unity: 'Do not ignore this one fact, beloved, that with the Lord one day is as a thousand years, and a thousand years as one day.' It is most unlikely that the author was literally expecting thousands of years of Christian history stretching ahead (he was developing a thought from Psalm 90: 'For a thousand years in thy sight are but as yesterday when it is past, or as a watch in the night'), but it is a good thought on the brink of the millennium that if we were to take such counting seriously we would now be on the brink of the third day, just a little while before daybreak. We know perfectly well that there is something arbitrary about the time which will see in a new millennium (in just over a year's time), and it is probably about two thousand and three years since the birth of Jesus, but to be on the brink of the Lord's

222

third day would be to be on the brink of the day of the Resurrection, on the brink of the Lord's 'new creation'.

Those to whom this letter was written clearly needed that reminder. Scattered through it are hints of doubt and discouragement as a new generation of Christians who lack the leadership of the Apostles takes over. It is written in the name of Peter to give the message authority, but it also speaks of Peter's imminent death and it already accords Paul's writings the authority of 'Scripture'. The scenario is one of persecution in which a remnant is called to remain faithful, following the example of Noah and Lot and heeding the warning that those who have known 'the way of righteousness' but then turned back 'from the holy commandment' would have been better off if they had never begun to follow Christ at all.

Our conference has been one of stocktaking at the end of 'the century of ecumenism'. It is clear that, by the grace of God and through the dedicated work of many, extraordinary things have been achieved and there is much for which we have to give thanks, but we are coming to the end of the century without the visible unity that many of the ecumenical pioneers must have hoped for, and there are places where the freshness seems to have gone out of ecumenical relations if it was ever there at all. We have been sharply reminded of the new threats to the unity some of the churches already enjoy and, after the optimism of the 1960s and 1970s, there is clearly a sense that new encouragement is needed for the ecumenical movement as a whole. As we pass into the third millennium of Christian history, there seems so far to go to attain the elusive goal of a visible unity that will embrace the great majority of Christians in and for the world. It is against this background that I turn back to 2 Peter for encouragement and help.

We might identify as the one dominant theme through the whole of this short epistle the theme of *time* – of our being in time, of God's sovereignty over time, of the time that Christians have allotted to God to keep his promises now running out, and the time that God allots to humanity being generously extended. The sharp question that is being put is a question about time: 'Where is the fulfilment of the promise of his coming?', and the answer is a sharp reminder that time in God's eyes is not the same as time in ours. The sense of time in the epistle leads rapidly to the conviction of the sovereignty of God, especially

God's sovereignty over time. It was God who 'long ago' formed the heavens and the earth by his word and who will, again through his word, bring the heavens and the earth to their end by fire. Thus the beginning and the end of time, the very existence and continuance of the universe, is at the behest of God. It is God who is the giver of time, and it is for his creatures to use time as God wills. We are invited to see the continuance of time as in itself a form of salvation, since by remaining in time we are saved from the terrible ending of time that is drawing so close.

However, if time itself cannot be experienced as the gift of God it is merely duration. A key word in 2 Peter is *promise*, which comes some five times. Time, for the Christian Church, is the interval between the utterance of the word of promise by God and the fulfilment of that promise:

> By the word of God heavens existed long ago, and an earth formed out of water and by means of water . . . By the same word the heavens and earth that now exist have been stored up for fire . . . According to his promise we wait for new heavens and a new earth in which righteousness dwells.

The Christians who are suffering in time are encouraged again and again to hold on to the promise of God. It is this that is to sustain them in time, and this which transforms their experience of time. Time and grace come together: 'The Lord is . . . forbearing toward you, not wishing that any should perish, but that all should reach repentance.' If it is difficult to withstand the pressure of persecution or of discouragement, then we should hold on to the promise of God that he will bring about an end to all these things in his own good time.

This is a short epistle, which nowhere delves into what is meant by the *promise* or *promises* of God. It is assumed that we know of the history of God's dealing with his creation, and after that with Noah and with Lot, both of them righteous men. The fundamental appeal is to God's dealing with Abraham, and then with the children of Abraham:

> Now the Lord said to Abram, 'Go from your country and your kindred and your father's house to the land that I will show you. And I will make of you a great nation, and I will bless you, and make your name great, so that you will be a blessing. I will bless those who bless you, and him who curses you I will curse; and by you all the families of the earth shall bless themselves.'

It is because of Abraham's response to the promise (holding on, as the Epistle to the Hebrews says, to 'the assurance of things hoped for, the conviction of things not seen'), that he became the type of the people that lives by faith, and the land of Israel became 'the land of promise'. If there is in 2 Peter an echo of God's covenant promise to Abraham, it is in the account of the Transfiguration, which is seen precisely in terms of promise and hope:

> We were eyewitnesses of his majesty. For when he received honour and glory from God the Father and the voice was borne to him by the Majestic Glory, 'This is my beloved Son, with whom I am well pleased', we heard this voice borne from heaven, for we were with him on the holy mountain. And we have the prophetic word made more sure. You will do well to pay attention to this as to a lamp shining in a dark place, until the day dawns and the morning star rises in your hearts.

The Transfiguration gives glorious confirmation of God's word of promise: 'This is my Son, my Beloved, with whom I am well pleased.' It fulfils the messianic promises in the Hebrew scriptures and it holds out promise of the future glory of Christ at the end of time. For the author of 2 Peter (as indeed for all the New Testament writers) ours is a time between covenant promise renewed in Christ and ultimate fulfilment. 'According to his promise we wait for new heavens and a new earth in which righteousness dwells.' Time for the Christian and for the churches is never merely duration: it is shaped from last to first by grace. It is the promise of God that gives time its meaning, for it is within time that we learn what it means to live in hope of the fulfilment of the promises of God.

There is one more thing I would take from this epistle which speaks so directly about the difficulties of being a Christian in a time of waiting. The writer is very clear how the period of waiting should be used: 'Therefore, beloved, while you are waiting for these things, strive to be found by him *at peace*, without spot or blemish.' This is by no means to be a passive waiting. The Christians are to take heart from the very fact that they have been given time in which to 'strive to be found at peace' and to hold on to the promises of God. Here there are for us further direct links with the work of ecumenism, first in the echo of the bridal imagery of Ephesians (cf. 5:27). Nothing less than perfection will do for the one Church, which is the bride of the Lamb.

225

It is because we are acutely aware of the divisions of the churches as 'spots' or 'blemishes' that we strive so hard to find God's way of reconciliation. Second, there is the injunction to be 'at peace', again echoing a key theme in Ephesians, where it is made clear that the real ground for peace among Christians is the reconciliation that has been brought about through the Cross (2:15–16). The thought is less developed in 2 Peter, but no less powerful. We have been given time; we are sustained by the promises of God; we are called to live in such a way that the divisions which mar the Church may be overcome. We are to strive to be men and women of true peace.

What, then, shall we take from 2 Peter for the work of ecumenism? First, a reminder that our time is in God's hands. We may set deadlines and targets and hope that certain things will have come about by the year 2000, but the pace at which things move is ultimately in the hands of God, and not to accept that will be a prescription for disappointment and stress. Time is not only the gift of God but also the sign of God's grace, in that he calls us to work with his Spirit in time for the peace and unity of the Church. By no means is this an end in itself. We are not called to be professional ecumenists or to concern ourselves with the business of the churches for its own sake. God has given us time, 'not wishing that any should perish, but that all should reach repentance'. If, by our disunity, we have failed to bear witness to the ministry of reconciliation that has been entrusted to us, then God has given us time for repentance and renewal. We are called by this epistle, again and again, to survive the pressure by tenaciously holding on to what the writer calls 'God's precious and very great promises'. We are called to live as *koinonoi*, as sharers in the very nature of God. To share in the nature of God is to be patient as God is patient, to 'strive' to be at one with God and with each other. This is the *koinonia* that the Centre for Ecumenical Studies has been founded to promote; this is the *koinonia* which makes us friends and, in Christ, more than friends; this is the *koinonia* which enables us to see the gift of a new millennium as time in which Christ the promised morning star may rise in our hearts and the unity of the Church be found afresh in him.

Appendix: the Charta Oecumenica

Guidelines for the Growing Cooperation among the Churches in Europe[1]

Glory be to the Father, and to the Son, and to the Holy Spirit.

As the Conference of European Churches (CEC) and the Council of European Bishops' Conferences (CCEE)[2] we are, in the spirit of the messages from the two European Ecumenical Assemblies of Basel (1989) and Graz (1997), firmly resolved to preserve and develop the fellowship that has grown up among us. We give thanks to the triune God for guiding our steps towards an ever deeper fellowship through the Holy Spirit.

Various forms of ecumenical cooperation have already proved themselves. Christ's prayer is 'that they may all be one. As you, Father, are in me and I am in you, may they also be in us, so that the world may believe that you have sent me' (John 17:21). If we are to be faithful to this prayer, we cannot be content with the present situation. Instead, aware of our guilt and ready to repent, we must strive to overcome the divisions still existing among us, so that together we may credibly proclaim the message of the Gospel among all people.

Listening together to God's word in Holy Scripture, challenged to confess our common faith and to act together in accordance with the perceived truth, let us bear witness to the love and hope which are for all people.

Europe – from the Atlantic to the Urals, from the North Cape to the Mediterranean – is today more pluralist in culture than ever before.

227

With the Gospel, we want to stand up for the dignity of the human person created in God's image and, as churches together, contribute towards reconciling peoples and cultures.

In this spirit, we adopt this charter as a common commitment to dialogue and cooperation. It describes fundamental ecumenical responsibilities, from which follow a number of guidelines and commitments. It is designed to promote an ecumenical culture of dialogue and cooperation at all levels of church life, and to provide agreed criteria for this. However, it has no magisterial or dogmatic character, nor is it legally binding under church law. Its authority will derive from the voluntary commitments of the European churches and ecumenical organizations. Building on this basic text, they can formulate their own local addenda, designed to meet their own specific challenges and resulting commitments.

I. We Believe in 'One Holy Catholic and Apostolic Church'

[Make] every effort to maintain the unity of the Spirit in the bond of peace. There is one body and one Spirit, just as you were called to the one hope of your calling, one Lord, one faith, one baptism, one God and Father of all, who is above all and through all and in all.

(Eph. 4:3–6)

1. Called together to unity in faith

With the Gospel of Jesus Christ, according to the witness of Holy Scripture and as expressed in the ecumenical Nicene-Constantinopolitan Creed of 381, we believe in the Triune God: the Father, Son and Holy Spirit. Because we here confess 'one, holy, Catholic and Apostolic Church' our paramount ecumenical task is to show forth this unity, which is always a gift of God.

Fundamental differences in faith are still barriers to visible unity. There are different views of the Church and its oneness, of the sacraments and ministries. We must not be satisfied with this situation.

228

Jesus Christ revealed to us on the Cross his love and the mystery of reconciliation; as his followers, we intend to do our utmost to overcome the problems and obstacles that still divide the churches.

We commit ourselves

- to follow the apostolic exhortation of the Letter to the Ephesians and persevere in seeking a common understanding of Christ's message of salvation in the Gospel;

- in the power of the Holy Spirit, to work towards the visible unity of the Church of Jesus Christ in the one faith, expressed in the mutual recognition of baptism and in eucharistic fellowship, as well as in common witness and service.

II. On the Way towards the Visible Fellowship of the Churches in Europe

> By this everyone will know that you are my disciples, if you have love for one another.
>
> (John 13:35)

2. Proclaiming the Gospel together

The most important task of the churches in Europe is the common proclamation of the Gospel, in both word and deed, for the salvation of all. The widespread lack of corporate and individual orientation and falling away from Christian values challenge Christians to testify to their faith, particularly in response to the quest for meaning which is being pursued in so many forms. This witness will require increased dedication to Christian education (e.g. catechism classes) and pastoral care in local congregations, with a sharing of experiences in these fields. It is equally important for the whole people of God together to communicate the Gospel in the public domain, which also means responsible commitments to social and political issues.

We commit ourselves

- to discuss our plans for evangelization with other churches, entering into agreements with them and thus avoiding harmful competition and the risk of fresh divisions;

- to recognize that every person can freely choose his or her religious and church affiliation as a matter of conscience, which means not inducing anyone to convert through moral pressure or material incentive, but also not hindering anyone from entering into conversion of his or her own free will.

3. Moving towards one another

In the spirit of the Gospel, we must reappraise together the history of the Christian churches, which has been marked by many beneficial experiences but also by schisms, hostilities and even armed conflicts. Human guilt, lack of love and the frequent abuse of faith and the Church for political interests have severely damaged the credibility of the Christian witness.

Ecumenism therefore begins for Christians with the renewal of our hearts and the willingness to repent and change our ways. The ecumenical movement has already helped to spread reconciliation.

It is important to acknowledge the spiritual riches of the different Christian traditions, to learn from one another and so to receive these gifts. For the ecumenical movement to flourish it is particularly necessary to integrate the experiences and expectations of young people and actively encourage their participation.

We commit ourselves

- to overcome the feeling of self-sufficiency within each church, and to eliminate prejudices; to seek mutual encounters and to be available to help one another;

- to promote ecumenical openness and cooperation in Christian education, and in theological training, continuing education and research.

4. Acting together

Various forms of shared activity are already ecumenical. Many Christians from different churches live side by side and interact in friendships, in their neighbourhoods, at work and in their families. Couples in interdenominational marriages especially should be supported in experiencing ecumenism in their daily lives.

We recommend that bilateral and multilateral ecumenical bodies be set up and maintained for cooperation at local, regional, national and international levels. At the European level it is necessary to strengthen cooperation between the Conference of European Churches and the Council of European Bishops' Conferences (CCEE) and to hold further European Ecumenical Assemblies.

In the event of conflicts between churches, efforts towards mediation and peace should be initiated and/or supported as needed.

We commit ourselves

- to act together at all levels of church life wherever conditions permit and there are no reasons of faith or overriding expediency mitigating against this;
- to defend the rights of minorities and to help reduce misunderstandings and prejudices between majority and minority churches in our countries.

5. Praying together

The ecumenical movement lives from our hearing God's word and letting the Holy Spirit work in us and through us. In the power of this grace, many different initiatives now seek, through services of prayer and worship, to deepen the spiritual fellowship among the churches and to pray for the visible unity of Christ's Church. A particularly painful sign of the divisions among many Christian churches is the lack of eucharistic fellowship.

In some churches reservations subsist regarding praying together in an ecumenical context. But we have many hymns and liturgical prayers in common, notably the Lord's Prayer, and ecumenical services have become a widespread practice: all of these are features of our Christian spirituality.

We commit ourselves

- to pray for one another and for Christian unity;
- to learn to know and appreciate the worship and other forms of spiritual life practised by other churches;
- to move towards the goal of eucharistic fellowship.

6. *Continuing in dialogue*

We belong together in Christ, and this is of fundamental significance in the face of our differing theological and ethical positions. Rather than seeing our diversity as a gift which enriches us, however, we have allowed differences of opinion on doctrine, ethics and church law to lead to separations between churches, with special historical circumstances and different cultural backgrounds often playing a crucial role.

In order to deepen ecumenical fellowship, endeavours to reach a consensus in faith must be continued at all cost. Only in this way can church communion be given a theological foundation. There is no alternative to dialogue.

We commit ourselves

- to continue in conscientious, intensive dialogue at different levels between our churches, and to examine the question of how official church bodies can receive and implement the findings gained in dialogue;
- in the event of controversies, particularly when divisions threaten in questions of faith and ethics, to seek dialogue and discuss the issues together in the light of the Gospel.

III. Our Common Responsibility in Europe

Blessed are the peacemakers, for they will be called children of God.

(Matt. 5:9)

7. Participating in the building of Europe

Through the centuries Europe has developed a primarily Christian character in religious and cultural terms. However, Christians have failed to prevent suffering and destruction from being inflicted by Europeans, both within Europe and beyond. We confess our share of responsibility for this guilt and ask God and our fellow human beings for forgiveness.

Our faith helps us to learn from the past and to make our Christian faith and love for our neighbours a source of hope for morality and ethics, for education and culture, and for political and economic life, in Europe and throughout the world.

The churches support an integration of the European continent. Without common values, unity cannot endure. We are convinced that the spiritual heritage of Christianity constitutes an empowering source of inspiration and enrichment for Europe. On the basis of our Christian faith, we work towards a humane, socially conscious Europe, in which human rights and the basic values of peace, justice, freedom, tolerance, participation and solidarity prevail. We likewise insist on the reverence for life, the value of marriage and the family, the preferential option for the poor, the readiness to forgive and, in all things, compassion.

As churches and as international communities we have to counteract the danger of Europe developing into an integrated West and a dis-integrated East, and also take account of the North–South divide within Europe. At the same time we must avoid Eurocentricity and heighten Europe's sense of responsibility for the whole of humanity, particularly for the poor all over the world.

We commit ourselves

- to seek agreement with one another on the substance and goals of our social responsibility, and to represent in concert, as far as possible, the concerns and visions of the churches *vis-à-vis* the secular European institutions;

- to defend basic values against infringements of every kind;

- to resist any attempt to misuse religion and the Church for ethnic or nationalist purposes.

8. *Reconciling peoples and cultures*

We consider the diversity of our regional, national, cultural and religious traditions to be enriching for Europe. In view of numerous conflicts, the churches are called upon to serve together the cause of reconciliation among peoples and cultures. We know that peace among the churches is an important prerequisite for this.

Our common endeavours are devoted to evaluating, and helping to resolve, political and social issues in the spirit of the Gospel. Because we value the person and dignity of every individual as made in the image of God, we defend the absolutely equal value of all human beings.

As churches we intend to join forces in promoting the process of democratization in Europe. We commit ourselves to work for structures of peace, based on the non-violent resolution of conflicts. We condemn any form of violence against the human person, particularly against women and children.

Reconciliation involves promoting social justice within and among all peoples; above all, this means closing the gap between rich and poor and overcoming unemployment. Together we will do our part towards giving migrants, refugees and asylum-seekers a humane reception in Europe.

We commit ourselves

- to counteract any form of nationalism which leads to the oppression of other peoples and national minorities and to engage ourselves for non-violent resolutions;

- to strengthen the position and equal rights of women in all areas of life, and to foster partnership in church and society between women and men.

9. Safeguarding the creation

Believing in the love of the Creator God, we give thanks for the gift of creation and the great value and beauty of nature. However, we are appalled to see natural resources being exploited without regard for their intrinsic value or consideration of their limits, and without regard for the well-being of future generations.

Together we want to help create sustainable living conditions for the whole of creation. It is our responsibility before God to put into effect common criteria for distinguishing between what human beings are scientifically and technologically capable of doing and what, ethically speaking, they should not do.

We recommend the introduction in European churches of an Ecumenical Day of Prayer for the Preservation of Creation.

We commit ourselves

- to strive to adopt a lifestyle free of economic pressures and consumerism and a quality of life informed by accountability and sustainability;

- to support church environmental organizations and ecumenical networks in their efforts for the safeguarding of creation.

10. Strengthening community with Judaism

We are bound up in a unique community with the people Israel, the people of the Covenant which God has never terminated. Our faith teaches us that our Jewish sisters and brothers 'are beloved, for the sake of their ancestors; for the gifts and the calling of God are irrevocable' (Rom. 11:28–29). And 'to them belong the adoption, the glory, the covenants, the giving of the law, the worship and the promises; to them belong the patriarchs, and from them, according to the flesh, comes the Messiah' (Rom. 9:4–5).

We deplore and condemn all manifestations of anti-Semitism, all outbreaks of hatred and persecutions. We ask God for forgiveness for anti-Jewish attitudes among Christians, and we ask our Jewish sisters and brothers for reconciliation.

It is urgently necessary, in the worship and teaching, doctrine and life of our churches, to raise awareness of the deep bond existing between the Christian faith and Judaism, and to support Christian–Jewish cooperation.

We commit ourselves

- to oppose all forms of anti-Semitism and anti-Judaism in the Church and in society;
- to seek and intensify dialogue with our Jewish sisters and brothers at all levels.

11. Cultivating relations with Islam

Muslims have lived in Europe for centuries. In some European countries they constitute strong minorities. While there have been plenty of good contacts and neighbourly relations between Muslims and Christians, and this remains the case, there are still strong reservations and prejudices on both sides. These are rooted in painful experiences throughout history and in the recent past.

We would like to intensify encounters between Christians and Muslims and enhance Christian–Islamic dialogue at all levels. We recommend, in particular, speaking with one another about our faith in one God, and clarifying ideas on human rights.

We commit ourselves

- to conduct ourselves towards Muslims with respect;
- to work together with Muslims on matters of common concern.

12. Encountering other religions and world-views

The plurality of religious and non-confessional beliefs and ways of life has become a feature of European culture. Eastern religions and new religious communities are spreading and also attracting the interest of many Christians. In addition, growing numbers of people reject the Christian faith, are indifferent to it or have other philosophies of life.

We want to take seriously the critical questions of others, and try together to conduct fair discussions with them. Yet a distinction must be made between the communities with which dialogues and encounters are to be sought, and those which should be warned against from the Christian standpoint.

We commit ourselves

- to recognize the freedom of religion and conscience of these individuals and communities and to defend their right to practise their faith or convictions, whether singly or in groups, privately or publicly, in the context of rights applicable to all;

- to be open to dialogue with all persons of goodwill, to pursue with them matters of common concern, and to bring a witness of our Christian faith to them.

*

Jesus Christ, the Lord of the one Church, is our greatest hope of reconciliation and peace. In his name we intend to continue on our common path in Europe. We pray for God's guidance through the power of the Holy Spirit.

> May the God of hope fill us with all joy and peace in believing, so that we may abound in hope by the power of the Holy Spirit.
>
> (Rom. 15:13)

As Presidents of the Conference of European Churches and the Council of European Bishops' Conferences, we commend this *Charta Oecumenica* as a basic text to all the churches and Bishops'

Conferences in Europe, to be adopted and adapted in each of their local contexts.

With this commendation we hereby sign the *Charta Oecumenica*, on the occasion of the European Ecumenical Encounter, on the first Sunday after the common celebration of Easter in the year 2001.

Strasbourg, 22 April 2001

Metropolitan Jérémie	*Cardinal Vlk*
President	President
Conference of European Churches	Council of European Bishops' Conferences

Notes

1. The original draft of the *Charta* was prepared in German; the final text was agreed at a meeting of CEC and CCEE at Strasbourg in April 2001.

2. To the Conference of European Churches (CEC) belong almost all Orthodox, Protestant, Anglican, Old Catholic and independent churches in Europe. In the Council of European Bishops' Conferences (CCEE) are represented all Roman Catholic Bishops' Conferences in Europe.

Index

Abidjan assembly (1969, AACC) 141, 144–8, 163
adiaphora 15, 25
Africa, ecumenism in 135–64
African Independent churches 146, 153, 200
Africanization 140
Alexei, Patriarch 122
All Africa Conference of Churches (AACC) xiv, 135, 141–53, 155f, 158–63
American Methodism 65, 68
Amin, Idi 143
Amsterdam assembly (1948, WCC) 129
anamnesis 37f, 41, 49
Anglican churches 26–51, 54, 57f, 66f, 69, 78, 87, 99, 105f, 108, 114, 125, 167f, 171, 180f, 184, 189, 191, 194, 200, 204, 206, 208–12
Anglican–Methodist Covenant (2001) 54, 73
Anglican–Roman Catholic International Commission (ARCIC I & II) 29f, 31–3, 27–51, 88, 181, 187
Antioch, synod of 23
Apostolic Canons 50
Apostolic Tradition, The (1991) 55
Apostolicae Curae (1896) 29, 49, 194, 207f

Apostolicity 34f, 40, 42, 63f, 69, 208f
Aquinas, Thomas 86
Association of African Theologians 144
Association of Evangelicals of Africa and Madagascar 147
Assumption, of Mary 29, 46
Augsburg Confession 82, 172
Augustine 22, 37, 84, 86, 139, 205
authority 33f, 106–10
Avis, Paul 103, 116

Baillie, John 78
Balandier, G. 136
Balcomb, Anthony 139
baptism 22
Baptism, Eucharist, Ministry ('Lima' document, 1982) xiv, 57, 68, 70, 92, 168
Baptist churches 67, 87, 99, 105, 127
Barth, Karl 85
Basle conference (1989, CEC) 124
Bediako, Kwame 139
Bell, George 207
Benin 148
Blaser, Klauspeter 158
Blyden, Edward 141
Bonhoeffer, Dietrich 120, 129
Bonn agreement (1931) 24, 66, 184, 207
Book of Common Prayer 59

239

Britain, ecumenism in 91–117
Bucer, Martin 78
Burundi 138
Butler, B. C. 115

Called to be One (1996) 72, 183
Called to Common Mission (1999) 167, 171
Called to Love and Praise (1999) 60
Called to Witness to the Gospel Today (1982) 81
Calvin, Jean 78f, 183f, 205
Camara, Dom Helder 213
Cambridge 105f, 109–11
Cambridge Theological Federation xv, 94, 108–10, 116
Canberra assembly (1991, WCC) 124, 170, 174, 182, 187
Carey, Archbishop George 27
Carr, Burgess 150–2, 156
Cassidy, Cardinal Edward 27
catholicity 10, 14, 44, 60f, 63, 80–2, 85, 88. 93, 102, 152, 211
Centre for Ecumenical Studies xiii, 221
Centre for Jewish–Christian Relations (Cambridge) 108
charismatic churches 197
Charta Oecumenica 132, 227–38
Christ the Cornerstone, Milton Keynes 98–101, 105f, 109
Church as Communion (1991) 31, 44, 211
Churches Together in England (CTE) 100
Clarifications (1994) 30, 40
Cock, Lovell 80
Cold Ash Report (1983) 170–2
Coleridge, S. T. 102f
Commission on Church and Society 131
Communion ecclesiology 23, 31, 66, 113
Communion in Mission (2000) 27
Conference of Catholic Episcopal Conferences (CCEE) 123f, 130–3, 227
Conference of European Churches (CEC) 123–33, 227

Confessing Church, the 84
Confessio Augustana 25
confessions, church 81f, 191
Congar, J. M. Y 102f
congregationalism 96
connexionalism 65f, 72, 97, 212
conscience 45
contextualism 103f, 111, 113, 173
Council of Europe 121
councils 34f, 49f, 94, 101, 112f, 115
Covenant service (1936) 60
covenants (local) 112f
Covenanting scheme (1982) 54, 68
Cranmer, Thomas 79
Cressey, Martin 84f, 186
Cyprian of Carthage 9, 17, 139

Davie, Grace 206
Dayton, Robert 149
Dei Verbum (Vatican II) 48, 71
Denmark, church of 126
diaconate 41
diakonia 6, 10
Dias, Bartholomew 136
Didache 68
diocese 96f
Disciples of Christ 78, 87
Divided Christendom (Congar, 1939) 102f
Donatists 139
Dulles, Cardinal Avery 205
Durber, Susan 104
Dutch Reformed church 214

East Barnwell 105f, 112
Eastern Europe 213
Ecumenical Assocation of Third World Theologians (EATWOT) 144
Edinburgh conference (1910) 146, 162
Eliot, T. S. 203, 217
Elucidations (ARCIC I) 38f
England, Church of 96, 109, 114f, 174, 196
Enugu consultation (1965) 144
episcopacy 17f, 26, 34, 40, 58, 60, 64, 67, 69, 88, 106, 206, 208–12

episcope 9, 11, 17–19, 26, 34f, 42f, 50, 64, 97, 106, 209, 213
essentials 15, 24f
Ethiopian Christianity 139
eucharist 6, 9f, 16, 22, 26, 30, 37–41, 49, 70
Eucharistic Doctrine (ARCIC I) 38f
Eucharistic ecclesiology 37f
Eucharisticum Mysterium (1967) 39
Europe, ecumenism in 119–33
European Union 120f
Evangelical Church of Germany 125
Evangelicalism 146f, 155f

Faith & Order xiv, 6, 67, 92, 181, 191, 196, 198
Fedorov, Vladimir 128
Field, Richard 49
Final Report (1982) 30, 181
First Vatican Council (1870) 4, 25
Fisher, Archbishop Geoffrey 54
Flew, R. Newton 53
Free Church Federal Council 53
fundamentals 112

Gama, Vasco de 136
Gassmann, Gunther 170, 182, 184
Gatu, John 150, 156
Germany, ecumenism in 126
Ghana 137, 141, 145
Gift of Authority (1999) 30, 33–5, 37, 42f, 62, 191, 196
Gill, Robin 206
Goodall, Norman 78
Gorbachov, Mikhail 120
Graham, Billy 155
Graz assembly (1997, CEC) 124, 128, 132
Great Schism 22
Gregory, Benjamin 58f, 62f, 67
Grindelwald conferences (1891–6) 53
Groupe des Dombes 204
Gruchy, John de 148

Halifax, Lord 207
Hanciles, Jehu 138

Hanson, Anthony 180
Harare assembly (1998, WCC) 181, 193, 195f, 202
Hastings, Adrian 137
Heidelberg Catechism 79
hierarchy of truths 25
Historic epsicopate 26, 64, 68f, 88, 212
Historic succession 25f, 66f, 70, 208
holiness 44, 73
homosexuality 210
Hooker, Richard 43, 49, 211
Hopkins, Paul 153–5
House of Bishops (Church of England) 109
Huddleston, Archbishop Trevor 213
Hughes, Hugh Price 53
Hume, Cardinal Basil 123
Hutu people 138
hymnody 56

Ibadan conference (1958, AACC) 142
Idowu, Bolaji 144
Ignatius of Antioch 9, 17
Immaculate Conception 29, 46
indefectibility 41f
indigenization 140
infallibility, of Church 42f, 49f
infallibility, papal 29, 42f
International Missionary Council (IMC) 142
Islam 138, 140f, 148f, 162, 215f
Italy, ecumenism in 127

Jerusalem, council of 34
John Paul II 30, 61, 120, 193, 206
John XXIII 202
Johnson, Samuel 221
Joint Declaration on the Doctrine of Justification (1997) 27f, 31, 35f, 103, 116, 167
Joshua, Samuel 183
Judaism 215f
justification 28, 35–7, 192

Kampala conference (1963, ACC) 142f, 146f, 163

Kenya 138, 141, 144
Kimbanguist church 153
Kingdom of Christ, The (Maurice, 1838) 102
Kissack, Rex 59
koinonia 5, 16, 31, 33f, 42f, 67, 69, 93f, 113, 116f, 135, 160, 170, 182, 226
Kosovo 121f, 129
Küng, Hans 114, 214

laity 35, 63, 67, 107, 197
Lambeth conference (1867) 212; (1920) 207; (1998) 48, 54, 171, 180, 189, 194
Laud, William 49
Lausanne conference (1974, International Congress on World Evangelization) 155f, 196
leitourgia 6, 10
Leuenberg agreement (1973) 87, 168
Liberation theology 213
Lidgett, John Scott 53
Life and Work xiv, 181
Life in Christ (1994) 44f
liturgical movement 16
Livingstone, David 150
local church, the 6–11, 13, 18f, 35, 37f, 50, 91–117, 209–12
Local Ecumenical Partnerships 54, 66, 94, 98–101, 183f
Lores, Ruben 153–5
Lumen Gentium (Vatican II) 7, 22, 31, 46, 107, 200
Lund principle 86, 202
Lusaka assembly (1974, AACC) 150, 163
Luther, Martin 7, 29, 48, 84, 86, 200, 205f
Lutheran churches 27f, 54, 59, 87, 96, 125, 167, 171–4, 184, 189, 191f, 199, 205
Lutheran World Federation (LWF) 167–9, 172

Mackay, John 78
Maddox, Randy 56
Malawi 144

Malaysia 217
Mana, Kä 159f
Manning, Bernard Lord 88
Mar Thoma church 184
marks of the church 80, 83
martyria 6, 10
Mary 29, 46, 51, 55
Mary, Sign of Grace, Faith and Holiness (1995) 55
Marx, Karl 107
Marxism 213
Maurice, F. D. 102f
Mbiti, John 139, 144, 161
Meissen agreement (1988) 125, 208
Methodism 53–75, 78, 87, 99, 105f, 108, 127, 149, 205, 207, 209
Methodist Worship Book (1998) 66
Meyer, Harding 170, 179–82, 184
Milton Keynes Christian Council 99
ministry 14, 17, 25f, 30, 40, 64, 69, 185f, 206, 208f
Ministry Division (Church of England) 109
missionary movement, the 139–41, 149f, 160
Mississauga meeting (2000) 27, 46f
Moehler, J. A. 103
Mohammed 216
Mombasa symposium (1991, AACC) 157f
Monnet, Jean 120
morality 44f
moratorium 149–57, 160, 163
Moravian churches 59
More, Thomas 221
Mott, John R. 53
Mozambique 148
M'Timkulu, Donald 141, 143
Mugambi, J. N. K. 157–60
Muzorewa, Gwinyai 152

Nairobi assembly (1975, WCC) 26, 189
National churches 97, 125f
nationalism 142
Nature and Purpose of the Church, The (1998) 23

Nature of the Christian Church, The
    (1937) 61, 92f
négritude movement 144
New Delhi assembly (1961, WCC) 169,
    173
New Zealand 210
Newbigin, Lesslie 72, 78, 91f, 131, 180
Nicaea, Council of (325) 23
Niceno-Constantinopolitan creed 7f
Nigeria 136, 145, 148, 162
Nigeria Inter-Religious Council 149
Nkrumah, Kwame 140f, 143
North India, Church of 182f
'Not Strangers but Pilgrims' process 70
Nthamburi, Zabulon 153
Nyerere, Julius 137

Old Catholic Church 3–6, 23f, 26, 184,
    207f
'On the Catholic Spirit' (Wesley) 59
Ordinals (Anglican) 49
Ordinatio Sacerdotalis (1994) 49
Origen 139
Orthodoxy (Eastern) 8, 12, 87, 108,
    115, 126–8, 130, 191–5, 199f, 206,
    208, 210
Orthodoxy (Oriental) 87, 115, 191
Oxford Movement 57, 61

Pan-African Christian Leadership
    Assembly (1994) 147
Panikkar, Raimundo 216f
parish 96, 99f
Pastor Aeternus (1870) 42
Pasztor, Janos 84
Paton, William 78
Paul 94f, 212
Payne, William 50
Pearson, John 49
Pentecostal churches 87, 127, 205f
Pobee, John 137
Poland 214
Portal, Abbé 207
Porvoo agreement (1993) 66, 125, 167,
    171, 184
priesthood 40f

primacy, papal 13, 23, 25, 30, 37f, 40,
    42f, 50, 55, 64, 66, 192, 209, 211
primacy, universal 50, 209, 211
Primitive Methodism 57

Raiser, Konrad 213
Ratzinger, Joseph 25
reception 12, 23, 70
Redemptoris Mater (1987) 46
Reformation 4, 28, 82, 85, 97, 168, 200,
    205
Reformed churches 26, 53f, 67, 77–90,
    96, 114, 167f, 174, 200, 205
re-reception 23, 32, 43, 48, 50, 62, 103
reservation of the sacrament 39f
Reuilly Common Statement (1999) 212
Ricci, Matteo 218
Rigg, James 61
Robertson, George 121
Roman Catholic Church 12, 23, 27–51,
    55, 63, 83, 87, 96, 99, 105, 108, 126f,
    130, 137, 147f, 162f, 174, 181, 189,
    191–3, 196–200, 205f, 209f, 219
Root, Michael 179–85, 187, 189
Runyon, Ted 56, 61
Russia, ecumenism in 128
Rwanda 138

sacrifice 41
Sagovsky, Nicholas 135, 160
salvation 36f
Salvation and the Church (1987) 36
sanctification 55
Sanneh, Lamin 140
Santiago de Compostela conference
    (1993, Faith and Order) 183
Schaff, Philip 78
Schumann, Robert 121
Scotland, Church of 79, 96
Scotland, ecumenism in 65
Second Vatican Council (1962–5) xiv,
    137, 147, 198, 204, 211
Sell, Alan 85, 89
Serbian Orthodox Church 129
Sharing in the Apostolic Communion
    (1996) 54

Shrewsbury, William James 58–60, 70f
South Africa 141, 213f
South India, Church of 69, 79, 99, 182f
Spain 215
Sudan 138, 148
Swahili 137
Sweden, Church of 207
Synod of European Catholic Bishops
    (1991) 126
synodality 35, 38, 42, 50, 109

Tanner, Mary 169, 172
Tanzania 137, 144
Tertullian 139
theiosis 55
Theodosius IV 120
Thirty-Nine Articles of Religion, The
    29, 31f, 39f, 43, 46, 48, 180, 205
Tillard, Jean Marie xvi, 47, 64, 71, 114,
    185
Toronto statement (1950) 210f
Towards a Statement on the Church
    (1986) 55
tradition 26, 32, 34f, 42, 49, 55, 66, 70,
    94f, 98, 114
transubstantiation 38f
Trent, Council of (1545–63) 28, 31f
Trinitarian theology 31, 216f
Truth and Reconciliation
    Commission 124
Tutsi people 138
Tutu, Desmond 147

Uganda 148
ultramontanism 97
Unitarian churches 63
Unitatis Redintegratio (Vatican II) 22,
    50, 192, 200f
united churches 79
United Methodist Church 57
United Reformed Church (URC) 58,
    79, 96, 99, 108, 183
United States, ecumenism in 175
Unity of the Church as Koinonia, The
    (1991) 170, 174, 182
Unity We Seek, The (1984) 172

Uppsala assembly (1968, WCC) 26, 122,
    169
Ut Unum Sint (1995) xiv, 13, 50
Utuk, Efiong 145

Virginia report (1997) 50
Vischer, Lukas 83, 170
Vishnu 218
Visser't Hooft, W. A. 78

Wagner, Peter C. 156f
Wainwright, Geoffrey 53, 61, 70, 186,
    211
Waldensian churches 127
Walls, Andrew 139, 144
Ward, Marcus 69
Waterloo declaration (1997) 168, 171
Webb, Pauline 53
Weber, Max 102
Wesley, Charles 62, 73
Wesley, John 55–7, 59, 62, 65
Wesleyan Methodist Church 57
Westcott House, Cambridge xv
Westminster confession 205
Willebrands, Cardinal 194
Williams, Archbishop Rowan 130f,
    216f
Willis, David 85, 90
women, ordination of xv, 29, 49, 193f,
    210
Word of Life, The (1996) 55
Workman, H. B. 60
World Alliance of Reformed Churches
    (WARC) 77, 86f
World Council of Churches (WCC) xiv,
    77, 86, 122, 127, 143, 151, 170, 195
World Methodist Council (WMC) 54

Yoruba people 136f

Zaïre 136
Zambia 145, 149
Zimbabwe 141
Zizioulas, Metropolitan John 50, 210
Zulu people 136
Zwingli, Ulrich 78